Queen Elizabeth in the Garden

Queen Elizabeth in the Garden

A Story of Love, Rivalry, and Spectacular Gardens

TREA MARTYN

BlueBridge

First published in Great Britain in 2008 under the title *Elizabeth in the Garden* by Faber and Faber Limited

Published in the United States of America in 2012 by
B l u e B r i d g e
An imprint of
United Tribes Media Inc.
Katonah, New York
www.bluebridgebooks.com

Library of Congress Cataloging-in-Publication Data
Martyn, Trea.
[Elizabeth in the garden]
Queen Elizabeth in the garden : a story of love, rivalry, and spectacular gardens / Trea Martyn.
p. cm.
"First published in Great Britain in 2008 under the title Elizabeth in the garden by Faber and Faber Limited"—T.p. verso.
Includes bibliographical references and index.
ISBN 978-1-933346-36-6
1. Gardens—England—History—16th century. 2. Elizabeth I, Queen of England, 1533-1603. 3. Burghley, William Cecil, Baron, 1520-1598—Homes and haunts. 4. Leicester, Robert Dudley, Earl of, 1532?-1588—Homes and haunts. 5. Theobalds (England) 6. Kenilworth Castle (Kenilworth, England) 7. Gardens—England—Design. I. Title.
SB466.G7M27 2011
635.0942—dc23
2011038798

Jacket design by Stefan Killen Design
Cover art top: Healy, George Peter Alexander (1813–1894), after Gerards Marcus the Younger (ca. 1561–1635): Queen Elizabeth I of England. 1844.
Photo credit: Réunion des Musées Nationaux / Art Resource, NY
Cover art bottom: Tapestry of the miracle of Saint Eligius (Eloy). French 16th c.
Photo credit: Erich Lessing / Art Resource, NY

Printed in the United States of America
10 9 8 7 6 5 4 3 2 1

For my mother and father

Contents

'Many strange herbs, plants and unusual fruits are daily
brought unto us'

Woodcut from Thomas Hill's *Most Briefe and Pleasaunt Treatyse*, 1558

Princely Pleasures

THIS IS THE STORY of spectacular gardens and the powerful men who created them in their battle for ascendancy. Queen Elizabeth I was their audience and muse. Inspired by her love of gardens, her favourite of the time Robert Dudley, Earl of Leicester, and her chief minister William Cecil, Lord Burghley, competed for her favour by laying out innovative and extravagant pleasure grounds at their palaces for when she came to visit – which was very often.

Dudley's garden at Kenilworth Castle, in Warwickshire, and Cecil's landscape at Theobalds Palace, in Hertfordshire, were masterpieces of Renaissance design. They also enticed Elizabeth to stay longer. Whereas most courtiers could count themselves lucky if she called on them for an afternoon, Dudley and Cecil entertained her for days and weeks at a time. As she played one off against the other, they created gorgeous palaces and landscapes that amazed the world.

The garden at Kenilworth Castle lay within tall stone walls, so that only the tops of the fruit trees and the wooden galleries could be seen from outside. If a passer-by asked what kind of garden it was, he was told that the paths were laid with gold. In fact, they were made of sand and glittered in the sunlight.

The head gardener locked the garden gate and surveyed the scene. His men were raking the sand on the paths, which were as firm to walk on as the seashore when the tide is out. They wore wide-brimmed hats, loose-fitting mantles tied at the waist over long-sleeved shirts and trousers, and soft leather shoes. Everything was looking its best, despite the recent downpours – the covers had just been removed from the flower beds.

It was the second fine day in a row: perfect weather for weeding. The ground was soft, and women were kneeling on the paths between the beds, casting away stones and pulling up weeds by the roots, so as not to damage the expensive plants.

The owner of the garden was away for a few days. The head gardener leant down to smooth greenfly from the petals of a crimson lily, a gift from the English ambassador in Constantinople. At the heart of a maze, a young gardener was trimming the low hedges with a sharp knife. The hedges were made of thyme, and the delicious-smelling cuttings piled up on grass that was planted with daisies and buttercups. This square-shaped labyrinth faced a circular maze with hyssop hedges. Both compartments were surrounded by low wooden fences, which men were repainting black and white.

Halfway down the central avenue, a boy was feeding the fish in the fountain basin. The fountain only played when there were visitors. All was quiet until a carp leapt to steal the bread from the boy's fingers. Suddenly, water blasted from the sundial at the top of the fountain and splashed from the highest dish to the bowl and basin below. It was a test run. Moments later, countless tiny jets exploded in all directions from the sides of the basin. Gardeners, painters, labourers and weeders turned to see a blurred shape inside a wall of water. The boy darted down the steps, drenched, but joined in the laughter. He was new to working in these grounds: almost everyone had been caught by the water jokes, at least once. Somewhere out of sight, the head gardener turned a stopcock, and the jets disappeared.

At the corners of the garden, the men returned to their work. They were winding vines around juniper poles which had been bent to form pumpkin-shaped enclosures. One of the bowers was covered with honeysuckle, damask roses and sweet briar. Inside it, a painter was coating a bench with a glistening jasper.

All of this splendour had been put together in less than a year. It followed a style that had now dominated gardens for over half a century. Criss-crossed with paths, the garden was a grid, enclosing geometrical shapes. The patterns were best viewed from the top-floor windows of the castle. The cloistered garden was still seen as the height of sophistication and elegance.

But gardens were about to change. Within a decade, England's pleasure grounds would look very different – the joke fountain was an early sign. This transformation would be brought about by the rivalry between the two most powerful men in the country.

On this blazing hot day in August 1572, the gossip in the garden concerned the Queen's repeated visits to the castle. She had been here twice within the last ten days. Out of the blue, in the middle of her official visit to nearby Warwick Castle, she had said that she desired to go to Kenilworth. She had left her household behind, bringing her Lord Treasurer, William Cecil, as her only companion. She had come to enjoy the 'princely pleasures' of Kenilworth: falconry, archery and hunting. Both times, she had stayed for several days, returning to Warwick late at night.

The head gardener did not say a word but kept one ear open to the conversations around him. Everyone knew that the Queen really came to see their master Robert Dudley. But this summer, her unscheduled appearances had caused a scandal. On a whim, she had invited a local official to accompany her and Cecil on her second excursion. The man had been so shocked by what he had witnessed at the castle that, on returning to Warwick, he had reported 'such things as, some for their untruths, and some for other causes, had been better untold'. The scandal had revived the rumours concerning the Queen and her favourite.

Rumours and reports, whether true or false, can play as important a part in men's lives as the things that they do. In 1572, Dudley was Earl of Leicester and Queen Elizabeth I's Master of the Horse. He was then about thirty-nine. Elizabeth had granted him Kenilworth Castle in 1563. It was said that they had been lovers for thirteen years – since the beginning of her reign.

In less than a week's time, the Queen would return to the castle for a state visit. The court would stay for five days, as a mark of special favour. The garden would be ready.

'God save my people!'

George Vertue's sketch of the Procession Portrait

Fireworks

ON THE LAST NIGHT of the entertainments at Warwick Castle before the court left for Kenilworth, in August 1572, the guests followed a zigzag path to the top of an artificial hill, which had once been a lookout post. At the summit stood a canvas pavilion decorated with roses and honeysuckle. Lanterns hung at the entrance, and, inside, candles lit up the walls, which were painted with flowers. From a ceiling painted with the moon, the stars and clouds, vines dangled baskets of apples, oranges and pears, some covered with gold leaf. Sweet-smelling herbs lined the floor.

At the back of the pavilion, Queen Elizabeth sat on a throne on a low platform, beneath a purple canopy embroidered with gold and studded with pearls. She was dressed in white, black and gold – so was Dudley, who was telling her a story, kneeling on a velvet cushion. Diamonds sparkled in her hair. She wore a ruby and diamond ring and ropes of pearls around her neck and wrists. Her ladies-in-waiting sat at her feet. Like all of her courtiers and servants, they wore black and white (her colours, which she had adopted as a princess, during her semi-exile from court).

Her host and hostess, Lord and Lady Warwick, stood near by (Warwick was Dudley's brother). Boys dressed in silk served candied fruits and spices on gold platters. The guests drank Gascony wine, and music played in the background. To one side, Cecil was talking to the official who had accompanied him and the Queen on her last scandalous visit to Kenilworth.

The guests of honour were two of France's highest-ranking diplomats: the distinguished-looking ambassador and his handsome young assistant. They stood out in the crowd as the only guests not in monochrome and looked overdressed in rich greens and yellows. They were there as representatives of the Duke of Alençon, brother of the French king and the Queen's latest suitor.

In 1572, England faced a formidable enemy in Spain, which was backed by Italy. There was also the threat of rebellion in Ireland. Elizabeth and her ministers had contrived an uneasy alliance with France. England's only allies, apart from the French, were the Protestant leaders of the Netherlands, who, lacking military strength, had desperately sought protection against their Spanish overlords. When the French diplomats caught her eye, Elizabeth smiled and drank their health.

Once the sky had turned an inky black, Dudley led Elizabeth into the torchlit garden. The grass was as soft as moss, and fruit trees and flowering shrubs scented the air. The countryside lay spread out before them, illuminated by great drums of burning pitch which lined the banks of the River Avon. A hundred feet below, there was a garden created by Dudley and his brother especially for the royal visit. The flower beds formed kaleidoscopic patterns.

A great crowd had gathered by the river to watch the entertainments: Across the river stood two small forts, one in the fields and the other on an island. Hundreds of soldiers were stationed at the fort in the fields, whereas the island fort was defended by just a handful of men. Both sides had plenty of weapons and artillery: as master of the Tower armoury, Lord Warwick had supplied cannons, firearms and ammunition for the mock battle.

First there was gunfire, followed by drum rolls. Then huge cannons shot fireworks and balls of fire high into the sky. The explosions were so loud that spectators felt as if they were on a real battlefield. The sky rained fire. Some of the fireworks flew off at angles, skimmed the surface of the river and sank below, only to shoot up again with violent flashes and explosions. The special effects delighted Elizabeth. It was a triumph for Dudley, who had commissioned them.

A huge green-and-gold dragon flew through the air, spouting fire, and scored a direct hit on the island fort. But, about the same time, a fireball shot off in the direction of the town, followed by three more. Fires broke out where the shots struck. Three houses caught fire on the bridge spanning the river.

The courtiers who had starred in the entertainments led the rescue operation. Soldiers, spectators and townspeople swarmed to the bridge. They rescued an elderly man and his wife who had been fast asleep inside the first house struck by a fireball – somehow, they had slept through the din of the mock battle. It had been a narrow escape. The fire had spread so quickly that it had engulfed the house, and there had been no time to save any of their possessions.

Meanwhile, four more houses in the town and suburbs had caught fire. One of the fireballs had sheared through two walls of a house, leaving holes the size of a man's head, as described by the town clerk:

And no marvel it was that so little harm was done for the fire balls and squibs cast up did so fly quite over the castle, and into the midst of the town, falling down, some on houses, some in courts . . . and some in the street, as far as almost to Saint Mary Church, to the great peril, or else great fear, of the inhabitants of this borough.

By midnight, the fires had been brought under control, and, despite the destruction, there were no reported casualties.

The next morning, Elizabeth sent for the elderly man and his wife whose house had burnt to the ground and consoled them. She gave them a sum of about £25 as compensation – twice their annual income – to be divided up between all those who had suffered losses.

But this was not enough to satisfy some of the townspeople. Too many fireballs had overshot and flown off target for them all to have been accidents. But if it had been foul play, who was to blame?

Later that day, Dudley rode behind the royal coach on the six-mile journey to his castle at Kenilworth. As Master of the Horse, he travelled closest to Elizabeth in the procession. He rode with the ease of a naturally gifted rider. His dark hair and tanned skin set him apart from the pale-faced courtiers who followed him. There were hundreds of coaches and carts in the royal convoy – his hospitality was going to be tested to the limit.

Elizabeth and Dudley had once been inseparable. They had known each other since childhood, when they may have been tutored together. As the son of leading courtier John Dudley, later Duke of Northumberland, Dudley had been placed in the household of Elizabeth's half-brother Prince Edward. The royal tutors had included renowned Cambridge scholars John Cheke, Regius Professor of Greek, and Roger Ascham, Lecturer and Public Orator of the University, with whom Dudley later developed a close friendship. Elizabeth and Dudley excelled in languages, especially Italian, which they used as a kind of code since few people at court could understand it. Since coming to power in 1558, she had showered him with gifts of offices and lands.

But she was equally close to her Lord Treasurer, Cecil. As a princess, she had made him her surveyor, trusting him to look after her properties while she had been in the Tower. More than ten years older than her and Dudley, Cecil was a classical scholar, a statesman and a tireless worker. He had been educated at Cambridge and at the Inns of Court; at Cambridge, he had employed a bellringer to wake him at four o'clock every morning. Elizabeth was entirely dependent on him for advice in matters of policy. Astonishingly for a man in such a high position, he did not come from the nobility: originally Welsh farmers, the Cecils had slowly achieved success at court. His star was still rising – just a year ago, Elizabeth had raised him to the peerage as Baron Burghley.

The two men could not have been more different. Whereas Dudley loved the outdoors, Cecil spent most of his time inside, working on state papers. Dudley was a magnificent sportsman, but Cecil's health had been ruined by relentless work. Cecil's first concern had always been to marry Elizabeth into one of the royal families of Europe and so gain England a powerful ally. If she chose Dudley, all would be lost. And Dudley's hopes were running high, judging by his lavish improvements to Kenilworth.

Both men were famous for their extravagant houses, gardens and parties, but they were equally reserved in manner. Elizabeth's affection for them meant that they had to proceed carefully in their dealings with each other. Their methods were subterfuge, cunning and deception. Their feud had already lasted for over fifteen years.

November 1558. According to legend, Elizabeth was walking beneath an ancient oak tree in the park at Hatfield Palace, where she was being held captive by her half-sister Mary, when messengers brought her the news that she was queen. That day, she appointed Cecil Secretary of State.

The next day, she made Dudley her Master of the Horse. He had arrived at the palace on a snow-white steed, entrancing her with his superb horsemanship (though this is possibly yet another legend). While Cecil became the most powerful politician in the country, Dudley was responsible for organising the transport for progresses and processions and for improving conditions in the royal studs. Most importantly, his duties also included accompanying Elizabeth whenever she was on horseback. He had to help her mount and dismount and so became the only man in England officially allowed to touch her. Her love of riding and hunting meant that she was soon seeing him more than any other courtier.

Dudley's friend the astrologer Dr John Dee won the commission to choose an auspicious day for the coronation (15 January). During December, Dudley whiled away the time by entertaining Elizabeth at suppers in marquees in St James's Park, at his own expense. The best musicians in the country played for them. Elizabeth was impressed and put him in charge of the coronation festivities.

Traditionally, on the day before the coronation, the monarch rode in procession through the City and Westminster. The City's merchants paid for the pageants performed along the route, as well as for decorations and gifts. This was always costly, but Dudley's spending broke all records.

The procession began at the Tower, where Elizabeth had been imprisoned by Mary just five years earlier. In an open litter of crimson velvet, with a canopy carried by knights, Elizabeth made a speech in which she compared her survival to Daniel's escape from the lion's den. Dead on cue, there was a great roar from the lions in the Tower menagerie.

As Elizabeth set out for the City in her horse-drawn carriage, Dudley rode behind her, leading her white palfrey, while Cecil headed the legion of senior courtiers dressed in crimson. Rich tapestries hung from the windows of every house on the route. There were streamers, banners and pictures celebrating Elizabeth. The great conduit at Cheapside flowed with wine.

Extravagant sets had been built for the pageants, in which all of the parts were played by children. In the first pageant, a triumphal arch garlanded with roses towered over a three-tiered stage which stretched the width of the street. On the lowest level, there was the figure of Henry VII, in the centre of a vast red rose, hand-in-hand with Elizabeth of York, inside a white rose, representing the union of the House of Lancaster with the House of York and the ending of the War of the Roses. On the next stage, Henry VIII and Anne Boleyn sat inside a giant Tudor rose. Two roses stretched up above them, joining in a single stem to reach Elizabeth, enthroned at the top of the pyramid. It was the first time in nearly thirty years that Anne's image had appeared in public. Her memory had until now brought disgrace – in the aftermath of her execution in 1536, Elizabeth had been exiled from court.

Dudley's Pageant of the Roses showed how well he knew Elizabeth. It was a daring move to place Anne Boleyn next to Henry VIII in the new royal family tree. Although, as one ambassador had put it, Elizabeth 'gloried in her father', she had been careful, as a princess, not to talk about her mother. But she had secretly adopted her emblem: the crowned white falcon, bearing a sceptre, on a blasted tree stump from which Tudor roses grew. And Elizabeth signed off her letters to Dudley with Anne's motto, *Semper eadem*. Ever the same.

The day after the coronation, Dudley impressed Elizabeth in the tilt-yard at Whitehall Palace, winning joint first place with Elizabeth's cousin the Duke of Norfolk. As well as his ability to devise entertainments, in which he acted and danced, what set him apart from other courtiers was his horsemanship, displayed in hunting and in the old chivalric arts of the manège and the jousts. His skill in martial arts, from archery to swordsmanship, made him a good bodyguard. Elizabeth nicknamed him 'Eyes' as much for his vigilance as his looks. In his letters to her, he signed himself 'o o'.

That first year of the reign, Dudley took part in every tournament, ran at the ring (an exercise in which a rider speared a ring with his lance), won contests in archery and shooting and beat his opponents at tennis. Such was his love of tennis that he personally supervised the renovation of the courts at Whitehall, which had fallen into disrepair.

In November, Dudley organised a tournament to entertain Duke John, Prince of Sweden, who had come to England as the representative of his elder brother Prince Eric, heir to the Swedish crown, one of Elizabeth's suitors. Dudley and Elizabeth's favourite cousin Henry Carey, Lord Hunsdon (Anne Boleyn's nephew) were the challengers and wore white and black scarves (Elizabeth's colours); Dudley's brother Ambrose led the eighteen defenders, who wore red and gold (the colours of the Earl of Warwick, which had been their father's title).

The two Dudley brothers wore badges decorated with ragged staffs (staffs roughly pruned of branches), another emblem of the Earls of Warwick. Dudley also had a shield showing an obelisk with a vine entwined around it – code for his love for Elizabeth. The Latin motto beneath translated: 'You standing I will flourish.' Dudley broke sixteen lances and scored two amazing hits, one of which was on the vizard, which counted as a broken lance. The climax of the tournament came when he hit the lance of one of his opponents 'coronal to coronal' (tip to tip) – the most difficult of all jousting feats. After that breathtaking performance, Elizabeth presented him with the prize: a diamond, symbol of love.

A set of commemorative drawings of the tournament was commissioned. There were two pictures of Dudley, one with his shield bearing the obelisk-and-vine emblem and the other showing him performing the tip-to-tip hit. As a further reward, Elizabeth made Dudley Constable of Windsor Castle. Since Windsor was her stronghold, this was a further sign of her trust, as well as her admiration – in an interview with the Spanish ambassador, she said that anyone who hoped to win her should not 'sit home all day amongst the cinders, but should in time of peace keep himself employed in warlike exercises'.

In return, Dudley gave her some gold buttons decorated with ragged staffs (in later years, she would also wear his other emblems, acorns and oak leaves, on her buttons and in the embroidery on her clothes). Later that month, he beat Duke John at tennis at Southwark and gave a great banquet in his honour at Whitehall. Finally, Elizabeth told the Duke that she could not accept his brother's offer of marriage.

The following March, Dudley won victories on the tennis court against his enemy the Earl of Sussex, who felt that his ancient lineage qualified him for greater prestige at court than Elizabeth's favourite. Sussex taunted Dudley, nicknaming him 'the gypsy' because of his dark skin, and plotted his downfall with his cousin Norfolk, who also resented Dudley's success. Although Norfolk held the highest-ranking post at court as Earl Marshal (commander of the armed forces) and was England's only duke, Elizabeth preferred to take counsel from newcomers Dudley and Cecil.

Norfolk had one of the grandest tennis courts in the country at his ancestral mansion at Norwich. In a tennis match at Whitehall, Dudley and Norfolk nearly came to blows when Dudley stopped the game and took Elizabeth's handkerchief to wipe his brow, which Norfolk thought an unpardonable liberty.

Cecil was carried in a litter on his third visit to Kenilworth within two weeks. His earlier trips on horseback, accompanying the Queen from Warwick to Kenilworth and back again, had taken their toll. His gout was worse than ever. As the convoy rolled onwards past fields which would yield poor harvests because of the poor summer, he was one of the few courtiers not puzzled by the unusual route they were taking to the castle. The main entrance lay to the south, but they were approaching from the north. His fellow courtiers expressed their fears, wondering if there had been a mistake. The coaches would never fit through the narrow back gates. And the bridge would surely collapse under the weight of the overloaded carts carrying everything from gold and silver plate to four-poster beds.

The royal coach was open on all sides, so that the people lining the route could see their queen. When Elizabeth passed by, some of them fell to their knees, as if she were a goddess. Every so often, she called out 'God save my people!' and the crowd responded 'God save your Grace!'

Months of preparations had gone into this visit in August 1572, but everything had only come together in the last few weeks. Not long before, Dudley had written to his steward, Anthony Forster, about buying tapestries for the dining chamber – his instructions had been to get hold of the best quality, whether from Holland or London, at the lowest possible price. Other urgent concerns had included spices and fireworks and the construction of a banqueting house in the garden.

I hope you have made the provision of spice for me and have had the officers of the Queen's household to help, who promised me all at the [Queen's] Majesty's price . . . I pray you send down with speed some such spice as is needful for all other matters against my chiefest day.

By striking bargains for luxury goods like tapestries, and paying subsidised prices for expensive spices, Dudley could afford to spend on the things that mattered. Experience had taught him that costly 'trifles', as he called them, like fireworks, worked wonders with Elizabeth. As did garden pavilions. He had left his steward and servants in no doubt as to the importance of the state visit. Everything that could be done would be done to ensure the success of his 'chiefest day'.

Until recently, the entire nation had been absorbed by events leading up to Norfolk's execution at the Tower. Dudley and Cecil had worked together to bring this about.

Norfolk had become increasingly isolated at court and had plotted to assassinate both Dudley and Cecil, as a prelude to marrying Elizabeth's cousin Mary, Queen of Scots and seizing the crown. When Dudley and Cecil had arranged his arrest, the lords of the northern counties had risen against Elizabeth in 1569. After he had spent almost a year in the Tower, Dudley and Cecil had finally persuaded Elizabeth to order his execution.

Dudley had gained the most from the events of this summer. His friend Lord Shrewsbury had been given Norfolk's post of Earl Marshal. Dudley had been appointed his deputy. Since Shrewsbury was away from court, as Mary, Queen of Scots's gaoler at Tutbury Castle in Derbyshire, Dudley had assumed his responsibilities. Dudley and his brother Warwick now had almost complete control of the military.

In the early years of the reign, Elizabeth had shown Dudley and his brother extraordinary favour by restoring to them many of the lands and titles which had belonged to their father (who had himself been executed for treason by her half-sister Mary). But Elizabeth had waited a few years before giving Kenilworth to Dudley.

Strategically located in the Midlands, Kenilworth's turbulent history encompassed siege warfare and violent insurrection: it had belonged to kings and noble statesmen, as well as would-be kings and kingmakers. Massively fortified and surrounded by an enormous lake that made it an island stronghold, the castle was also palatial, with its Great Hall and private apartments. So far, Dudley had downplayed the castle's military might, modernising the accommodation and enhancing its dramatic setting.

On a royal progress, the court travelled slowly, covering about twelve miles a day. The gardeners at Kenilworth had until nightfall.

The warmth of the last few days had made the air heavy with the exotic scents of tobacco and sweet marjoram, which over-powered more familiar fragrances such as mint, lavender and honeysuckle. Peacocks stalked the paths, watched by Dudley's steward, Forster, and the head gardener, who were talking about the arrangements for that night's entertainment.

Painters were applying a special gum to the rosemary covering the thirteenth-century keep on the south side of the garden. They laid gold leaf on the needle-like leaves – in a few hours, the heat of the sun would harden the gum and bind the gold to it, so that the rosemary would stay gilded in the event of further rain. The finishing touches were being put on the fleet of barges. Carpenters were fitting them with frames draped with scarlet canopies surmounted by golden plumes. In the veiled interiors, women were smoothing down velvet seats and covering them with silk cushions.

The castle came into view – a vision of massive russet towers reflected in shimmering water. The gaping windows were lit, one by one, by great fires, and lanterns were placed on the banks of the lake. But what amazed the courtiers was that Dudley had turned the castle upside down: there was now a grand entrance to the north, replacing the old southern one. On the new highway, the castle loomed above them, and they caught tantalising glimpses of tall trees above the garden walls. Dudley had changed the entire layout of the castle so that the garden lay at the new northern entrance: one of the writers hired to describe the festivities would later joke that since the rearrangement of the castle to make the garden the main attraction, the keep's outer wall now 'guards the garden, as the garden the castle'.

They crossed a splendid new bridge and passed beneath a monumental arch to arrive at a neo-medieval stone gatehouse

decorated with Dudley's initials and armorial emblems, cinque-
foils (five-petalled flowers) and ragged staffs, as well as shells
(symbols of Venus, goddess of love and gardens). Dudley helped
Elizabeth down from her coach and led her through the gatehouse and along labyrinthine paths to the garden. The first thing
she saw was the wall of rosemary spangled with gold, glowing in
the torchlight.

Gilded rosemary was worn at weddings. It was believed to be
good for the memory and so considered an aid in remembering
marriage vows. With the French diplomats as special guests,
marriage was the theme of this year's royal progress to
Warwickshire. On her arrival at Warwick a few weeks earlier, an
official had presented Elizabeth with a petition. Assuming it to
be a request for money, she had promised to read it later. The
scroll had turned out to be a poem urging her to marry. But a
match with the French prince was unpopular with her people. So
who could the Warwickshire townsmen have had in mind, except
her long-time suitor Dudley?

At about nine o'clock, Elizabeth, Dudley, her favourites, including Cecil, and her French guests approached the garden at
Kenilworth through an Italianate arcade. A stone staircase led
down to the pleasure grounds where they were welcomed by
wild men covered with ivy, carrying clubs that scattered fireworks. Their guides led them along the perimeter path to an
octagonal stone banqueting house overlooking the lake.

Elizabeth climbed a spiral staircase past luxuriously fur-
nished rooms and emerged on to the roof, where there was a
red-marble table set with platters of sweets and blue-glass

flagons full of wine. Musicians entertained them until darkness fell. Geysers of white light erupted from fountains of fire beautifully reflected in the lake and exploded high into the impenetrable blackness. Accompanied by fanfares and cannon-fire, great fire-wheels span into life, and huge mortars were launched. The explosions shook the castle. Three enormous sprays of fireworks filled the heavens. When the smoke had at last cleared, a final set of fireworks detonated in furious blasts of light. It was as if the stars were falling out of the sky.

A few days later, Elizabeth summoned the French ambassador and told him that she could not marry the Duke of Alençon. It was a great victory for Dudley and for Kenilworth.

The court moved on to the palace of Woodstock, in Oxford-shire (later the site of Blenheim Palace). While Elizabeth was hunting, news reached her of the massacre of St Bartholomew's Day, 24 August, in Paris. More than three thousand Protestants had been killed by royalist forces; within a few days, the death toll rose to ten thousand. Cecil called it the most terrible crime since the Crucifixion.

At the beginning of the summer, there had still been a chance that Elizabeth would accept Alençon. So Dudley had pretended to help the French and had even suggested that, after the marriage, they could reward him by setting him up with an eligible French lady.

After St Bartholomew's Day, it seemed that relations between the English and the French would never recover. For the first time ever, Dudley was Elizabeth's only suitor. In recent years, his attempts to persuade her to marry him had become little more than play-acting. But with him as her only lover, who could tell what would happen?

Kenilworth had worked its magic. When Elizabeth next came to stay, in 1575, Dudley would throw the party of the century for her. The festivities would be sensational and the fireworks unforgettable. Understanding her as well as he did, he knew that she had an uncommon love of gardens. So he set about transforming Kenilworth and its landscape in amazing new ways.

3

'I covet three or four [days] here for myself at my house
at Theobalds'

Woodcut from Thomas Hill's *Gardener's Labyrinth*, 1577

A Leave of Absence

THREE YEARS LATER, in 1575, Cecil was walking in the long avenue in his garden at Theobalds Palace when his secretary brought him two letters. The secretary set a stool beneath the canopy of a young elm tree. The delicate leaves appeared translucent in the sunlight. On a lovely May morning, it was very pleasant to sit there, listening to the birds, looking at the wild flowers and taking in the scents of the herbs.

The first letter was from Dudley, thanking him 'very heartily that your Lordship is pleased to help me that I may have some stone toward the making of a little banqueting house in my garden'. Cecil had instructed his architect, Henry Hawthorne, to send Dudley some stone from Theobalds.

Dudley's new banqueting house was going up in the southeastern corner of his London garden on the Strand, near the river. He hinted that it would be a modest building compared with Cecil's magnificent palace and sumptuous pavilions. But Cecil knew that Dudley had other plans.

The second letter was a note from the Secretary of State, Sir Francis Walsingham. Elizabeth had granted Cecil permission to stay on at Theobalds for a while. Her summer progress had already begun – Theobalds had been one of the first visits.

Elizabeth's progresses lasted much longer than those of earlier kings and queens. This year, she had left London in May and would return to Windsor in October. She often made two progresses a year: a short tour in spring, followed by a long summer expedition. More than any previous monarch, she loved to meet her people, often leaving her carriage to walk amongst them, making herself even more popular.

Each year, her courtiers anxiously awaited news of the 'gites' (the houses where she and the entire court would stay, for as little as one night or as long as three weeks). While they had a good idea of which counties she would visit, often the list of places where she would stay was not fixed until a few weeks beforehand. The tour was an opportunity for her courtiers, local politicians and townsmen to present her with petitions and win favour. In return, she expected to be fêted with lavish hospitality in magnificent surroundings.

Theobalds Palace had won Cecil a reputation as one of the country's greatest builders. But getting it ready for the royal visit had been a struggle. Even now, he had no time to rest. Tomorrow, he was going to London to attend to some business at the Royal Exchequer which would take a few days.

Elizabeth had been expecting him to join her in the Midlands as soon as possible. Cecil had suggested to Walsingham that for the time being he could be of more use to her at Theobalds. A leave of absence would give him a chance to make some improvements to his house and its grounds, if he could find the money. As he had admitted, however, his motives were not entirely selfless:

I covet three or four [days] here for myself at my house at Theobalds,

30

where, though my wife and children are, yet have I not been but two nights since her Majesty went from there, a hard case to bridle my desire.

Cecil's 'desire' for his wife – and Theobalds – won him a holiday, but it was a dangerous strategy to deploy. Elizabeth was bound to become jealous.

Cecil was right to be suspicious about Dudley's motives for asking him for help with his banqueting house. Earlier in the year, Dudley had written to Elizabeth, urging her to spend as much time outside as possible for the sake of her health:

So good a medicine I have always found exercise with the open good air as it hath ever been my best remedy against those delicate diseases gotten about your dainty city of London, which place but for necessity Lord he knoweth how sorry I am to see your Majesty remain, being persuaded it is a piece of the sacrifice you do for your people's sake.

A few weeks later, he had repeated his advice in a letter about arrangements for the progress. He had been overseeing the renovations to her palace at Grafton, in Northamptonshire, and had assured her that they would be finished by the end of May (he would welcome her there, as her host, in June):

Meanwhile, other good places shall see you, which if they could speak, would show how sorry they are that you have been so long from them.

Before the summer was over, he planned to show the world that the place that was most devoted to her was Kenilworth. In preparation for her visit, he had expanded the magnificent hunting park, and within the castle walls there would soon be new walks, gardens and courtyards.

Cecil disapproved of Dudley's spendthrift habits and, as Treasurer, resented his eagerness to lure Elizabeth on long and costly journeys to lavish palaces. Two years earlier, compiling the royal accounts, Cecil had warned of the 'increase of charges in the time of progress' to the extent of £1,034, 'which should not be if her Majesty remained at her standing houses 20 miles of London'. Elizabeth's nearby 'standing houses' included royal palaces such as Greenwich and Richmond as well as Cecil's Theobalds; his proposed twenty-mile limit would put Grafton and Kenilworth out of reach.

At the end of June, Cecil was still at Theobalds, where Dudley wrote to him from Grafton. All was going well, and Elizabeth was in good health:

And for her liking of this house, I assure your Lordship I think she never came to place in her life she liked better, or commended more; and since her coming hither, as oft as weather serves, she has not been within doors.

Dudley had charmed Elizabeth with his garden and park at Grafton. She was hunting twice a day.

But, on their arrival, there had been a near-disaster. It had been a scorchingly hot day, and there had been no decent drink available:

But we were fain to send to London with bottles, to Kenilworth, to divers other places where ale was. Her own here was such, as there was no man able to drink it; it had been as good to have drunk malmsey [a strong sweet wine]; and yet was it laid in about three days before her Majesty came. It did put her very far out of temper, and almost all the company beside so: for none of us was able to drink either beer or ale here.

Luckily, Dudley had managed to get hold of some new supplies.

There was just a week to go before Elizabeth came to Kenilworth, where the festivities would be the culmination of his life's work. His steward had personally supervised all the arrangements, down to the last detail. Everything was in place.

In the peace and tranquillity of Theobalds, Cecil had been making his own meticulous preparations. For some time now, he had been gathering intelligence about every aspect of Dudley's activities – from his household expenses to his improvements to the castle and its grounds. Cecil's spies had sent him profiles of Dudley's servants and close friends and had supplied details of the guest list and programme of events at Kenilworth. Judging by this information, the entertainments would be phenomenal.

Cecil was determined to turn the tables on his rival. If all went well, he alone would profit from the royal visit. He was planning to join Elizabeth on the day of her arrival at the castle. That way, he would gain the advantage of surprise.

4

'The Queen's Majesty thanks be to God is in very good health
and is now become a great huntress'

Elizabeth being offered the hunting knife, from George Turberville's
Noble Arte of Venerie or Hunting, 1575

Rivals

WHEN DUDLEY HAD asked Cecil for help with his London banqueting house that May of 1575, he had hoped to divert attention from his more exciting projects at Grafton and Kenilworth. Later that month, his friend Henry Killigrew had written to tell him that he had commissioned a master craftsman to create a new fountain for the garden at Kenilworth. Killigrew had reported that the craftsman intended to present to the Queen 'a singular piece of work whereof the like was never seen in these parts'. Kenilworth would have the first authentically Italian fountain in England.

The Italian's fee was £50 – the fountain alone cost £7. The rest of the money was for more novelties for the garden and landscape and for the fireworks. Killigrew had enclosed the man's outline for the display, which promised many 'wonderful and pleasing things . . . worth seeing' for their 'marvellous fireworks'.

Renaissance Italy had the most advanced gardens in the world. The grounds of Italian palaces displayed statues from antiquity side by side with new masterpieces by sculptors such as Michelangelo, and medieval emblems were recast in a modern and often humorous way. There were fountains in the shape of gods, goddesses and mythical creatures, which demonstrated their art together with the ability of Italian engineers to harness the forces of nature and the power of their patrons.

Gardens were laid out on different levels so as to expand space and intensify depth, increasing the impact of the fountains and the geometrical patterns of compartments and paths. Unlike the enclosed retreats of the Middle Ages, these gardens were open; many were constructed on hillsides by means of terraces, maximising views of the wider landscape.

The concept of the garden designer as architect and engineer originated in Italy; in the case of the gardens of the Villa d'Este, the designer, Pirro Ligorio, was also an archaeologist inspired by the remains of Roman pleasure grounds and a scholar of classical literature and mythology.

Dudley's love of Italy gave him a huge advantage over Cecil. Although Cecil admired classical architecture, he secretly despised modern Italy. In 1564, he had written with advice to his eldest son Thomas, on the occasion of his marriage, warning him never to let his sons 'pass the Alps, for they shall learn nothing there but pride, blasphemy and atheism'. Nor should they set much value on learning languages:

And if by travel they get a few broken languages, that shall profit them nothing more than to have one meat served in diverse dishes.

While Cecil vetoed Italy for his grandsons, Elizabeth and Dudley created a cosmopolitan culture at court. Foreign visitors were welcome, and a knowledge of modern languages, especially Italian, could do a lot for a courtier. Dudley's circle included many Italian exiles: merchants, writers, translators, engineers, doctors, sculptors, pyrotechnicians, garden designers and painters.

His close friends, like Lord North, also became aficionados of all things Italian.

Dudley had secured places for his new allies at court. Giovanni Battista Castiglione had become Elizabeth's Italian tutor and a Groom of the Presence Chamber, and Giulio Borgarucci had been appointed her physician. Dudley had also gained commissions for the distinguished military engineer Giacomo Concio and had become a close confederate of financier Benedict Spinola, who had a famous pleasure garden on Bishopsgate Street, describing him in a letter to Walsingham in 1572 as 'my dear friend and the best Italian I know in England'.

As Master of the Horse, Dudley had invited the Neapolitan horse trainers Claudio Corte and Prospero d'Osma to England. D'Osma had founded a school of manège at Mile End and had carried out an investigation into the royal studs, suggesting improvements. In his love of horses, Dudley was his father's son. Northumberland's superb ability in martial sports had delighted Henry VIII, who had made him Master of the Horse to Anne of Cleves, Master of the Tower Armoury and Lord High Admiral; Northumberland had become the greatest soldier of his age, famous for his naval victories against France.

Dudley had also inherited from his father a love of classical and Italian Renaissance architecture: Northumberland had financed artist and architect John Shute's travels in Italy, commissioning him to write the first book on classical architecture published in England, *The First and Chief Grounds of Architecture* (1563). In 1550, the year that Cecil had become Elizabeth's surveyor, Dudley had impressed her with his talent for interior design, when his father had put him in charge of refitting the classical-style palace Somerset House for her (he had spent the princely sum of £900). His library at Leicester House would include works in Italian by Machiavelli, scholar and poet Trissino and humanist historian Sabellico.

In the spirit of the times, Dudley combined his love of architecture with a delight in creating gardens. When Elizabeth had given him a house on the river at Kew, shortly after becoming queen, he had wasted no time in hiring a French gardener to redesign the garden and had taken advice from Cecil's gardener at Wimbledon and the Royal Gardener at Whitehall. Dudley's rooms at court were always filled with flowers, herbs and boughs.

By the 1570s, Dudley knew that the gardens of France, which had long set the fashion, could not compare with those of Italy. No longer the champion of the tilt-yard, he needed a new arena (since his unofficial retirement, jousting had gone into such a decline that Elizabeth had called on her younger courtiers to revive the tournament which had 'of late fallen asleep'). In his spacious and luxurious garden at his riverside house on the Strand, there was an orchard, a banqueting house, a tennis court and a distilling house for making perfumes and herbal remedies; he now added an Italianate terrace. Elizabeth was a frequent visitor.

When Elizabeth went hunting, Dudley gave extravagant outdoor feasts and commissioned celebratory engravings of them. He entertained her most important guests, mainly French aristocrats and diplomats, with lavish banquets and masques which took place alfresco in the royal parks and gardens and on the terraces of Windsor and Whitehall. It was impossible to compete with him, so Cecil had resorted to underhand ways of making gardens further his own interests.

[5]

'Then she entered in to discern whether my queen's hair or hers
was the best; and which of them two was fairest'

Elizabeth encircled by Tudor roses and eglantine, wood engraving, 1588

From Princess to Queen

IN THE FIRST SPRING of her reign, in 1559, Elizabeth commissioned her gardeners to create a new orchard at Whitehall. The orchard lay to the south of the main garden, which she also remodelled as her private garden. In the late 1560s, she laid out a knot garden and private walk at Hampton Court. To enhance the pleasure of looking at the garden, a bay window was built into her bedroom wall.

The geometrical patterns of Tudor knot gardens, made up of interlacing bands of hyssop and thyme enclosing flowers such as violets, marigolds or pinks, were best seen from above, where, as gardening expert Thomas Hill commented, they gave 'comfort and delight' to the viewer's 'wearied mind'. Hill added that a knot garden should 'give such grace to the garden, that the place will seem like a tapestry of flowers'.

Elizabeth's bay window still survives. Carved into one of its stone facings are her initials and the date that it was made: 'ER 1568'. By that time, the knot, symbol of love and devotion, had become one of her emblems: that year, her Champion, Sir Henry Lee, had his portrait painted wearing a black-and-white shirt (her colours) with a pattern of true love knots and armillary spheres (another of her emblems, representing the universe).

By 1575, gardens and architecture were the best way to impress the Queen. Although she commissioned no new palaces and only a few gardens, Elizabeth loved her courtiers to create them for her. Her love of gardens and nature was lifelong: as a girl, she took long walks in gardens and showed an unusual appreciation of plants. On her extensive progresses, she especially enjoyed visiting courtiers who had wonderful pleasure grounds.

Elizabeth's childhood home was Hatfield, but she occasionally visited her father at Hampton Court. The Great Garden at Hampton Court was a mesmerising place. From the first-floor windows of the palace, it resembled a giant chessboard, with alternating green, red and gold squares made of grass, brick-dust and sand. There were about twenty golden sundials placed at intervals along paths lined with over a hundred green-and-white poles bearing brightly coloured and gilded kings' and queens' beasts, a few feet tall and carved out of wood, holding colourful metal flags. Green and white were the Tudor colours, and the myriad beasts, including greyhounds, leopards, panthers, griffins and unicorns, represented the great families of England converging in the Tudor dynasty.

Banqueting houses with battlements and turrets lined an avenue that led from the palace to the watergate. The most innovative building in the pleasure grounds was Henry VIII's Great Round Arbour, or Tower of Babylon: a three-storey pavilion made almost entirely of glass and crowned with a gilded, onion-shaped dome. This pavilion stood on a small hill planted with holly, pear trees and service trees. A cockleshell path lined with rosemary and stone kings' and queens' beasts spiralled up to the top, where there were stunning views of the gardens, the park and the river. There was impressive topiary: centaurs, sirens and serving maids with baskets adorned the gardens, while in the park topiary hounds chased hares which were so lifelike that, from a distance, visitors thought they were real. A raised walkway led from the glass pavilion to the watergate, a two-storey building with a gallery, where important guests were welcomed with grand receptions.

Until his creation of the pleasure grounds at Hampton Court, Henry had not paid much attention to gardens: he had been more interested in staging glittering contests in the tilt-yard. But he had famously competed against the French king François I, and it was this rivalry that led to his change of heart. On the Field of the Cloth of Gold, in 1520, Henry and François had vied with each other in everything from jousting to pavilion design – at Henry's headquarters, there had been a makeshift fairy-tale palace and an elaborate fountain which had spouted wine.

So when the French king dazzled Europe with his extravagant programme of building and garden design, seen to best effect at Fontainebleau – with its spectacular trapezoid lake and formal gardens designed by Italian artists and architects, featuring a grotto and a statue of Hercules by Michelangelo – Henry took up the challenge. His new garden at Hampton Court aptly resembled a chessboard: Henry and François can well be imagined as garden grandmasters.

Although the garden was Henry's counter-attack against François's Italianate pleasure grounds, it was not particularly

Italian. Cardinal Wolsey had made a few Italianate additions to the palace (the roundels in the courtyards carved by Italian stonemasons still survive), but the garden was a strange mixture of English heraldry and French design. The dazzling rows of beasts took centre stage, and Henry's shimmering squares in a grid were a simplified version of French flower beds enclosing geometrical patterns – his gardener was a French priest. The pleasure grounds, though bizarre, must have been immensely impressive, especially to a child. Henry's bestial army would have been a formidable sight.

The Great Garden was a symbol of power, but Henry had originally created it as a present for his fiancée Anne Boleyn. It was decorated with true love knots which entwined their initials: a honeymooners' paradise. Anne's leopards stood on the posts, but would be re-carved to make the unicorns and panthers of Jane Seymour (today, a single leopard survives on a hard-to-reach corner-turret of the Great Hall). There were also carvings of Anne's other emblem, the crowned white falcon.

In Elizabeth's reign, the garden at Hampton Court continued to be a place of romance. Elizabeth met her first royal suitor there – in secret. The Earl of Arran (heir to the Scottish throne if Mary, Queen of Scots died childless) was Cecil's choice. Cecil sent his spies to France to help Arran escape from prison and brought him to England. In September 1559, Cecil and Arran arrived at Hampton Court by barge and entered the garden via the water-gate. Although the meeting with Elizabeth was not a success, the garden emerged as the perfect place for secret assignations. It was where Cecil arranged for Elizabeth to see foreign diplomats early in the morning – it would be another twenty years before her next official meeting with a royal suitor in a garden. In the afternoons and evenings, she rendezvoused there with Dudley.

Cecil was behind a second secret meeting about a royal marriage in the grounds of Hampton Court. In 1564, he arranged for Elizabeth to meet James Melville, the agent of her cousin Mary, Queen of Scots, in one of the avenues in the garden to discuss a match between Mary and Dudley. In return for agreeing to the proposal, Mary hoped to gain Elizabeth's recognition of her place in the succession. But Elizabeth was just playing along – she was still set against Dudley marrying anyone but herself. And she had used the marriage plans as an excuse to grant Kenilworth to Dudley: in order to wed Mary, he needed a castle fit for a king.

Although doomed from the start, the clandestine negotiations could have rid Cecil of the two major threats to his position: Dudley and Mary, who, as a successor to Elizabeth, would restore England to Catholicism. Like Norfolk before him, Dudley had already secretly made overtures to Mary and planned to marry her (whoever succeeded in winning her hand could one day lay claim to the crowns of both Scotland and England). Cecil hoped to expose him.

Dudley was godfather to the son of the ambassador to Scotland, Sir Nicholas Throckmorton, who had briefed Mary's agent Melville on 'how to proceed with the Queen and every courtier in particular'. A former friend of Cecil who had switched allegiance to Dudley, Throckmorton resented both men for having ensured his transfer from Paris to Scotland against his wishes. In his advice to Melville, Throckmorton had acknowledged their power: 'Albeit he had no liking for the time either of my Lord

Robert or of Master Cecil, yet he knew that then nothing could be done without them.'

Dudley believed that he could count on Melville as an ally and sent his servant to Melville's lodging early in the morning on the first day of his stay at Hampton Court to bring him to the Queen, who was waiting for him in the garden. The servant had brought Melville a gift from Dudley: a horse and a velvet riding mantle laced with gold. All the while that Melville was at court, Dudley's servant waited on him with the horse, and, by means of this ploy, listened in on his conversations with Elizabeth, relaying them to his master.

Elizabeth was charmed by Melville and met with him several times a day. He soon discovered, however, that she was interested in talking to him about almost anything but the proposed match between Mary and Dudley. In one of their conversations, they discussed the different fashions he had seen on his travels, and she revealed that she had clothes cut in the style of every country in Europe. Each day for the remainder of Melville's stay, Elizabeth changed her dress, one day wearing English clothes, the next French, then Italian, German and Polish. When she asked him 'which of them became her best', he answered, 'The Italian dress.' Since the queen 'delighted to show her golden-coloured hair, wearing a caul and bonnet as they do in Italy', as he later reflected in his journal, this was the correct answer. Elizabeth then teased Melville by entering his chamber with another set of questions, 'whether my queen's hair or hers was best, and which of them two was fairest', before interrogating him about Mary's looks, diet, exercise regime, and musical and dancing skills.

*

48

Over 250 years later, Sir Walter Scott would mention in his journal a telling moment in this exchange:

Queen Bess, when questioning Melville sharply and closely whether Queen [Mary was] taller than her, and, extracting an answer in the affirmative, she replied, 'Then your Queen is too tall for I am just the proper height.'

When Melville decided to leave early, Elizabeth reproached him, saying that he was weary sooner of her company than she was of his, and joked that he had to stay for a few more days to see her dance. He agreed to extend his visit to witness the ceremony in which she would make Dudley Earl of Leicester: as with Kenilworth, the official purpose was to make him a fit husband for Mary.

The ceremony took place in the Presence Chamber at Whitehall, and Melville remarked on the 'great solemnity' of the occasion and Dudley's 'great gravity and discreet behaviour'. Cecil escorted Dudley up to the platform, where he knelt before Elizabeth. But as she fastened the ermine-lined mantle around his shoulders, she tickled his neck, in full view of everyone. Melville commented that she did this 'smilingly, the French ambassador and I standing by'. The audience also included Darnley, Lady Lennox's good-looking son. Towards the end of the ceremony, in conversation with Melville, Elizabeth hinted at her knowledge of Mary's desire to marry Darnley.

Melville's *Memoirs* reveal the hostility between Cecil and Dudley. When Melville finally left Hampton Court, Dudley accompanied him to London on his barge and confided that the match had been the work of his 'Mr Cecil, his secret enemy'. Dudley added that, if he had seemed at all interested, he would have lost 'the favour of both the queens'. Cecil's attempt to trap Dudley had failed, but he still gave Melville a grand send-off from his 'palace', as Melville described it, on the Strand.

We also discover from this strange episode a practical side to Elizabeth's love of gardens. Melville's first encounter with her took place at eight o'clock in the morning in the garden because, apart from its advantages as a place to meet in secret, this was where, as she said, she walked to 'catch her a heat in the cold mornings'. Melville was struck by how briskly she walked in the morning, compared with later in the day, when 'she who was the very image of majesty and magnificence, went slowly and marched with leisure'. Elizabeth's habit of walking several times a day for exercise and pleasure was something that resourceful courtiers like Cecil and Dudley would exploit to the full.

But, as her confidant, Dudley was the first to recognise the hold that gardens and flowers had on Elizabeth: her memories of her early life were full of them.

As a princess, Elizabeth's love of flowers and their meanings found expression in embroidery. Like many of her contemporaries, she set great store by the language of flowers. Her New Year's presents for her father and stepmother Katherine Parr were her own translations of religious works, specially bound and decorated with embroidery, including 'hearteases' in violet, yellow and green silk (wild pansies – *viola tricolor* – also known as 'pensées', meaning 'thoughts': as a gift from a friend or lover, they meant 'think of me' or 'you are in my thoughts'), forget-me-nots (true love and affection), Tudor roses and Henry's and Katherine's initials, HR and KP, in a gold-and-silver true love knot.

Henry's death in 1547 left Elizabeth vulnerable to her stepmother and to the Lord Admiral Thomas Seymour. Tall and handsome, Seymour had been the idol of the court and one of Henry's favourites. Henry's generous gifts of monastic lands had made him rich, and he had become one of the court's biggest gamblers. But his dalliance with Katherine Parr had resulted in Henry's sending him to the Netherlands to make way for his own courtship.

Seymour was the younger brother of Lord Somerset, regent to Elizabeth's half-brother, the young King Edward VI. Their sister had been Henry's third wife, Jane Seymour – Edward's mother. With his brother in power as regent, though, Seymour could only rise so far.

After Henry's death, the thirty-eight-year-old Seymour was free to marry Katherine; however, his first choice was Elizabeth, then fourteen. When he secretly wrote to ask for her hand in marriage, she reproached him for his hastiness: 'I can never have believed that anyone can have spoken to me of nuptials, at a time when I ought to think nothing but sorrow for the death of my father.' At the same time, she assured him that there was no one 'who sees you with more pleasure'. Yet they could not marry without the consent of the Privy Council, which was controlled by Somerset, who would never approve of the match.

Seymour then secretly revived his love affair with Katherine, who was living with Elizabeth at Chelsea Palace, situated by the Thames. Stretching to the north and the east were beautiful gardens, with pools, and planted with cherry trees, damask roses and lavender. It was Katherine's favourite residence: as she put it, 'Weeks are shorter at Chelsea than in other places.' Seymour slipped in and out through the back gate of the gardens at Chelsea late at night and early in the morning. Elizabeth was one of the few observers. He married Katherine in a clandestine ceremony in May 1547, just a few months after Henry's death. In retaliation, Somerset seized the jewels that Henry had left Katherine in his will.

Despite his marriage to Katherine, Seymour continued to flirt with Elizabeth. At Chelsea, he let himself into her room early in the morning, and, at night, she joined him on his barge on the Thames. At his town house, Seymour Place, he appeared at her door every morning, wearing only his nightgown and slippers.

In addition to Chelsea, Henry had left Katherine the royal manors of Wimbledon and Hanworth, in Middlesex. Hanworth was a moated manor house, with bridges leading to a garden famous for its strawberries. There were pools, an aviary and a well-stocked orchard backing on to the hunting park which had made it one of Henry's favourite manors.

At Hanworth, on two occasions, Katherine accompanied Seymour to Elizabeth's room, and they both tickled her in her bed. When Elizabeth's governess challenged Katherine about Seymour's behaviour, Katherine made light of it.

Shortly afterwards, Seymour's sexual advances culminated in a terrifying scene in the garden. He romped with Elizabeth, while Katherine stood near by, and then Katherine held Elizabeth while he cut her dress into tiny pieces.

Elizabeth ran to the house and, coming up the stairs, met her governess, who scolded her for being 'so trimmed', asking, 'What have you done to your gown?'

Elizabeth answered, 'I could not do with all', meaning that she could not struggle against both of her step-parents: 'The Queen held me while my Lord did so dress it.' Not long afterwards, Katherine sent Elizabeth away to Cheshunt, in Hertfordshire – close to where Cecil would build Theobalds Palace. Gardens were entrancing but potentially dangerous places.

Tragedy followed separation: Katherine died soon after giving birth to her first child, and Seymour was executed for treason – he was accused of planning to marry Elizabeth, in defiance of the Council, and conspiring against the life of King Edward.

Although Somerset had orchestrated Seymour's death, Elizabeth sought his protection and visited him at Syon House, by the Thames. Somerset's physician and gardener was the great William Turner, who had studied medicine and herbalism in Italy and Germany. The garden at Syon was celebrated for its rare plants, including pomegranates, figs, almonds, apricots and black mulberries grown against south-facing brick walls.

In 1551, Turner dedicated his *New Herbal* to Elizabeth: it was the first herbal written in English, with records of 238 native plants, the result of his many travels all over England. In his preface, he mentioned his conversations with Elizabeth, which they had conducted in Latin, and defended his decision to dedicate his herbal to her against possible suggestions that 'a book of weeds or grass (as some will call precious herbs) is a right unmeet [unsuitable] gift for such a Prince'. His dedication revealed both Elizabeth's unusual interest in botany and her increasing prestige. Somerset's secretary, at the time, was none other than Cecil, who, like Elizabeth, must have been impressed by the garden and gardener at Syon House.

It is no accident that some of the most successful gardeners of her reign were trained herbalists. Herbal cures fascinated Elizabeth – she took after her father, who had his own collection of herbal potions. Elizabeth once sent her tonic for heart and brain to the Emperor Rudolf II: it contained amber, musk, and civet dissolved in a spirit of roses. She was fiercely opposed to physic (more akin to what we would now call conventional medicine), refusing to take it even when close to death. This gave her something in common with her people, most of whom relied on herbal remedies, if only because English physicians charged the highest fees in Europe.

In 1581, Elizabeth intervened in a dispute between the Royal College of Physicians and a poor woman apothecary. In their attempt to gain a monopoly on herbal medicine, the physicians had ruled that no one except members of the Royal College could practise it. They wrote to Elizabeth to complain about an illegal apothecary, 'one Margaret Kennix, an outlandish, ignorant, sorry woman', who had been supplying her friends and neighbours with herbal remedies. Elizabeth astonished them by defending her, in a letter written by Walsingham:

It is her Majesty's pleasure that the poor woman should be permitted by you quietly to practise and minister to the curing of diseases and wounds, by the means of certain simples [medicinal plants], in the application whereof it seems God hath given her an especial knowledge. I shall therefore desire you to take order amongst yourselves for the readmitting of her into the quiet exercise of her small talent, lest by the renewing of her complaint to her Majesty through your hard dealing towards her, you procure further inconvenience thereby to your selves.

In their reply, the physicians drew Elizabeth's attention to the dangers of letting unlicensed practitioners dispense remedies to patients. In their view, she was setting a dangerous precedent. But they took her warning seriously, and Margaret Kennix was allowed to continue with her practice.

During her imprisonment in the Tower by her half-sister Mary, in the wake of the Wyatt rebellion in 1554, Elizabeth fell ill and asked to be allowed into the garden to 'take the air'. While she was in the garden, security measures were doubled: all the shutters that looked towards the garden were closed, and strict instructions were given that no other prisoner should look in her direction.

At the time, Dudley was also in the Tower, with his four brothers (after their father's failed coup against Mary), and was allowed to take exercise by 'walking the leads' on the Tower ramparts – although unlikely, it is possible that he caught a glimpse of Elizabeth in the garden, despite the strict security.

In their room in the Beauchamp Tower, the Dudley brothers left a record of their imprisonment which can still be seen today. On the wall to the right of the fireplace, Dudley's eldest brother John employed one of their servants to carve their family emblems: the bear and ragged staff (badge of the Earls of Warwick, showing the ragged staff as the stake to which baited bears were tethered) and the double-tailed lion of the Dudleys.

Below these heraldic beasts, John Dudley's name appears in capital letters, with a poem in the form of a riddle about the names of his four brothers:

> You that these beasts do well behold and see
> May deem with ease wherefore here made they be
> With borders eke wherein [there may be found]
> Four brothers names who list to search the ground.

The borders of the carving are filled with flowers, leaves and acorns which pun on each brother's name: roses for Ambrose; honeysuckle for Henry; oak leaves and acorns for Robert (a pun on the Latin *robur*, meaning 'oak') and gillyflowers (pinks) for Guildford. In the wainscot to the right of the window, which looked down on to the scaffold on Tower Green, Dudley carved his emblems a second time. In the middle of other prisoners' names, there is a small, clearly carved oak branch, with leaves and acorns, and his initials 'RD'. As a third record of his time in the Tower, on a wall in the room below, he carved his name in faint, slanting capitals: this last record looks as if it was carved in haste.

Although Elizabeth was supposed to be alone in the garden at the Tower, a five-year-old boy, the son of a warder, brought her flowers. Afterwards, the Lord Chamberlain questioned the boy and banned him from meeting her, but he returned to the garden the next day. Although the gate was locked, he could see Elizabeth through a hole in it and called, 'Mistress, I can bring you no more flowers.' This episode signalled her popularity and her innocence: as the Catholic Emperor's informant reported, 'The lawyers can find no matter for her condemnation. Already she has the liberty to walk in the Tower garden.'

Elizabeth left the Tower in May, only to be placed under house arrest first at Woodstock and, later, at Hatfield. At Woodstock, she asked her guard, Sir Henry Bedingfield, for permission to take exercise in the garden. He granted it but insisted on accompanying her, opening and locking the six garden gates. As he was locking one of them, she called him her 'gaoler'. He fell to his knees and begged her not to call him 'that harsh name', saying that he was only there to protect her since her enemies had hired assassins to murder her.

On the window in her room at Woodstock, she famously carved, with a diamond ring,

> Much suspected by me,
> Nothing proved can be,
> *Quod* Elizabeth the prisoner

Watching milkmaids from this window, she envied them their freedom. Walking in the garden, she heard one of them singing and told Bedingfield that she wished she could change places with her.

*

When the Swiss tourist Thomas Platter visited Woodstock in 1599, the keeper told him about Elizabeth's return visit to the palace in 1592. During her stay, she had wept on remembering that, as a prisoner there, she had not even been allowed to walk in the garden:

The overseer of the residence told us that when the Queen was last at Woodstock . . . with tears in her eyes she related how strict they had been then, allowing her neither paper nor ink. And when she entered the garden she wept again, and told how the gardener's boy had often brought her flowers from the garden to her prison, and how this was immediately forbidden him although he was only an innocent child.

The keeper's anecdote gives the impression that, on her return to Woodstock thirty-eight years after her imprisonment, her memories of that time had been as vivid as ever.

It would seem, however, that over the years the stories about Elizabeth in the gardens at the Tower and at Woodstock became blurred. After his tour of the palace at Woodstock, Platter was taken around the grounds by the gardener, who repeated the keeper's tale about how 'the gardener's boy' had given Elizabeth flowers. As far as we know, a warder's son brought her flowers in the garden at the Tower, not at Woodstock, although something similar could have happened at both places. Whatever happened, the stories about her in these gardens had become legends in her own lifetime.

[6]

'As soon as he is seen anywhere, they say I am at hand'

Antoine Caron, court ball and the gardens of the Tuileries, 1573

Deep Desire

DEEP IN THE Kenilworth woods, the men were making arched bowers out of willow branches. They were surrounded by a circle of hawthorn bushes. It was three in the afternoon. The last two bowers under construction were different from anything they had seen before. Instead of the usual vines and roses, the frames supported a laurel tree and a holly bush. Binding the holly to the frame was the unenviable task of the head gardener and his son: they were under instructions to take special care with this bower.

The way-maker and his team of labourers were sweltering in the heat on the dusty highway. After the Queen's last visit three years before, in 1572, the approach routes to the castle had fallen into disrepair. They had filled in the potholes and relaid and levelled the surfaces, making the highways nearly as smooth as glass.

At the southern gate, carpenters were nailing together planks of wood to make platforms, which they lowered on to the lake. Actors stepped on board and recited long speeches to their manager, who stood in the middle of a bridge. Musicians rehearsed in rowing boats which circled the floating stages. Acrobats performed somersaults on the paths in the garden, and, in the Great Hall, costumiers sheared through reams of blue silk to make long, flowing robes for the performers.

A clockmaker stood at the top of a tall ladder to reach a gold-and-blue-enamelled clock on a turret of the keep. He was moving the hands so that they pointed to exactly two o'clock. The dial faced towards the town. There was an identical dial on the same turret, facing the inner court. It told the same time. The clockmaker climbed down and checked his work. No sign of any movement. Both clocks had stopped.

During the royal visit, time stood still – a tribute to Elizabeth's magical presence, as well as Dudley's talents as a host. Two o'clock was when people usually dined, so at Kenilworth it was always the most hospitable hour of the day. There was gossip that Dudley's choice of hour hinted at his desire to wed Elizabeth (taking 'two' to mean 'couple').

Fourteen earls and seventeen barons were staying at the castle, as well as privy councillors and foreign ambassadors. Great tents had been erected in the grounds for the lesser courtiers. The remaining members of the royal household had been assigned lodgings in Warwick.

For a few weeks at Kenilworth, fortunes would be won or lost, depending on the favour of the Queen.

⁂

On Saturday 9 July 1575, the royal progress stopped at Long Itchington, about seven miles from Kenilworth. Dudley led Elizabeth inside a vast tent decorated with colourful streamers, flags and banners, where they dined. He showed her one of nature's marvels: a six-year-old boy who was four feet four inches tall (a prodigious height for his age). Afterwards, Dudley and Elizabeth went hunting. It was about eight o'clock by the time the royal convoy reached Kenilworth.

The procession entered the castle grounds from the south.

The courtiers were kept guessing, again. No one could tell why they were heading for the old gates, instead of the modern northern entrance.

In the park, a short distance from the castle, a sibyl dressed in white silk stepped out of a bower and hailed Elizabeth with 'You shall be called the Prince of Peace'. By associating her with Christ, the sibyl hinted at miracles yet to come, during her stay. She also assured Elizabeth that, while she was at Kenilworth,

> Nothing shall rest unsought
> That may bring pleasure to your mind,
> Or quiet to your thought.

But at the gate to the tilt-yard, Elizabeth met Hercules, the porter – a towering figure, wielding an enormous club. Instead of welcoming her, he started ranting about the noise and commotion (Dudley had set this up, as a joke). Hercules claimed that he had never seen or heard anything like it. There were hundreds of guests, but no one had given him a hint of warning. As he came closer, however, he saw Elizabeth and realised who she was. Mortified, he laid his club at her feet, as a sign of submission, offered her his keys of office and begged her pardon. She graciously forgave him.

Hercules called on his 'harmonious blasters' to sound a welcome. Elizabeth and her courtiers looked up to see six eight-foot-tall musicians with five-foot-long trumpets behind the battlements. Everything at Kenilworth was larger-than-life – as she would discover, Hercules and his trumpeters on stilts, with their outsize trumpets, were the signs that she was stepping into the heroic world.

As Elizabeth rode through the tilt-yard towards the castle's inner gate, the Lady of the Lake and her nymphs floated over on an island lit by torches to greet her. Dressed in silk, which heightened the dreamlike effect, the Lady of the Lake told her the history of the castle from its original ownership by 'great King Arthur' up to the present day. One implication was that Dudley was Arthur's heir and, also, a giant among men. Then the Lady made Elizabeth a present of the lake. Elizabeth thanked her but added, 'We had thought indeed the lake had been ours, and do you call it yours now? Well, we will herein commune more with you hereafter.'

The lake made a magnificent stage: at III acres, it was the largest artificial stretch of water in the country. An entire village had been evacuated to make way for it and now lay drowned in its depths. At Kenilworth, Dudley held the first marine entertainments of the age. By transforming the great lake into a colossal theatre, he fused the English tradition of seafaring with Continental water festivals based on the ancient Roman custom of flooding amphitheatres for mock naval battles.

Elizabeth passed through the inner gate to the sound of loud wind instruments and crossed a bridge that had been specially designed for her visit. The bridge had seven pairs of magical posts bearing gifts from the gods, including fruit from the nymph Pomona, wheat and barley from Ceres, armour and weapons from Mars, many different kinds of fish and waterfowl from Neptune and musical instruments from Apollo. What really captured her courtiers' attention was a post that sprouted glasses of red and white wine, gifts from Bacchus. The evening was so hot and the wine was 'so fresh of colour' and 'so lovely smiling', according to one observer, that they leered at it and imagined themselves kissing it. But there were just two glasses: one for Elizabeth and another for Dudley.

In the inner court, Dudley helped Elizabeth down from her palfrey and showed her up to her rooms. As she entered the royal suite, there was a round of gunfire and fireworks exploded above the castle.

On the next day, there was a lavish feast in the Great Hall. Elizabeth dined with Dudley in a private chamber with a magnificent oriel window, separated from the hall by a screen of giant obelisks. At the start of the feast, a servant dressed in blue silk placed an immense silver salt cellar in the shape of a ship in front of her.

Elizabeth's supper usually consisted of about twenty-four dishes for each course. At Kenilworth, there was so much variety that it seemed as if every kind of animal, bird and fish had been included. For the first course, there was sliced beef, sirloin steak, roast veal, lamb, wild boar, stag, buck, partridge, capon, pullet, roast and boiled mutton and chicken, gammon, cock, tongue and venison pies and pasties. The carvers served the guests according to their status, reserving the best cuts for Elizabeth and her favourites. Early in his career, Dudley had been a royal carver and, at Kenilworth, his men were masters of the Italian art of carving 'in the air': juggling slices of meat with incredible skill as part of the entertainment and ensuring that they made perfect landings on the right plates.

The second course consisted mainly of fish and fowl, some from the castle's great lake. The seafood included salmon, sturgeon, turbot, porpoise, anchovies, perch, dace, roach, cod, gudgeon, flounder, barbel, tench, pike, red herring, carp, lobster, crayfish, shrimp and oysters. The range of fowl was especially impressive: heron, crane, goose, swan, stork, peacock, pheasant, pigeon, baked lark, duck, duckling, turkey, plover, peewit, gull, bustard, lapwing, shoveler, woodcock, snipe, bittern, quail and curlew. There was also rabbit and a variety of tarts and fritters.

In a memorandum for the royal visit, Dudley had ordered 'wine of all sorts' from London and had specified that if 'the ale of the country' did not 'please the Queen's Majesty', it would have to be brought from London, or else a local brewer would need to be engaged to brew London ale. Elizabeth and her favourites drank wine from Venetian glasses etched with diamond patterns. Most of her courtiers and guests drank ale and beer – in enormous quantities (nearly three hundred hogsheads in just three days).

During the feast, two life-size portraits of Elizabeth and Dudley were unveiled. Dudley was shown in battle armour, but wearing a hat. His helmet and breastplate lay on the ground, and he had a relaxed but self-mocking expression. He still hoped to lead Elizabeth's armies in battle, but what chance was there, when she refused to let him fight? Later in the festivities, he planned to appear in a masque as Elizabeth's knight, rescuing the Lady of the Lake from a cruel suitor. His costume was a splendid new suit of armour decorated with ragged staffs. As fate would have it, however, the show would not be performed.

In her portrait, Elizabeth wore a diaphanous veil and a gossamer dress. She was smiling, as if sharing a private joke. In the background stood a column encircled by a snake (symbolising wisdom) and surmounted by an ermine and a little dog. Her emblems – the column, symbol of stability, and the ermine, representing purity – were well known. Only insiders could fully account for the presence of the dog, symbol of fidelity.

When Dudley had last asked for her permission to go to war, ten years earlier, she had refused, teasing him by saying that then she 'would be without a groom'. She had gone on to tell her courtiers: 'I cannot live without seeing him every day. He is like my lapdog – as soon as he is seen anywhere, they say I am at hand; and wherever I am seen, it may be said, that he is there also.' The painting of ermine and lapdog could be interpreted as showing Elizabeth and Dudley together, at the top of her world.

The two portraits were by Frederico Zuccaro, a famous painter whom Dudley had invited to England about four months before. Zuccaro had been recommended to Dudley by Chiappino Vitelli, Marquis of Cetona, a general in the Spanish army in the Netherlands. Vitelli had described Zuccaro as 'one of the most excellent and remarkable painters to be found in Italy'.

Elizabeth admired Italian painters. In conversation with Nicholas Hilliard, she remarked on their reputation as the best in the world. She added that she liked the way that they painted in 'the open light', so that there were no shadows – an iconic look that she chose for her own portraits. In his treatise on the art of painting miniatures, Hilliard mentions that she liked to sit for her portrait 'in an open alley of a goodly garden, where no tree was near nor any shadow at all'.

Apart from the advantages of the light, Hilliard recommended painting portraits in a garden because, as he wrote, 'sweet odours comfort the brain, and open the understanding, augmenting the delight' of the experience for painter and sitter. One of his miniatures of Elizabeth shows her looking radiant in the sunlight, gazing away from the viewer. The background is bright blue, like a cloudless summer sky. She wears a black dress with white sleeves embroidered with colourful flowers. A single white rose is pinned to her dress, while others adorn her hair.

What lies beyond Hilliard's spyglass boundaries is left to our imagination. Tantalisingly, the miniature may well be a painting of Elizabeth in a garden, although it is not shown. Possibly, Elizabeth is sitting in one of the broad alleys of a princely garden belonging to Dudley or Cecil, while musicians play to her to pass the time; near by, exotic flowers make intricate maze patterns and, beyond, arched arbours or close-clipped hedges interplanted with fruit trees lead to a fountain at the intersection of two paths.

❧

In the heat of the afternoon at Kenilworth, a huge pump sent up diamond drops of light which fell to the ground like fine rain. It took the strongest man at the castle to operate the pump, which stood in a tub near the entrance to the garden.

During the summer months, the most difficult task was keeping the garden watered. That year's drought had made the job harder than ever. And, as gardener Thomas Hill warned, mid-July was the worst of times:

The youngest of any discretion know that the beds chiefly require watering after a drought, or when many hot days have chanced together, as the like especially cometh to pass in the summer time, about the cosmic rising of the canicular or dog star (which with us commonly happeneth about the seventeenth day of July).

The dog star raged and the sun beat down mercilessly, but Dudley's men were equal to anything. There were sophisticated new techniques to cope with drought. Hill listed over ten different methods of irrigation, including Kenilworth's massive pump, which he called 'the great squirt'. He pointed out that the best location for a garden was between two rivers or expanses of water and, amongst other things, recommended building a well in the garden, or at least a small reservoir. Surrounded by the great lake, the garden at Kenilworth was perfectly located.

Pots filled with water stood next to the most delicate flowers. Scraps of cloth twisted to make sharp tongues dripped water from the pots to the plants all day long. And the entire garden was watered morning and evening – men patrolled the plot, carrying copper watering pots with big bellies and long, narrow necks.

The garden was an oasis: its greenness and freshness astonished visitors.

❧

Later that evening, a vast array of sweets was served in the banqueting house in the garden. Although Elizabeth ate very little at any time, she had a sweet tooth. Her favourite sweetmeats were candies containing aniseed, caraway or coriander seeds (which freshen the breath). At Kenilworth, these sweets were dyed red and white, and there was marzipan and sugar-work in many different shapes, including birds, fish, animals and angels. But the star attractions were sugar-work bears holding ragged staffs (Dudley's emblem) and a gilded marzipan model of the castle, made by Elizabeth's master cook.

The banquet also included candied flowers, red-and-white gingerbread, almond macaroons, fruit tarts and conserves and Dutch cheese, served with biscuits and wafers. Everything was presented on sugar plates, and Elizabeth, Dudley and their guests drank spiced wine in sugar glasses – at the end of the night, if they liked, they could smash and eat them.

There was a squadron of writers at Kenilworth. Dudley's young nephew Philip Sidney was back from his tour of the Continent, bringing news of court festivities in Venice, Paris and Vienna.

Sidney was Dudley's heir – his mother was Dudley's favourite sister and one of Elizabeth's best-loved ladies-in-waiting, and his father was Lord Deputy of Ireland. Dudley had sponsored Sidney's European tour: they were very close. It had been an exciting and, at times, terrifying three years. Sidney had been in Paris during the Massacre of St Bartholomew's Day and had taken refuge in the English embassy. He was also much loved by Cecil, one of his father's oldest friends. Years earlier, a match had been proposed between Sidney and Cecil's favourite daughter. At the time, in his letters to Sir Henry Sidney, Cecil had called his son his 'darling Philip'. But the betrothal had been broken off. As Cecil had risen in the world, he had cooled towards the idea, probably because of the Sidneys' lack of money.

From an early age, Sidney had been trained in fighting and in statesmanship. Now twenty, he was beginning to establish a reputation as a diplomat but had yet to make his mark as a man of letters or as a soldier. Nevertheless, he was the only first-rate poet at Kenilworth, joining Dudley's motley crew of ageing professional entertainers, masque-writers and storytellers. Great things were expected of Sidney, but not that summer, when more seasoned entertainers were running the show.

George Gascoigne was in charge of the masques and pageants. He had been educated at Cambridge and at the Inns of Court. On his arrival in London, he had set up as a poet but had led a dissolute life, and his father had disinherited him. Gascoigne had left the country in order to escape from his creditors. After disastrous military service in the Netherlands and imprisonment in a Spanish gaol, he had returned to England.

During his absence, one of his friends had published a collection of his poems. The book had caused controversy: critics had claimed that his poems were lascivious and scandalous (the Privy Council had called him 'a notorious ruffian . . . an atheist and godless person'). That had not, however, deterred Dudley from commissioning him to write pageants for Elizabeth's visits to Kenilworth and Woodstock.

Gascoigne was in his late thirties and still heavily in debt. He was also suffering from an illness that would lead to his death two years later. But Dudley's patronage had given him a new lease of life. Earlier that year, he had published a series of comic poems starring the Green Knight (his nickname as a soldier) about turning over a new leaf. The poems had appeared in a section called 'Weeds' in his collected verse (the titles of other sections were 'Flowers' and 'Herbs'). With Dudley's help, Gascoigne hoped that they might bring him to the attention of the Queen.

In his 'Farewell to Fancy', the Green Knight said goodbye to all of life's vanities, including gardening:

> To plant strange country fruits, to sow such seeds likewise,
> To dig and delve for new found roots, where old might well suffice;
> To prune the water boughs, to pick the mossy trees,
> Oh how it pleased my fancy once to kneel upon my knees,
> To griff [graft] a pippin stock, when sap begins to swell;
> But since the gains scarce quit the cost, *Fancy* (quoth he) *farewell.*

The 'pippin' apple had been introduced from France in about 1525. Grafting its stock, growing exotics and pruning trees in a water garden were sure signs of a gentleman's expertise in gardening. Gascoigne's knight bade farewell to horticulture as his second-to-last pleasure, after the love of women, courts, farming, hunting, poetry and music. Finally, he gave up soldiery: gardening and warfare were his worst obsessions.

Despite the Green Knight's farewell to arms, Gascoigne still saw himself as a soldier as well as a poet: he was as likely to win fame and fortune by fighting for Dudley as by writing for him. Gascoigne's motto was *Tam Marti quam Mercurio* (As much Mars as Mercury). In his portraits, he wore battle armour. Like his patron Dudley, he was hoping that success at Kenilworth would help him to relaunch his military career.

George Ferrers, a celebrated 'lord of misrule' at court entertainments, and William Hunnis, the famous choirmaster, were Gascoigne's assistants. Hunnis had known Dudley since they had been sent to the Tower by Elizabeth's half-sister Mary. On her accession, Elizabeth had restored Hunnis to his former office, the Mastership of the Children of the Chapel Royal. Other star writers and performers at Kenilworth included Richard Mulcaster, Headmaster of the Merchant Taylors' School; Master Badger, Beadle of Oxford University, who played Hercules; and Captain Cox, a well-known storyteller.

Dudley's actors were the best in the country, and enjoyed special privileges. They had overcome fierce opposition from the Puritans, who had accused them of lewdness and had attempted to ban them. In 1572, Cecil had passed legislation that had threatened their livelihood by placing restrictions on the movements of all servants, including actors, for reasons of national security. But Elizabeth had made an exception for Dudley's men, whom she saw as above suspicion. They had become the only actors free to tour the country at will and so earn a living, which made them the first professional actors in England. The master of the company, James Burbage, would later build the first theatre in London – Shakespeare would become one of his actors, and Elizabeth would steal his stars when she formed the Queen's Company in 1583.

Dudley was planning to make his festivities famous by publishing glamorous descriptions soon afterwards. Gascoigne was writing *The Princely Pleasures at the Court at Kenilworth*, which would include transcripts of the masques. There would be two other accounts: *The Pastime of the Progress* by an unknown writer and a detailed description of events supposedly written by

Dudley's servant Robert Langham, Keeper of the Council Chamber at Kenilworth.

The activity at Kenilworth was frantic. As usual, Elizabeth had given little notice of her visit. According to Gascoigne, everything – writing, rehearsing, sets and costumes – was put together at the last minute.

Kenilworth would turn out to be a far cry from the polished court entertainments of Europe. Just the year before, Sidney had watched the Venetians welcome Henri III in style. There had been water pageants and, at the Lido, a specially commissioned triumphal arch designed by Palladio and adorned with paintings by Tintoretto and Paolo Veronese. At Kenilworth, although considerable efforts would be made to emulate grand Continental pageantry, the clowns would ultimately rule. Everything depended on Elizabeth's entering into the spirit of things. She would be both star and audience.

The most extravagant festivities at Kenilworth took place outside, after dark. The pageants looked best by torchlight, and the heatwave meant that everything had to start late. On some days, it was so hot that Elizabeth stayed inside, in the cool of the castle, until five o'clock, when she went hunting.

The total cost of Elizabeth's nineteen-day visit was rumoured to be a phenomenal £1,700. It was said that Dudley had spent over £60,000 (nearly £10 million today) on improvements to the castle and its grounds. The medieval keep had a new flat roof for parties, and the courtyards had been cleared of old buildings, creating wide-open spaces which resembled piazzas. There were new towers with de luxe suites, and Dudley had blasted through the castle's ancient stone walls to put in modern rectangular windows. The handsome stables with their ogee arches would have made suitable accommodation for people.

A three-storey tower for Elizabeth and her favourites had been designed so that the bedrooms faced towards the east, for the sunrise. Elizabeth's apartments at the top had the biggest windows and best views, while Dudley occupied the floor below so that no one could see her without his knowledge. There is a story that on her arrival, however, Elizabeth mentioned that she could not see the garden from her suite, so Dudley's men worked around the clock to create an additional, private garden below her bedroom window.

Not all of the improvements were ornamental. In recent years, Dudley had employed thousands of men to fortify the castle, building up an immense armoury with enough weapons and ammunition to withstand any siege. He had made many enemies in his twenty-five years as the Queen's favourite.

At night-time, the festivities were open to all, and the crowds were enormous (according to one observer, there were between three and four thousand visitors each day). Great fires were lit inside the castle, which glowed from within because of its giant windows. Seen from a distance, some said that it resembled the ancient lighthouse of Alexandria, one of the Seven Wonders of the World.

There was every kind of entertainment on offer – dancing, storytelling, pageants, masques, plays, bear-baiting, performances by minstrels, and fireworks. According to 'Langham', an Italian acrobat performed such incredible 'feats of agility, in goings, turnings, tumblings, castings, hops, jumps, leaps, skips, springs, gambols, somersaults, capers and flights: forward, backward, side-wise, downward, upward and with sundry windings, gyrings, and circumflexions: also lightly and with such easiness', that people wondered whether he was 'a man or a spirit'. Or else, perhaps, he had a lute-string for a backbone.

The firework displays lasted over two hours and could be seen and heard twenty miles away. On the first night, dragons, serpents and birds flew into the sky and exploded high above the lake, as promised by Dudley's Italian pyrotechnician. Firework dogs fought spitting, sparkling cats. A rocket shot up to the heavens like a golden ribbon, curved and, as if shattering against the sky, spilled sparks across the whole expanse of night. The crowd gave a gigantic cheer. In the inner court, there were three wonderfully scented green, white and purple fire-wheels and a magnificent fountain with jets of water and wine, which also shot fireworks.

On the second night, Gascoigne described how some of the 'strange and well-executed' fireworks passed beneath the water for a long time and then rose and mounted 'out of the water again' and burnt 'very furiously' until they were 'utterly consumed'. Hard to believe? But this was Kenilworth and so not beyond the bounds of possibility. And, three years earlier, Dudley had showcased similar pyrotechnics at Warwick.

But a few of the shows did not go according to plan. On Monday 11 July, on her return from hunting, Elizabeth encountered a wild man covered in moss and ivy, carrying a young oak tree. The part was played by Gascoigne, who lived up to his reputation for bawdy humour with some verses about Dudley's love for Elizabeth. The wild man summoned Echo, and they talked about the events that had taken place during the first three days of the royal visit. Their conversation was more like the gossip of courtiers than the talk of innocent woodland spirits.

They speculated that the presents given to Elizabeth on her arrival at the castle were not really the gifts of the gods but 'tokens of true love'. So who was Elizabeth's secret admirer? The wild man thought that he knew the answer:

> Was it not he, who (but of late)
> this building here did lay?
> *Echo.*   *Dudley.*
> O *Dudley*, so methought:
> He gave himself and all,
> A worthy gift to be received,
> And so I trust it shall.

Dudley was known for the marvellous presents he had given Elizabeth, especially for the New Year: in 1572, a diamond and ruby bracelet set with a clock (an early wristwatch); in 1574, a fan of white feathers with a gold handle studded with emeralds, diamonds and rubies, and, on each side, a white bear, two pearls and a lion with a white muzzled bear at its feet; and on New Year's

Day 1575, a white satin doublet embroidered with gold thread and fastened with eighteen pairs of gold clasps decorated with diamonds and rubies (Elizabeth would wear this doublet in a portrait painted that year).

There were more double meanings when the wild man remembered the astonishing fireworks that had flown through the water the night before:

> What meant the fiery flames,
> Which through the waves so flew?
> Can no cold answers quench desire?
> Is that experience true?

The unquenchable fireworks that had so delighted Elizabeth were revealed as symbols of Dudley's enduring passion.

At the end of the performance, Gascoigne broke his tree in half, as a sign of submission, but when he went to throw it away one of the halves shot off in the wrong direction and nearly hit Elizabeth's horse, which reared up. She calmed her horse and called out 'No hurt, no hurt!', which Gascoigne called the best part of the play.

At the fireworks that night, Elizabeth's courtiers gossiped about the near-accident. Some dared to ask if it could have been mere carelessness. Someone repeated the slander that Dudley had murdered his wife. (He had married young, while, as a princess, Elizabeth was living at Hatfield. But, a year and a half into her reign, his wife had died in mysterious circumstances – found with a broken neck at the foot of a staircase. Although there were rumours that he had tried to poison her and had hired an assassin to kill her, the coroner had returned a verdict of death by misadventure.) The gossip died away as a dragon as big as an ox flew three times the height of the castle, where it burnt out and firework dogs, cats and birds issued from its body, scattering fire on all sides. Each night's display had been more spectacular than the last.

Shortly afterwards, the Spanish ambassador reported that while Elizabeth had been hunting in the woods, a dart from a crossbow had narrowly missed her. Was this an exaggerated account of the wild man's misadventure or had there really been an attempt on her life? Towards the end of her reign, Elizabeth would claim that Philip II had tried to have her assassinated fifteen times.

Out of all the amazing entertainments laid on for Elizabeth at Kenilworth, 'Langham' gave highest praise to the sensational new garden. Dudley had redesigned it in the latest Italian style, making it almost unrecognisable since her last visit three years earlier. 'Langham' described it as 'worthy to be called paradise', though he pointed out that it fell short of Eden because it lacked rivers. But, as a castle garden, it was necessarily limited in scale, and the great lake lay just beyond its walls. 'Langham' nevertheless went on to pay his master the highest possible compliment, saying that the garden was evidence of a 'right noble mind, that in this sort could have thus all contrived'.

Cool and shady, the garden was a haven. The day after the pageant starring the wild man, in the still intense heat of the afternoon, Elizabeth walked with Dudley along the arcaded gallery that led from the inner court through the Norman keep to the garden gate, usually kept locked by the head gardener. The gate opened on to a grassy terrace about ten feet high and twelve feet broad, backed by the keep's northern wall and bordered by a balustrade. There were statues of white bears and stone spheres, as well as fifteen-foot-high obelisks. They heard the sounds of a fountain playing and exotic birdsong below.

The terrace was a viewing platform for the sixteen compartments in which lines of herbs, flowers and fruit trees formed patterns, such as circles within squares (representing eternity within mortality, body and soul or heaven upon earth). There was a cool breeze, and Elizabeth and Dudley enjoyed views of the lake, the park and the countryside. To the east, the terrace looked down on the castle's outer court, where they watched people coming and going.

They reached the lower level by one of two stone staircases in the shape of a diamond and arrived at a huge tunnel arbour of sweet-smelling trees intertwined with roses and honeysuckle, at the east side of the garden. Here, they rested for a while. Once inside, they could see out, but no one could see in. At the other end of the garden stood a second bower which led to Dudley's octagonal stone banqueting house overlooking the lake, in the north-west corner.

Refreshed by the shade, they followed a sandy path to the white-marble fountain in the middle of the garden. The fountain had two Atlases standing back to back, holding up a globe that spurted water in all directions. The globe was crowned by an alert-looking bear with a ragged staff, Dudley's emblem. The Atlases represented Dudley and Warwick, the last remaining brothers holding up the Dudley dynasty – and Elizabeth's world.

(Famous for supporting the heavens – his punishment for having participated in the rebellion of the Titans against the Olympian gods – Atlas was also associated with the Garden of the Hesperides, with its tree bearing golden apples, through the story of Hercules. Dudley's choice of the god recalled François I's Italianate grotto at Fontainebleau, where four Atlases emerged from rough stone to hold up three rusticated arches.)

The fountain basin was full of fish: carp, tench, bream, perch and eels. Its eight sides showed scenes from Ovid's *Metamorphoses*: there was Neptune on his throne, driving his marine horses, and Thetis in her chariot drawn by dolphins. This brought to mind the first night's water pageant and heralded the return of the golden age. (During the first era of human history, according to Ovid, people lived in harmony with nature, before the rapacious ages of bronze and iron: after the chaos of Mary's reign, Elizabeth had been credited with its return.) Some of the carvings were provocative. 'Here were things, you see, might inflame any mind to long after looking,' joked 'Langham'. The return of the golden age for Dudley depended on his ability to inflame his queen. (But, at the turning of a cock by the head gardener, myriad surprise jets caught out anyone mesmerised by the carvings who stood too close.)

Elizabeth and Dudley walked along a grass path flanked by streams that sprang up from the ground, as if by magic (more early English experiments with hydraulics). They passed beds of exotic flowers and aromatic herbs on their way to the orchard. The garden was divided into quarters, which were further subdivided into compartments. At the heart of each quarter stood a gleaming porphyry obelisk topped by a sphere. (Obelisks reflected the Renaissance fascination with ancient Egypt and recalled one of Dudley's emblems, an obelisk encircled by a vine, symbol of his love for Elizabeth.)

Further on, they entered the orchard of cherry, apple and pear trees. Beyond lay beds of strawberries – Dudley stopped to pick one for Elizabeth. At the end of the path, they passed through the western arbour, leaving it by a sandy path that lined the castle's outer wall. The birdsong grew louder. Halfway up the path, on the fountain axis, there was a classical-style aviary based on a first-century BC design by Varro. It was full of colourful birds, some European and others from the Canary Islands and Africa, perching on clipped holly bushes. Elizabeth was amazed to discover that the brilliant jewels that decorated the aviary, just beneath the cornice, were, in fact, *trompe l'œil* paintings. Replicating the exact way a jeweller would cut it, each jewel had been so skilfully painted that it looked like the real thing. When the sunlight caught the gems and the birds' plumage the effect was dazzling.

The garden bombarded the senses. Could this siege succeed where so many had failed?

One of the last entertainments held at Kenilworth was the most boisterous to date: a mock wedding performed by country people from the surrounding areas. This took place in the tilt-yard, about halfway through Elizabeth's stay, on Sunday the 17th, and opened with performances by morris dancers, a Maid Marion and a jester. Then the bride and groom arrived.

The groom was young but walked with a limp – he had broken his leg playing football as a boy. Football, played on a

Sunday, was the most violent sport in England: according to contemporary commentator Philip Stubbes, serious injuries and even fatalities were common:

It may rather be called a friendly kind of fight, than a play or recreation; a bloody and murdering practice, than a fellowly sport or pastime.... But whosover escapes away the best, goes not scot-free, but is either sore wounded, grazed and bruised, so as he dies of it, or else escapes very hardly. And no marvel, for they have the sleights to meet one between two, to dash him against the heart with their elbows, to hit him under the short ribs with their clenched fists, and with their knees to catch him upon the hip, and to pitch him on his neck with a hundred such murdering devices.

The bride was old and ugly, according to 'Langham', who tactlessly mentioned that she and her bridesmaids were about thirty – Elizabeth was in her forties. Putting together the shortcomings of the bride and groom, it looked as if Dudley was joking about the two things that had ruined Elizabeth's chances with Alençon's good-looking older brother (now the King of France) a few years earlier and that she had been particularly sensitive about: her age and her temporary lameness (the result of an ulcer on her leg). The bride's ugliness also appeared to mock her vanity.

No one could believe what they were seeing, but Elizabeth remained calm. By making fun of her history of disastrous courtships, Dudley seemed to be living dangerously. But perhaps he knew what she would tolerate; despite the savage humour, was this a last desperate appeal to her to marry him, before it was too late? If so, he could not have come up with a less flattering proposal.

The show ended in chaos, with the bridegroom and his friends on horseback charging at each other, and horses and riders tumbling to the ground. 'Langham' commented that the sight would have 'moved any man to a right merry mood, though he had been told his wife lay dying'. But at the feast that night, Elizabeth ate almost nothing. Although this was not unusual for her, 'Langham' hinted that something was wrong and suggested that she might have been offended by the poor service and the coarse way in which her fellow guests had devoured each course. It was as likely that the grotesque wedding had spoilt her appetite.

On the night of Monday the 18th, as she returned from hunting, Elizabeth saw an eighteen-foot-long mermaid swimming over to her. Triton was riding the mermaid, sounding a horn in the shape of a whelk. Elizabeth reached the bridge first, and Triton made his mermaid swim faster to catch her up, so that he could tell her the sad story of the Lady of the Lake, kept prisoner in the lake by a villainous knight, Sir Bruce 'Sans Pitié', because she had refused to marry him. Triton revealed that Neptune had sent him to beg Elizabeth to free the Lady by the sheer force of her magical presence.

The Lady was freed, as Neptune had predicted. As a token of her thanks, she presented Elizabeth with the gift of Arion (played by a famous singer wearing a mask), riding a twenty-four-foot-long dolphin. Accompanied by exquisite music coming from inside the giant dolphin, Arion began to sing but soon became hoarse and tore off his mask, crying out that he was not really Arion 'but even honest Harry Goldingham'. This discovery pleased Elizabeth better than if the performance had gone perfectly.

It was lucky that she had a sense of humour. But then Goldingham was her favourite singer because he was as well known for his wit and extravagant costumes as his voice. (Goldingham had a tiny wife, and a story had it that when one of his noble patrons had arrived at his house, on horseback, Goldingham had offered to save him the trouble of dismounting to greet his wife by setting her up beside him. As soon as she had been seated, Goldingham had slapped the horse to get it moving, calling out that someone was carrying off his wife.)

While Dudley's last water pageant was a great success, Cecil had done even better. Earlier that day, Elizabeth had knighted his eldest son Thomas, along with five other gentlemen. Cecil's family was well on the way to becoming a great dynasty, whereas Dudley was still without an heir, apart from his nephew Sidney (his brother Warwick was also childless).

But two days later, the castle was in chaos. Everyone was in a state of acute anxiety, as Gascoigne later told Elizabeth:

There was nothing but weeping and wailing, crying and howling, dole, desperation, mourning and moan . . . The which sudden change I plainly perceived to be, for that they understood . . . that your Majesty would shortly (and too speedily) depart out of this country.

It was the party of the decade, thrown in her honour, but she was about to leave early. How could anything drive her away?

Dudley's complicated love life held the answer.

The most important members of the nobility and the entire royal household were with Elizabeth at Kenilworth. One of her principal ladies-in-waiting was Lady Laetitia 'Lettice' Devereux, Countess of Essex; her husband had returned from service in Ireland especially for the festivities.

In the early years of the reign, Elizabeth and Lettice had been very close. The Spanish ambassador had described Lettice as 'one of the best-looking ladies of the court' and Elizabeth's favourite. Elizabeth and Lettice were cousins – Lettice's grandmother was Anne Boleyn's sister – and they closely resembled each other, with their pale skin and red hair. They were both charming and vivacious. But Lettice was younger and prettier (in the summer of 1575, she was thirty-four).

When she was not at court, Lettice lived alone at Chartley in Staffordshire with her three sons and two daughters. Her eldest son, Robert, probably named after his godfather Dudley, would become famous as Elizabeth's doomed last favourite, the Earl of Essex. (Sidney would fall in love, unrequitedly, with Lettice's daughter Penelope and would immortalise her as 'Stella' in his poems. Lettice and her children possessed a dangerous magnetism.)

About ten years earlier, Elizabeth had begun an infatuation with a good-looking young Gentleman of the Bedchamber, Sir Thomas Heneage, and, according to the Spanish ambassador, Dudley had retaliated by paying court to Lettice, as a way of making her jealous. Heneage had challenged him to a duel, but he had refused, on the grounds that Heneage was not his equal.

Dudley's relationship with Lettice had seemed to have run its course when in the early 1570s he had fallen for Lady Douglas Sheffield, a famous beauty and another of Elizabeth's ladies, despite the fact that ladies-in-waiting were forbidden to have affairs. In 1573, Dudley had written to Lady Douglas about his most troubling dilemma. He longed for an heir, but Elizabeth would not allow him to marry another and showed no real interest in taking him as a husband:

Yet is there nothing in the world next that favour [the Queen's] that I would not give to be in hope of leaving some children behind me, being now the last of our house.

In his darkest moods, he had felt that he had wasted the best years of his life trying to win Elizabeth's hand. Yet Lettice had by then come back into his life and had eclipsed Douglas in his affections. Possibly, they had met again at court in 1572, and, in 1573, he had sent her deer from Kenilworth. At last, he was ready to risk everything.

Dudley and Lettice's affair was a double betrayal for Elizabeth. But she laid the blame almost entirely on Lettice (although Dudley had arranged for Lettice's husband Essex to be sent to fight in Ireland and kept him posted there). Dudley had fallen in love with Lettice, even as he remained a widower and continued to woo Elizabeth.

At the time of the entertainments at Kenilworth in 1575, Shakespeare was eleven years old. He was living in nearby Stratford, so it is possible that he was amongst the crowd that came to watch the pageants and firework displays. In any case, he would have heard all about them.

A Midsummer Night's Dream, written twenty years later, evokes the secret romance between Dudley and Lettice. Oberon describes a scene directly recalling Dudley's fabulous water pageants for Elizabeth, featuring a mermaid, a dolphin and fireworks, before hinting at the love affair between Dudley and Lettice. Cupid (Dudley) failed to win the heart of the chaste moon goddess (Elizabeth), but his arrow pierced a little white flower, transforming it into 'Love-in-idleness' (Lettice):

> Yet marked I where the bolt of Cupid fell:
> It fell upon a little western flower,
> Before milk-white, now purple with love's wound:
> And maidens call it 'love-in-idleness' [the wild pansy].

In *A Midsummer Night's Dream*, Love-in-idleness is the flower of love and enchantment. It was also Elizabeth's favourite flower and, in folklore, a symbol of unrequited love. Said quickly, however, 'Love-in-idleness' sounds like 'Lettice'.

Such elision seems a feature of the period. There is a passage in John Aubrey's *Brief Life* of Raleigh in which a park, or perhaps a garden, plays a part:

He loved a wench well; and one time getting up one of the maids of honour up against a tree in a wood ('twas his first lady) who seemed at first boarding to be something fearful of her honour, and modest, she cried, 'Sweet Sir Walter, what do you ask me? Will you undo me? Nay, sweet Sir Walter! Sweet Sir Walter! Sir Walter!' At last, as the danger and the pleasure at the same time grew higher, she cried in the ecstasy, 'Swisser Swatter Swisser Swatter.' She proved with child, and I doubt not but this hero took care of them both, as also that the product was more than an ordinary mortal.

Shakespeare's mention of the events that took place at Kenilworth in *A Midsummer Night's Dream* probably drew on John Lyly's *Endymion, or The Man in the Moon*, performed at court on New Year's Day, 1585. The play was about the shepherd Endymion's love for Cynthia, the moon goddess (representing Dudley's impossible love for Elizabeth). Endymion was loved by two other ladies: Tellus, who was in love with his looks (probably Lady Douglas) and Floscula ('little flower'), who loved him for his 'virtues' (Lettice).

Until now, Elizabeth had refused to acknowledge Dudley's affair with Lettice. The relationship had been a court secret. In May 1573, Gilbert Talbot had linked Dudley to two women, Lady Douglas and her sister Lady Frances Howard, in a letter to his father Lord Shrewsbury, but had made no mention of Lettice:

There are two sisters now in the court that are very far in love with him, as they have long been; my Lady Sheffield and Frances Howard; they of like striving who shall love him better are at great war together, and the Queen thinketh not well of them, and not the better of him; by this means there are spies over him.

Talbot, however, had also reported that Elizabeth had been showing 'the same great good affection she was wont' towards Dudley and that lately he had 'endeavoured to please her more than heretofore'.

At Kenilworth in 1575, someone had dared to break the silence about Dudley and Lettice. The rumours had probably included reports about secret love-children and marriage plans. But who had leaked the story? There were numerous suspects, ranging from supporters of Elizabeth's foreign suitors to Dudley's political rivals.

❧

Over four hundred years later, we know little more about Elizabeth's private life than her contemporaries did. Many historians believe that, in her own words, she 'lived and died a virgin', while others allege that she and Dudley were lovers. However, much about their relationship remains puzzling – not least, her tolerance of his affairs, as long as they did not disturb her own relationship with him, and her affairs with other men, all of which would seem to contradict her reputation for chastity. There is also the question of her lack of children.

During her lifetime, Elizabeth's enemies said that she had several children with Dudley, but no convincing evidence has emerged to support this claim. Early in the reign, Cecil alleged that Dudley was sterile, like his brother Warwick, and so was unfit to be Elizabeth's suitor. But Cecil was proved wrong: although Dudley's first wife died childless, his mistresses Douglas and Lettice each bore him a son.

It is possible, as some historians have speculated, that Elizabeth was barren. Alternatively, others have proposed that she took precautions so as to avoid pregnancy.

*

Although Elizabeth was celebrated by her people as their Virgin Queen, in private she liked to provoke her courtiers and foreign diplomats with behaviour that was potentially scandalous.

In 1560, in his jealousy of Dudley, Cecil told the Spanish ambassador, Álvaro de Quadra, about Elizabeth's 'intimacy with my Lord Robert', which he feared would ruin her. He had planned to resign because Dudley had made himself 'master of the business of the state and of the person of the Queen, to the extreme injury of the realm, with the intention of marrying her, and she herself was shutting herself up in the palace to the peril of her health and life'. In what was probably his most outlandish scheme to marry Elizabeth, Dudley was then secretly attempting to secure Spain's support for his plan to elope with her to France in exchange for restoring England to Catholicism, after their triumphant return as king and queen. While Elizabeth must have known about Dudley's plot, she treated it lightly. Later that year, when de Quadra sounded her out about her relationship with Dudley, she admitted that he was her favourite suitor and that she was 'no angel', but wondered what King Philip would think if she were to marry one of her subjects.

In the summer of 1561, on a barge during a great water festival on the Thames at Greenwich, Elizabeth jokingly encouraged Dudley in his appeal to de Quadra (who was also the Bishop of Ávila) to marry them, there and then, although she added: 'I am not sure if my Lord [de Quadra] knows enough English to perform the ceremony.' De Quadra revenged himself on Elizabeth and Dudley for their raillery by writing letters full of salacious details about their affair to Philip II; in a further twist, these letters were intercepted by Cecil, with the result that de Quadra was disgraced and Dudley's negotiations with the Spanish were brought to an abrupt end.

When Elizabeth gave Kenilworth to Dudley in 1563, gossip about their relationship was rife: early that year, Edmund Baxter of Suffolk dared to call her a 'naughty woman' who was 'kept' by Dudley (perhaps, in hindsight, it was really the other way around), and, that summer, Lady Willoughby said that she looked 'like one lately come out of childbed'. Two years later, piqued by the failure of the match between Mary, Queen of Scots and Dudley (amongst other things), the French ambassador claimed that, on New Year's Eve, Elizabeth and Dudley spent the night together: this was supposedly after Elizabeth had forgiven Dudley for his flirtation with Lettice and his threats to Heneage. But the Spanish ambassador wrote to Philip II that he doubted that the story was true because he had heard it 'from a Frenchman'.

Former lady-in-waiting Bess Talbot (Bess of Hardwick, the wife of the Earl of Shrewsbury – Mary, Queen of Scots's gaoler) told how she had come into Elizabeth's bedroom on several occasions and found her in flagrante delicto with Dudley. However, Bess's jealousy of Elizabeth was well known, and furthermore, she conspired with Dudley in various schemes to gain power: Dudley sought to marry his illegitimate son by Lady Douglas to Bess's granddaughter, who was Henry VII's great-great-granddaughter. Success in this scheme might have made Dudley a kingmaker.

At Kenilworth, after hearing the latest gossip about Dudley's affair with Lettice, Elizabeth refused to attend a special supper and show arranged for her and got ready to leave, after one last afternoon's hunting. 'Langham' blamed the bad weather for the cancellation of the play but hinted that there was more to it. Gascoigne said that the rain was the 'tears of the gods' because Elizabeth was leaving.

The show that was never performed contained lines urging her to marry, so it would not have gone down well in the circumstances:

> How necessary it were
> For worthy queens to wed,
> That know you well, whose life always
> In learning hath been led.
> ... O Queen, O worthy Queen,
> Yet never wight [creature] felt perfect bliss,
> But such as wedded been.

The scandal had robbed Dudley of the chance to make a last-ditch appeal to Elizabeth to marry him.

Gascoigne had to bring his farewell speech forward by a week. As Sylvanus, god of the woods, he escorted Elizabeth as she rode back to the castle, delivering his speech while running alongside her. Traditionally, the farewell masque was a plea to the Queen to stay longer, but this time the appeal was in earnest. At one point, Elizabeth pulled up and told him that he would be out of breath long before her horse. As long as he was not offending her, he replied, he could keep going for another twenty miles.

Half joking and half flattering her, he talked about the heavenly way in which she had transformed her surroundings. Since her arrival, the trees flourished, the grass was greener and the deer were happier than ever. When she began to ride away, he apologised for boring her with his tedious tales, describing himself as a flea in her ear and playing the fool.

Just before the final farewell song, he steered her into a shady holly-bush arbour. There, he told her the story of Zabeta (Elizabeth), one of Diana's favourite nymphs, who turned her most annoying suitors into beasts, birds and plants. The worst offenders were two brothers (who may have been figures for the Dudley brothers): Zabeta had transformed one of them into a laurel tree, said Sylvanus, pointing to a nearby bower. The holly-bush arbour where they sat appeared to be the other brother, Deep Desire, the lover who had plagued Zabeta more than any other (Dudley had long been associated, in court entertainments, with the figure of Desire). Sylvanus joked that he was not sure if it was a he-bush or a she-bush, although 'some will say, that she-holly hath no pricks, but thereof I intermeddle not'.

At that moment, the arbour began to shake and strange music came from within it. Then a voice spoke:

> Stay, stay your hasty steps,
> O Queen without compare.

The voice inside the quivering holly bush belonged to Dudley.

> Live here, good Queen, live here,
> You are amongst your friends:
> Their comfort comes when you approach,
> And when you part, it ends.

Elizabeth stayed another week. As a lovesick holly-bush bower, Dudley was irresistible. He was her perfect 'garden-in-miniature': at once wild, civilised and delicious.

The first description of the Kenilworth entertainments appeared in September, when the court had moved to Woodstock. The book was attributed to Dudley's servant Langham; it caused immediate offence and was banned as soon as it was published. Every copy was recalled. Shocked by the news, Langham denied all knowledge of the book.

On first impressions, the book seemed harmless enough, taking the form of a letter supposedly from Langham to his friend in London. As it turned out, this behind-the-scenes account made a mockery of the entertainments. There were so many embarrassing details that it could only have been written by an insider. But if Langham was not the author, who was?

In the weeks leading up to and during the festivities, Kenilworth had a huge floating population. Temporary workers hired for the season included builders, gardeners, caterers, carters, actors, dancers, singers, acrobats, pyrotechnicians, costume-makers, stage-designers and writers. One of the hacks paid to write a few verses was William Patten, a friend of both Dudley and Cecil. Patten had known Cecil since 1544, when they had travelled to Scotland together on a diplomatic mission.

At the age of sixty-five, Patten was down on his luck. He had once been very successful, rising to become lord of the manor of

Stoke Newington, a Teller of the Exchequer and a Justice of the Peace, but, along the way, had contracted huge debts. He had lost everything: all his offices and possessions, including his house, had gone to his creditors. A brilliant linguist and the first serious student of Armenian in England, he had published works on a diverse range of subjects, including an account of an early expedition to Scotland with Cecil and books on the Armenian language and English place names. By 1575, all he had left was his pen, which he hired out to the highest bidder.

It has been thought that, as an insider at the castle, Patten's services had become more valuable and that Cecil had paid him to turn double agent and to write a lurid account of events. Patten has been advanced as the author of the 'Langham' letter, and some think that Cecil and Patten chose Langham as their fictitious author because, given his reputation as a fop and a rogue, it was plausible that he could have written a book that unwittingly sent up his master Dudley. Full of colourful episodes and focusing on the personalities involved in the festivities, the *Letter* read like an unauthorised biography.

By commissioning this spoof, Cecil had hoped to sabotage Dudley's publicity. Cecil was conscious of the success of Dudley's earlier commissions: in 1561, a glamorous description of his masque at the Inner Temple on Twelfth Night had helped to make it legendary. This extravagant masque had starred Dudley as Prince Pallaphilos (lover of Pallas, goddess of Wisdom), accompanied by his twenty-four Knights of the Order of Pegasus; Elizabeth had watched the show from the gallery. In the second part, Dudley had played a knight called Desire who travelled to the Temple of Pallas where the goddess gave him permission to marry his beloved, Lady Beauty. At the end of the festivities, Dudley had invited Elizabeth, as Lady Beauty, to dance with him. By dancing together, Elizabeth and Dudley had celebrated the betrothal of their fictional characters; the audience had wondered if this was a prologue to the real thing.

Dudley's entertainments for Twelfth Night had recalled a masque performed for Henry VIII, *The Siege of Lady Beauty*. In the finale, Anne Boleyn had made her stage debut as one of Beauty's Dames, who had welcomed the Knights of Ardent Desire to the Chateau Vert, after their defeat of Disdain and Scorn. In Dudley's masque, Elizabeth's ladies had played Beauty's Dames, following Elizabeth and Dudley's lead in the dancing. After Dudley's swift publication of the description of his masque, Elizabeth had called for a second performance at Whitehall, twelve days later.

If all went well, Patten's *Letter* would make Kenilworth unforgettable, for all the wrong reasons.

Patten mocked Dudley's lavish improvements to the park in purple prose, describing it as 'beautified with many delectable, fresh and umbrageous bowers, arbours, seats, and walks, that with great art, cost and diligence, were very pleasantly appointed'. But even Patten was charmed by the 'beautiful garden', describing it with genuine astonishment and admiration.

Cecil's plan had been to publish the *Letter* to coincide with the second round of Gascoigne's pageants, at Woodstock. Cecil had left Kenilworth on the 20th: it was no coincidence that this had been the day that the scandal about Dudley and Lettice had broken. Cecil had travelled to his ancestral mansion of Burghley, in Lincolnshire, where he had stayed for a week before returning to Kenilworth in time for the court's removal to Woodstock.

Cecil was at Woodstock when he received a letter from Patten, dated 10 September. Reading between the lines, it was all good news. Patten reported that he had heard from his 'good friend the Master of Requests how the book was to be suppressed for that Langham had complained about it, and otherwise that the honourable entertainment be not turned into a jest'. But it was too late: he had already sent more than sixty copies to their distributor, including one for Langham because, if he could not get hold of a copy, he would complain about it even more. Patten pretended to be sorry that Langham was taking it so badly and closed by 'beseeching the continuance of [Cecil's] favour, whereof my poor estate has so much need, God help me'. The *Letter* had been a complete success. They could not have hoped for a better result.

Dudley knew who was responsible for the *Letter*, but he was too caught up with other things to do more than enforce the ban. The exposure of his affair with Lettice meant that he had to deal first with Elizabeth and second with Lettice's husband, the Earl of Essex. There would be more embarrassment towards the end of the summer progress at Chartley, where Lettice would have to play hostess to Elizabeth.

'Walk into yonder garden'

Flowers planted in raised beds, from *The Gardener's Labyrinth*

'Worthy to Be Called Paradise'

ENGLAND'S ISOLATION from Europe meant that, until Kenilworth, its gardens were based on French and Dutch designs derived from Italian models – translations of translations. Thanks to his many contacts overseas and his patronage of artists and designers from the Continent, Dudley was in a unique position to introduce new ideas into garden design. In particular, his patronage of Frederico Zuccaro makes it likely that Kenilworth was modelled on Cardinal Gambara's contemporary garden at the Villa Lante, at Bagnaia in Lazio (Zuccaro is believed to have painted the frescoes at Bagnaia).

Both villa and garden survive at Bagnaia and have been attributed to the great architect Giacomo da Vignola, who designed the ultimate Renaissance palace, the Villa Farnese at nearby Caprarola, as well as François I's gardens. At the Villa Lante, Vignola used geometry and terraces to create the illusion of space in a confined area. The garden, villa and park form a single, unified landscape; in a similar way, the garden, park, woods, lake and castle at Kenilworth were designed to be viewed as a whole.

It is the Villa Lante that offers a clue as to how Dudley came up with his spectacular Italianate garden at Kenilworth in 1575. There are crayfish everywhere at the Villa Lante (Cardinal Gambara's emblem – *gambero* means 'crayfish'), just as, at Kenilworth, it was hard to get away from Dudley's emblem of the bear and ragged staff. In the middle of the garden at the Villa Lante, Vignola created a wonderful crayfish-shaped water-chain, leading down to a dining table made of stone, with a narrow central trough for cooling wine and stone seats concealing water-jets, so that the Cardinal could soak his unsuspecting guests halfway through dinner. Dudley's trick fountain showed that he had a similar sense of humour.

At the Villa Lante, fountains and statues told stories from Ovid's *Metamorphoses*. Visitors left the golden age in the park with its fountains dedicated to Pegasus and Bacchus and featuring ducks and acorns (during the golden age, according to Ovid, 'wine ran everywhere in streams', and people fed on 'acorns which had fallen from the broad tree of juniper') and entered the garden at the top of a hill, where they discovered the Grotto of the Deluge and the Fountain of the Dolphins. Lower down, they came across the water-table, water-chain, statues of river gods bearing cornucopias and the Fountain of the Lights with its exquisite jets, watercourses and water jokes (representing man's harnessing of the forces of nature). Originally, on the lowest level there was a fountain in the shape of a pyramid which, according to Montaigne (writing in 1580), spouted water 'in different ways: now up and now down'. This fountain was surrounded by four pools, in which there were stone trumpets spouting water (symbols of fame) and stone boats containing small soldiers firing water-guns (reminders of the Roman tradition of mock sea battles).

Dudley's Italianate fountain at Kenilworth was decorated with scenes from the *Metamorphoses*: the Elizabethans also loved 'wanton Ovid', as Gascoigne called him. And Dudley was the patron of Arthur Golding, the first English translator of the

Metamorphoses. Golding dedicated his translation to Dudley; the first part appeared in 1564 and the second in 1567. It was so popular that there were six more editions by 1612.

Cardinal Gambara only completed one of the two buildings forming his palace. (In the seventeenth century, a matching *palazzino* was built on the opposite side of the garden's central staircase.) One of the most striking things about the design at the Villa Lante was that the palace took second place to the garden and park: by the sixteenth century, a garden could be more impressive than a house.

When Pope Gregory XIII came to stay at the Villa Lante in 1578, he brought an entourage of eighty light horsemen and 180 Swiss Guards. The visit cost the Cardinal 4,000 *scudi*. Twenty years later, for the entertainment of Clement VIII, there were fireworks and a mock battle, with gunfire, flares and statues of animals which shot fire.

Montaigne called the Villa Lante 'one of the most richly ornamented places I ever saw. It is so well provided with fountains that it surpasses Pratolino and Tivoli.' High praise indeed: he was referring to the extravagant water park of Francesco I, the Medici Grand Duke, at his palace at the foot of the Apennines near Florence, and the magnificent terraced water garden of Cardinal Ippolito d'Este outside Rome.

Dudley's garden at Kenilworth had one of the first terraces seen in England: Patten's description of its raised walk as a 'terrace' in 1575 is the earliest recorded usage of that word. As one of the first Italianate Englishmen, Dudley would have drawn inspiration from the marvellous new terraced gardens of Italy.

For all their Renaissance trappings, however, the castle and garden at Kenilworth remained medieval at heart. The garden's arcade was balanced with a neo-Gothic gatehouse, and the Italian fountain stood in the centre, at the intersection of two paths, as in a medieval plot. There were old-fashioned tunnel arbours, and the statues mainly consisted of Dudley's bears and obelisks (an updating of medieval sundials and poles bearing emblems), instead of the classical gods, goddesses and heroes that populated the gardens of Florence and Rome. The sculptures of Atlas on the fountain took second place to Dudley's heraldic crest, the endearing-looking bear chained to a ragged staff.

As far as we know, just one sixteenth-century painting of the garden has survived, *Queen Elizabeth at Kenilworth*, dated around 1575 and attributed to Marcus Gheeraerts the Elder. The painting shows a gorgeous garden by a beautiful lake with pleasure boats, including a gondola. At the far end of the garden, steep steps lead up to a spectacular banqueting house. The statues on the fountain are Hercules and Antaeus. (According to ancient myth, the wrestler Antaeus was invincible until Hercules discovered his weakness: as a Giant, Antaeus drew his power from his mother, the Earth, and so Hercules lifted him up from the ground and strangled him.)

In the foreground, Elizabeth is shown walking along a terrace, arm in arm with Dudley and Sidney. Cecil is nowhere to be seen. But is this the real Kenilworth or a wonderfully enhanced version of reality? It is possible that the image does not record any actual garden but was based on Continental engravings.

Seventeenth-century depictions of the castle provide more clues. There is an imaginative reconstruction of Kenilworth at the time of the 1575 festivities attributed to Dirck Hals and entitled *Queen Elizabeth I and the Earl of Leicester at Kenilworth*. The setting is the castle's outer courtyard, and there is a tantalising glimpse of a garden through a stone archway. On a terrace in the foreground, Elizabeth plays the virginals (an early kind of harpsichord), her back turned towards us, while Dudley stands next to her.

The painting gives the impression that the atmosphere in princely gardens could be surprisingly informal. During the summer progress of 1565, Elizabeth's cousin Norfolk described a scene at Sir William More's Loseley Park, in Surrey, which reveals this aspect of life at court. Norfolk had gone in search of Elizabeth, hoping for a private meeting in which he might assure her of his loyalty, and was startled to come across her sitting on the threshold of the Privy Chamber with, on one side, one of More's children playing a lute and singing to her, and, on the other, Dudley kneeling next to her. We might equally imagine such a scene taking place in a garden.

In the background of Hals's painting, we see the tops of tall trees and an elaborate building with turrets and towers above the garden wall. Through the archway, a flight of steps leads up to a triumphal arch. The steps appear to be identical to those in the sixteenth-century painting of the garden at Kenilworth attributed to Gheeraerts. But neither of these images corresponds to the geography of the castle, and it is possible that both are fantasies.

The two most reliable visual sources are a painting and an engraving of the castle and its landscape, both based on a seventeenth-century fresco, now lost. The identity of the original painter is unknown. A copy of the fresco shows the garden in the seventeenth century, but only in broad outline: nevertheless, there is a three-storey octagonal banqueting house overlooking the lake, a fountain of Atlas in the centre and an arcade near the keep. It is possible that this arcade was part of Henry V's banqueting pavilion, which once stood in the park and was dismantled and moved into the castle garden.

To this day, the garden's layout remains mysterious. Until recently, archaeological investigations had yielded hardly anything to support either written or visual representations. In the 1970s (before the first modern re-creation of the garden), archaeologists discovered signs of the terrace that ran alongside the keep, but little else – there was no evidence of any hydraulics. But an inventory drawn up by the Parliamentary Surveyors in 1649 includes an elaborate fountain carved 'with story work', matching Patten's description. Also listed was 'the Queen's seat of freestone', which stood in the garden. In the last few years, there have been two archaeological excavations. Evidence has been found of an eight-sided fountain base, a baluster (possibly part of a balustrade) and a timber beam, which could have supported one of the arbours, leading to the second modern re-creation of the garden. Other finds include fragments of marble from the fountain, most likely from the northern Italian

Carrara quarries, and shards of high-quality ceramics, probably from Pisa.

Whether fantasy or reality, the sixteenth- and seventeenth-century paintings and Patten's contemporary description have one thing in common: they all give the impression that Elizabeth and Dudley's Kenilworth was an amazingly romantic place. Even so, Dudley still awaited his reward.

⌈8⌉

'As she was walking in the garden that morning
she found a letter'

Illustrations for the rose, from John Parkinson's
Paradisi in Sole Paradisus Terrestris

The Lady of May

IT WAS MAY 1578. Elizabeth was walking with her courtiers in the garden at Wanstead, in Essex. Her favourite little white dogs chased each other along the paths. She took the central path to the small fountain in the middle, passing flower beds edged with aromatic herbs. Honeybees wove patterns around the hedges made of hyssop, and the first roses had bloomed in the borders.

Dudley had bought Wanstead just a few months earlier. One of the first things that he had done was to invite Elizabeth to visit him. But when she had arrived, he had not been there to welcome her. She was missing him.

At the end of the garden, Elizabeth entered the grove. Old elm and ash trees lined the paths. She was in deep shadow when she saw a group of satyrs in a clearing. She came closer. When they saw her, they looked terrified (a comical way of acknowledging her 'dread' presence). Before she knew it, she was in a play by Sidney called *The Lady of May*.

Sidney was standing in as host. After the Kenilworth festivities of 1575, he had begun a career in diplomacy at the Emperor Rudolf II's court at Prague. Dudley had recalled him – after Gascoigne's untimely death, he had needed a new masque-writer. The play in the grove at Wanstead was Sidney's first major commission.

A country woman suddenly appeared in the midst of Elizabeth's courtiers and, falling to her knees, begged her for help.

The woman's daughter was 'oppressed' by two suitors, who detested each other. Their rivalry would probably end in murder, unless Elizabeth intervened. The woman asked her to choose one of them as a husband for her daughter (the Lady of May). Then she handed her a petition and said, 'I dare stay here no longer, for our men say here in the country, the sight of you is infectious' (a joke about Elizabeth's fear of the plague, one of the reasons for her frequent progresses, and the opposite of the usual praise for her royal healing powers).

The suitors for the Lady of May were a virile and handsome forester and a pale and doleful-looking shepherd. The audience soon recognised them as Dudley and Cecil, while Elizabeth was the Lady of May, torn between them.

The Lady of May stepped forward and called Elizabeth 'the beautifullest lady these woods have ever received'. She introduced her suitors, mentioning that although the shepherd was richer, the forester was livelier, then described the forester as a man of 'many deserts and many faults', whereas the shepherd was a man of 'very small deserts and no faults'.

The forester challenged his rival to a singing contest. The shepherd accepted and, accompanied by his friends on their pipes, sang a song in praise of Elizabeth's beauty:

> Two thousand sheep I have as white as milk,
> Though not so white as is thy lovely face.

Her complexion was famously fair, but no one had ever described it quite like that. If the prize had been for originality in flattery, there would have been no contest. As a last word, the shepherd warned her not to

> submit
> To one that hath no wealth, and wants [lacks] his wit.

It was well known that Dudley's extravagant lifestyle had left him penniless, and his reckless behaviour had led people to question his sanity.

The forester was accompanied by his fellow foresters, who played cornets which were hung around their necks like hunting horns.

> Two thousand deer in wildest woods I have,
> Them can I take, but you I cannot hold.

The forester's lines recalled Sir Thomas Wyatt's poem about his unrequited love for Anne Boleyn ('Whoso list to hunt, I know where is an hind'). Elizabeth's suitors pursued her in vain.

Although he did not challenge the shepherd's claim that he had lost his mind, the forester denied that he was destitute:

> Bound but to you, no wealth but you I would:
> But take this beast, if beasts you fear to miss,
> For of his beasts the greatest beast he is.

Dudley had always portrayed himself as Elizabeth's most loyal beast: her chained and muzzled bear.

But which suitor would she choose for her fictional character the Lady of May? The shepherd represented peace and the forester war. At the end of the play, a schoolmaster gave her a gift from Dudley: a necklace of agates that resembled a set of rosary beads (contraband goods, since rosary beads had been banned in 1571). He told her that Dudley had been saying his prayers every day – with a difference. After each 'Our Father', he had added 'and Elizabeth'.

Everything had been set up for her to choose the forester. But she favoured the shepherd. It was a victory for Cecil, although he was not there to see it. And everyone was still wondering, where was Dudley?

So far, Dudley's ambition to become a great military leader had come to nothing. Elizabeth still kept to Cecil's peace policy. Sidney's play about an insipid shepherd and a vigorous forester was yet another attempt to make her see that the time had come for intervention in the Netherlands. Dudley's lifestyle and excessive gambling had left him with huge debts, and the fate of the Netherlands would have a direct impact on his finances. While he enjoyed a salary of £1,000 a year from Elizabeth and received considerable revenues from his lands, most of his income came from his control of the licences for trading in textiles – a trade now in jeopardy, since the Merchant Adventurers who bought his licences conducted so much of their business in the Netherlands.

But Sidney's play was about more than Dudley's dreams of military glory, his desire to protect his business interests or his long-standing rivalry with Cecil. In the opening scene, the country woman described her daughter the Lady of May as 'troubled with that notable matter, which we in the country call matrimony'. She went on to say that because of the marriage plans she feared 'the loss of her wits' or, 'at least, of her honesty' (punning on 'honesty' as meaning truthfulness and chastity). Elizabeth knew very well the toll that marriage negotiations could take. And, in recent years, Dudley's own love life had brought him close to madness.

After the Kenilworth festivities of 1575, Lettice's husband Essex had sworn revenge on Dudley. Like Heneage before him, he had challenged him to a duel, but Dudley had again refused. The Spanish ambassador had reported that their feud was the subject of malicious gossip:

> As the thing is publicly talked about in the streets there is no objection to my writing openly about the great enmity which exists between the Earl of Leicester and the Earl of Essex in consequence, it is said, of the fact that while Essex was in Ireland his wife had two children by Leicester. Great discord is expected in consequence.

Essex had eventually returned to Ireland in June 1576.

That summer, Dudley's friend Thomas Wood had written to warn him about the many 'very common' and 'very dishonourable and ungodly' rumours about his affairs with court ladies. Then, in September, Essex had collapsed and died. Poison had been suspected, and there had been a public inquiry into the cause of his death. But the commission, chaired by Sir Henry Sidney (Dudley's brother-in-law), had ruled out foul play.

As Master of the Court of Wards, Cecil had gained the wardship of Lettice's eldest son Robert, the new Earl of Essex (becoming his legal guardian and adding him to his brood of wealthy young men who had lost their fathers). It had been quite a victory over his rival Dudley. Essex had come to live with Cecil at his magnificent house on the Strand, following in the illustrious footsteps of previous wards Lord Zouche (later an avid plant-collector, whose obsession with creating fabulous gardens would eventually bankrupt him) and the hot-headed Earl of Oxford, one of Elizabeth's favourites and, by now, Cecil's son-in-law. The combined income of Cecil's wardships was at least £30,000 a year (roughly £4.5 million today). And, with careful handling, his protégés might one day make a formidable power base.

Faced with Cecil's ascendancy at court, Dudley had turned to exploration as a way of impressing Elizabeth, becoming Sir Francis Drake's main backer for his most dangerous project to date: the circumnavigation of the globe. Elizabeth, Walsingham and Sir Christopher Hatton, one of her favourites, were also heavily involved. The official purpose of the voyage begun in 1577 was trade – after sailing around the world, Drake's ships were bound for Alexandria with a cargo of currants. (In 1575, Dudley's friend Acerbo Velutelli had been granted a monopoly for the import of currants. Since Dudley controlled the trade, which he had delegated to his Italian friends, currants made a good cover for piracy.)

The real mission was to capture Spanish treasure ships on the silver bullion route from Peru to Panama. Everyone in Elizabeth's inner circle had known, except Cecil: she had told Drake, 'Of all men my Lord Treasurer must not know of it.' Drake's ship for the expedition, the *Pelican* (one of Elizabeth's emblems), would later be renamed the *Golden Hind* (Hatton's emblem) to hide her involvement in the piracy. The details of the expedition had been finalised while, on Dudley's recommendation, Cecil had visited the spa town of Buxton, in Derbyshire.

In Cecil's view, Drake's piracy threatened the safety of the realm: it was folly to provoke as powerful an enemy as Spain. When Cecil had at last learnt the real object of the voyage, he had planted a spy on board one of Drake's ships (on his discovery, the spy would be executed, in South America).

To coincide with Drake's venture, Dudley's friend and astrologer John Dee had published his *General and Rare Memorials Pertaining to the Perfect Art of Navigation*, in which he claimed that, during the Middle Ages, King Arthur's knights had discovered America. Since it was believed that Elizabeth was descended from King Arthur, her claim on the Americas pre-dated that of Philip II. Dee not only urged her to assert her Arthurian rights but suggested that, since she could claim descent from the mythical founders of Rome (through the Trojan hero Brutus, who was believed to have travelled to England), an English assault on America would mark the beginning of a new Roman empire. Cecil strongly disapproved of the book – unfortunately for Dee, Cecil's lifelong enmity would have serious repercussions on his career.

Three years later, Drake would make his triumphant return with the *Golden Hind* and half a million pounds in Spanish booty (a staggering £80 million today): Peruvian gold, silver and jewels and Indonesian spices. His backers would receive a phenomenal return of £47 for every £1 invested. (Dudley and Elizabeth would make thousands, but Cecil would refuse to accept a share of the profits from the piracy, rejecting a gift of ten bars of gold and urging that the treasure be returned to the Spanish.)

Although Dudley had won back ground by launching a pirates' expedition behind Cecil's back, the events of 1578 had again forced his retreat. Early in the year, the widowed Lettice had told him that she was pregnant. Her father Sir Francis Knollys, a member of the Privy Council, had insisted that he marry her.

But first he had needed to deal with his ex-lover Lady Douglas (who had given birth to his son four years earlier and whom he had secretly married, while making sure that the ceremony was not legal). He had summoned her to a clandestine meeting in the gardens of Greenwich Palace, where he had bribed her to disavow their relationship and give him custody of their son. Later, he would arrange for her to marry Edward Stafford, a distant relation of the Duke of Buckingham.

With Lady Douglas taken care of, his secret wedding to Lettice had taken place at Kenilworth in the spring. At about that time, Dudley had bought Wanstead for Lettice so that he could visit her when he was at court. (Later that year, no doubt for her own peace of mind, she would insist on a second marriage ceremony, assembling a new chaplain and different witnesses in one of the garden arcades at Wanstead.)

In April 1578, the new Spanish ambassador had reported that Elizabeth had cancelled a meeting with him, saying that she was unwell, so that she could go to see Dudley at his house on the Strand:

As she was walking in the garden that morning she found a letter which had been thrown into the doorway, which she took and read, and immediately came secretly to the house of the Earl of Leicester [Dudley] who is ill here.

Dudley had also just been pretending to be unwell. When Elizabeth had come to his bedside he had confessed all. No one knew how Elizabeth had taken the news of his secret marriage, but she had stayed with him until ten o'clock that night.

After Elizabeth had sided with 'the shepherd' Cecil at Wanstead in May, Dudley had left London for the spa town of Buxton. The journey north was a further tactical retreat, but this time he really was ill.

Dudley had first drunk Buxton's mineral waters in 1575, while suffering from aches, especially in his legs. His physicians had prescribed taking the waters and a strict diet – difficult advice to follow in that busy year of revels. Elizabeth had done all she could to help, even arranging her progress to take in Ashby-de-la-Zouch, in Leicestershire, where she had stayed longer than planned so that, as Gilbert Talbot had told his father Lord Shrewsbury, who owned the spa, 'the water of Buxton might have been daily brought hither for my Lord of Leicester' because his physicians had 'fully resolved that wheresoever my Lord of Leicester be, he must drink and use Buxton water twenty days together'. The following July, Dudley had travelled to Buxton for the first time, bathing in as well as drinking the water – he had returned the next two summers.

John Jones, one of Dudley's physicians, was a great advocate of the healing powers of mineral waters. Although Elizabeth was sceptical, she would do anything to help restore Dudley's health. When Dudley and Warwick had visited Buxton together in 1577, she had joked about the powers of the 'sacred water', teasing them about the Spartan regime, which was good for those of 'more replete' figures, such as Warwick (although by that time Dudley had also been putting on weight).

On 18 June 1578, Elizabeth's younger favourite, Sir Christopher Hatton, wrote to Dudley: 'Since your Lordship's departure, the Queen is found in continual and great melancholy.' The royal progress was in serious trouble:

This court wanteth [lacks] your presence. Her majesty is unaccompanied and, I assure you, the chambers are almost empty.

Hatton begged him to return. Elizabeth and her court could not do without him.

But Dudley had no intention of leaving early, as shown by his letter to Walsingham of 24 June:

I find great good in this bath already for the swelling you felt in my leg, not by drinking but by going into the bath . . . I would fain write to Lord Cobham, but I am pulled away from this, being forbidden to write much, as this day I have to her Majesty and others.

Finally, on 7 July, Dudley replied to Hatton, promising to return soon:

I hope now, ere long, to be with you, to enjoy that blessed sight which I have been so long kept from [Elizabeth]. A few of these days seem many years, and I think I shall feel a worse grief ere I seek so far a remedy again. I thank God, I have found hitherto great ease by this bath.

He would not travel to Buxton for another six years.

*

But while Dudley proved that his absence made Elizabeth's heart grow fonder, Cecil's improvements to Theobalds won him more fame. Elizabeth had paid him a visit earlier in the year (before going to Wanstead), and, by the summer, the Scottish ambassador was angling for an invitation. He had heard that the palace and gardens were the most impressive in England. Cecil downplayed them, saying that there was nothing at Theobalds 'worth your desire, considering your foreign travels; although percase [perhaps], you may see as much to content you as in Muscovia [Russia]. With no other I will offer any comparison'.

Although it might not yet have been in the same league as the palaces and gardens of Italy, Theobalds had eclipsed Kenilworth as the most exciting place in the kingdom.

During her summer progress of 1564, Elizabeth paid her first visits both to Theobalds and to Cambridge University, where Cecil was Chancellor. She greatly admired the college buildings, describing them as 'sumptuous edifices erected by most noble kings', and promised to leave a comparable monument of her own. But, as she added, 'Rome was not built in a day.' Her love of classical and Italian Renaissance architecture galvanised her courtiers, and especially Cecil, into looking to antiquity for inspiration.

Cecil had only just begun his improvements to the original moated manor house. As there was no suitable accommodation for her, she stayed the night at her own house at Enfield. Although Cecil had bought Theobalds for his younger son, Elizabeth had other plans.

After the royal visit, Cecil built a new house on a site closer to the roads leading to London and St Albans and enlarged his estate, enclosing part of the common fields of Cheshunt and Northaw. This provoked a riot by the people of those parishes, which was quelled by Dudley's brother Warwick and his troops.

Elizabeth came to Theobalds for three successive years (it was conveniently close both to London and to the great hunting parks of Enfield and Waltham Forest). During her fourth stay, in 1571, Cecil presented her with some verses and a portrait of the house. Although, according to one commentator, she was impressed by his 'curious buildings, delightful walks, and pleasant conceits [witty and ingenious works] within and without', she complained that her bedroom was too small. The following year, work commenced on the palatial Fountain Court, to the west of the original court and outer courtyard.

The Fountain Court at Theobalds was a new departure in Cecil's buildings. Burghley House and his house on the Strand incorporated classical-style features such as arcades and arches, but Theobalds drew inspiration directly from Renaissance Italian designs. With its four square towers and garden arcades, the Fountain Court bore a striking resemblance to one of the earliest Renaissance palaces, Poggio Reale ('Royal Hill'), near Naples, built by Florentine architect Giuliano da Maiano for King Alfonso II.

Part-fortress and part-palace, Poggio Reale was the prototype for some of the greatest European palaces of the fifteenth and sixteenth centuries. Cecil would have known it from Sebastiano Serlio's *Third Book of Architecture*, published in 1566. In the late 1540s, Serlio described the palace as 'among the many pleasant and charming spots' outside the city of Naples. Serlio drew an improved elevation of the palace, with outside arcades 'because of the greater utility and ornament they could give to the building' and a flat roof 'since I personally would like a building such as this to be uncovered, such that it could be used for the pleasure of looking at the countryside'. Poggio Reale had spectacular views of the Bay of Naples.

According to Moravian tourist Baron Waldstein, from the rooftop gallery at Theobalds visitors could see the Tower of London. The Astronomer's Walk at Theobalds was a development of the roof at Burghley House, which is full of fantastical architecture, including balustrades with obelisks, elaborate turrets, stone enclosures forming little rooms, plinths bearing carved fireballs and chimneys in the shape of classical columns topped with miniature castles. The Fountain Court's 330-foot-long three-storey south front surpassed its Neapolitan prototype in its use of enormous windows stretching from floor to ceiling.

By 1575, the Fountain Court at Theobalds was nearly complete, and so Cecil turned his attention to the gardens. Sparing no expense, he planned to make them as luxurious as the palace. Neapolitan gardens were strongly influenced by Moorish and, ultimately, Persian designs (dating from the Moors' occupation of Sicily and much of southern Italy). At Poggio Reale, the most arresting garden had a Moorish-style rectangular pool overlooked by an elaborate arcade. The early gardens of the Italian Renaissance were essentially water gardens; likewise, at Theobalds, fountains, pools and watercourses would provide a refreshing coolness in the heat and give life and movement to stone and greenery.

In 1579, Dudley was faced with a new threat when Cecil revived the match between Elizabeth and the Duke of Alençon, brother of the French king – seven years after she had rejected him at Kenilworth. Alençon made plans to come to England, and Dudley stayed away from court, as a sign of his unhappiness. Behind Elizabeth's back, he persuaded the majority of her privy councillors to vote against the visit. But in July, she granted Alençon a passport.

On his return to court, Dudley threw himself at her feet, begging her not to see her French suitor and shedding 'many tears', according to an observer. But she would not listen, and it looked as if nothing could stop Alençon's visit. Dudley left court again, accompanied by his sister Mary.

When Alençon finally came to England in August, he secretly stayed at Greenwich. Although he was ignored at court, his visit was an unexpected success: Elizabeth favoured his suit and treated him affectionately, nicknaming him her 'dear frog'. Although there was no talk of an official engagement, Alençon presented her with a huge diamond ring. Since the beginning of the reign, Elizabeth had kept a miniature of Dudley in her prayer book: she now added one of Alençon.

Dudley once more enlisted his writers in an attempt to ruin the match. That spring, Edmund Spenser had become poet-in-residence at Leicester House. In December, he made his poetical debut with *The Shepherd's Calendar*, which he dedicated to Dudley's nephew Sidney, 'the president / Of noblesse and of chivalry'. With Dudley and Sidney as his patrons, Spenser looked forward to a brilliant career in poetry and at court. But within six months, he had moved to Ireland.

In his *Shepherd's Calendar*, Spenser celebrated Elizabeth as a goddess of love and 'Queen of shepherds':

> See, where she sits upon the grassy green,
>   (O seemly sight!)
> Yclad in scarlet like a maiden queen,
>   And ermines white.
> Upon her head a crimson coronet,
> With damask roses and daffadillies set:
>   Bayleaves between,
>   And primroses green,
> Embellish the sweet violet.

The spring flowers in her crown were her emblems and symbolised eternal youth: expected praise. But, in the list of flowers that the shepherds' daughters brought as offerings, Spenser included a 'flower delice' (the fleur-de-lis or iris, emblem of the French royal family), which diplomatically hinted at her proposed marriage to Alençon:

> Bring hither the pink and purple columbine,
>   With gillyflowers:
> Bring coronations [carnations], and sops in wine,
>   Worn of paramours.
> Strew me the ground with daffadowndillies,
> And cowslips, and kingcups, and lovéd lilies:
>   The pretty paunce [pansy],
>   And the chevisaunce,
> Shall match with the fair flower delice.

Spenser's *Shepherd's Calendar* was published to acclaim. It has been suggested that Dudley also secretly commissioned him to write *Mother Hubbard's Tale*, an animal fable which satirised Alençon's courtship. Although the fable was circulated anonymously and in manuscript, everyone knew who was behind it. Spenser depicted Cecil as a wily old fox who was attempting to trick a noble lion (Elizabeth) into marriage. Alençon's agent Jean de Simier appeared in the story as an ape (a play on 'Simier'/'simian' and a reference to Elizabeth's nickname for him, 'monkey'). Some think that, as Dudley had intended, the fable created the worst kind of publicity for Elizabeth's projected marriage – and it seems likely to have enraged Cecil.

It was a reckless venture, especially in view of the fact that Elizabeth had cruelly punished the publisher and author of an anonymous pamphlet lambasting her match with Alençon, and stirring up anti-Catholic feeling, which had appeared in September. The author had openly mocked her, saying that she was too old for marriage. She had ordered the arrest of the printer, publisher and author. Although she had pardoned the printer because he was elderly, the publisher William Page and the author John Stubbs had each lost his right hand, but not before Stubbs had made a joke about it: 'Pray for me, now my calamity is at hand.' Afterwards, he had raised his hat with his left hand, shouting, 'God save the Queen!' and had then fainted. A year and a half later, Elizabeth would realise that she had acted harshly and would free Stubbs from prison, helping him to build a career in politics.

Some have conjectured that, in the wake of the furore created by Spenser's writings, Dudley dismissed him from his post as poet-in-residence but took the trouble to find him a new position as secretary to Lord Grey, the Lord Deputy of Ireland. However, it seems likely that his posting was a career move – the starting salary was £10 half-yearly.

According to rumour, Spenser had offended Dudley with a foolish joke about his wife's earlier reputation as a louche court lady in *The Shepherd's Calendar*. In 'March', a shepherd tells his friend that, when May comes,

> Then shall we sporten in delight
> And learn with Lettice to wax light [become wanton].

In the poem, Lettice was supposed to be the name of a fictitious country girl, but the most famous Lettice in the country was Lady Dudley. (Things were made worse when some saw an ill-judged pun in the line, since lettuce was believed to stimulate the appetite.) And soon after the mention of Dudley's wife, Spenser brought back painful memories of Elizabeth's visit to Kenilworth in 1575, when another shepherd told how he was wounded by love on accidentally surprising Cupid, who had been hiding in a 'bustling' and 'rustling' ivy bush. The scene recalled Dudley's performance as Deep Desire, hidden inside a quivering holly bush in the Kenilworth woods. Although at the time Dudley's pageant had saved the day, his triumph had been short-lived. And Spenser's substitution of ivy for holly might also have been unfortunate, since ivy symbolised lust.

Philip Sidney was also drawn into Dudley's anti-Alençon propaganda, with equally disastrous result. During Alençon's stay, he had quarrelled with Cecil's haughty son-in-law Oxford on the tennis court at Whitehall, in the presence of the French ambassadors. (Oxford had married Cecil's favourite daughter, whom Cecil had originally intended for Sidney.) In December, at Dudley's request and to coincide with the appearance of Spenser's *Shepherd's Calendar* and animal fable, Sidney wrote a letter to Elizabeth, attacking her match with Alençon. Elizabeth was furious with Sidney for daring to tell her what to do. In January he left the court in disgrace. But the court's loss would be poetry's gain, since, in retirement at his sister's house at Wilton, he would begin work on his pastoral romance the *Arcadia*.

[9]

'Lives the man and speaks he English that you highly esteem
and love at this day?'

Illustrations for the lily, from *Paradisi in Sole Paradisus Terrestris*

A Melancholy Mood

SOME OF THE EVENTS of these years appear to be reflected in a painting of Elizabeth by Gheeraerts, which Dudley may have commissioned in the mid-1580s. Elizabeth stands in front of a garden traditionally identified as belonging to Wanstead.

The portrait seems to offer the viewer a rare glimpse of Elizabeth's private life. She looks troubled. Commentators have speculated that the portrait might have been painted to record the visit that she paid to Wanstead when Dudley was not there: she is missing him.

Elizabeth is wearing a dress cut in the Polish style, embroidered with her emblematic flowers, including lilies, briar roses, gillyflowers and honeysuckle. She holds an olive branch, and a sword lies at her feet (symbols of peace and justice). In the garden behind her, two ladies and a gentleman are talking to each other, in a close group. In the distance, a lady is being welcomed into the garden by a yeoman of the guard, who stands next to an arcade – it is possible that this figure is Elizabeth, because a lady-in-waiting carries her train.

There are two small white dogs in the painting: one sits at Elizabeth's feet in the foreground, on a Turkish rug, while the other runs down a path, away from the ladies in the background. The garden is only shown in outline and consists of large rectangular beds bordered by herbs. It appears old-fashioned, apart from the Italianate arcade. As garden historian Paula Henderson has pointed out, however, the striking patterns of the Turkish rug on which Elizabeth stands resemble those found in contemporary gardens.

The painting is mysterious. What is Elizabeth thinking? Who are the courtiers standing behind her? The gentleman resembles Hatton, but the ladies have not been identified. What are they talking about? Their expressions suggest that there is some kind of intrigue going on, and the painting's sombre colours create an ominous atmosphere. Who is the lady in the background, at the garden gate? Is this a portrait in miniature, showing Elizabeth arriving at Wanstead, before she discovers that Dudley is not there?

❧

With his marriage to Lettice, Dudley had jeopardised his position as favourite. Even Kenilworth had lost its charm: after 1575, Elizabeth would never return. But Dudley maintained the castle as a military stronghold: according to one commentator, there was enough 'of all things necessary for horse and man . . . to furnish 10,000 soldiers . . . beside all munition and artillery brought thither when her Majesty was there, never carried back again'.

Cecil seized the opportunity to turn Elizabeth against Dudley. Whereas Dudley sought to destroy her cherished match with Alençon, Cecil pretended to support it. But, secretly, he held meetings of the Privy Council against it, during which one councillor commented that 'in years the Queen may be his mother' (Elizabeth was twenty years older than Alençon) and warned of the dangers of childbirth which 'few old maids escape'. Cecil put forward the greatest obstacle to the marriage: 'Monsieur is a Frenchman' and 'the people of this realm naturally hate that nation.'

He also wrote Elizabeth a long letter which must have compounded her confusion about Alençon. All of her life, she had lived for 'the sweet dew of pleasure and delight'. But she now needed a companion: if she were to continue with her hedonistic lifestyle, her senses would become 'so full that the satisfaction makes an end of pleasure'. Cecil appeared to recommend Alençon, while mocking the idea that she might still prefer Dudley: 'Or lives the man and speaks he English that you highly esteem and love at this day?' He warned her that, if she bowed to Dudley's wishes and remained single, she might never again be happy, while reminding her that, as queen, she was free to do as she liked: 'And doubt [fear] not, lady, for when lions make a leap, the bears [a reference to Dudley's emblem] and other beasts lie down.'

Dudley was well aware of Cecil's machinations and had confronted him in September 1578, in a letter ostensibly written to remonstrate with Cecil over his failure to consult him about some proposed changes in coinage:

We began our service with our sovereign together and have long continued hitherto together. And touching your fortune I am sure yourself cannot have a thought that ever I was enemy to it. How often and how far I have offered myself always in good dealing towards you – as for what friends have slipped from me and I have shaked from also, chiefly in respect of your Lordship, I know best myself. If I have not both long since and of late perceived your opinion, by your entire conference and dealings, better settled in others than in me, I could little perceive anything. Yet this may I say and boldly think, that all them never deserved so well at your hands as myself, except in such secret friendship as the world cannot judge of.

You may suppose this to be a strange humour in me to write thus and in this sort to you, having never done the like before, although I must confess I have had more cause of unkindness (as I have thought) than by this trifling occasion.

Your Lordship is more acquainted by years with the world than I am. And yet I, by reason we live in a worse world where more cunning and less fidelity is used, may judge of bad and good dealing as well as an elder man, and the one being so common and the other so scant must make the proof of the better the more precious whensoever it is found. And surely, my Lord, where I profess, I will be found both a faithful and a just, honest friend.

Dudley and Cecil had long maintained a show of friendship, despite their opposition, but it seemed that Cecil's mask was slipping.

In the first decade of the reign, as Wallace MacCaffrey points out, they 'devoted much of their energy . . . to attacking each other'. More than once, according to rumours, Dudley had tried to have Cecil killed: after Cecil had blocked Elizabeth's attempt to make Dudley Lord Protector (when she had been dangerously ill from smallpox, in 1562), Dudley had told the Spanish ambassador that 'if Cecil were out of the way the affairs of our Majesty would be more favourably dealt with and religious questions as well'. According to one story, Cecil had escaped from a Spanish assassin who had been waiting with a dagger at the foot of a staircase by taking a different one. Both Dudley and Cecil had long memories, and, from then onwards, Cecil had detected Dudley's hand in every new plot against his life.

Cecil had chosen a different method of eliminating his rival: scandal. In the first year of her reign, he had reminded Elizabeth that Dudley was the son and grandson of traitors and, for several years, had barred his appointment to the Privy Council. Notoriously, Cecil had spread rumours that Dudley was an expert poisoner who had murdered his wife. Dudley's love of Italy was taken as incriminating evidence, since the Italians were the best poisoners in the world. There were reports of schools for poisoners in Rome and Florence, and the whole of Europe was fascinated by the legendary poison of the Borgias, concealed in a signet ring and easily slipped into a victim's cup. One of Cecil's greatest fears was that Elizabeth would herself be 'Italianated', as he put it – a frightening possibility since she was in the care of an Italian doctor recommended by Dudley.

When Dudley had seemed close to marrying Elizabeth, in the mid-1560s, challenging Cecil's candidate the Archduke Charles of Austria, Cecil had drawn up a list of the pros and cons for each suitor. Charles had everything to offer England: as a Habsburg, he would bring with him the friendship of the King of Spain. 'Nothing', Cecil had written bluntly, 'is increased by marriage' to Dudley, whom he had described as a man 'infamed by the death of his wife', 'far in debt' and attentive to 'enhance only his particular friends to wealth, to offices, to lands'. In 1584, the anonymous author of *Leicester's Commonwealth* would accuse Dudley of many crimes, including murder and attempted murder by poison, describing him as 'Signor Machiavel' and as a man 'of no religion but what brings him gain, like Machiavelli, his master'.

Yet Dudley and Cecil had collaborated with each other when it had suited them, conspiring against Norfolk and Mary, Queen of Scots, and had even gone into business together, founding gold and silver mines. During their scheme against Norfolk, Dudley had stayed with Cecil at Theobalds, and they seemed to have enjoyed each other's company, judging from Cecil's letter to Sir Henry Sidney: 'At the writing hereof my Lord of Leicester is in my house at dice and merry, where he hath taken pains to be evil lodged these two nights. And tomorrow we return both to the court.' As usual, Cecil was being self-deprecating – with the completion of the Fountain Court, Theobalds was one of the most luxurious palaces in England. Both men owed their position to Elizabeth: as Dudley reminded Cecil, they had begun their service at the same time.

Despite their rivalry, Elizabeth's reliance on them both and their shared concern for her well-being had encouraged an uneasy truce. Her reluctance to make decisions, when faced with such issues as military intervention in the Netherlands and the fate of Mary, Queen of Scots, further served to unite her councillors. (Current historians think that the competition for her favour between Dudley and Cecil might have been overstated in earlier accounts and that it certainly contrasted with the more vexed rivalries that would develop in her court.)

In 1581, Dudley and Cecil once again buried their differences. Their favour with the Queen was in jeopardy – Alençon had renewed his suit and, despite their joint opposition, Elizabeth had invited him to return to England.

Whereas Cecil had initially supported the match as a way of distracting Elizabeth from Dudley and forming diplomatic ties with France, the situation had completely changed. Elizabeth appeared to have fallen for Alençon. For the first time, Cecil found himself in the same position as Dudley: he too stood to lose everything if Elizabeth took a husband. In April of 1581, when Alençon's agents came to England to prepare the ground for his arrival in November, Dudley and Cecil united against their common enemy.

Dudley provided transport for the huge party (five hundred French noblemen and women) from Dover to Somerset House. On St George's Day, he gave a feast at Whitehall which surpassed the legendary Whitehall celebrations of 1572 for the visit of the Duke of Montmorency, who had come to sign a new peace treaty and to present Alençon's first proposal of marriage. A new banqueting house, specially commissioned for the feast, stood in the gardens, near the river.

The banqueting house had been completed in three weeks and three days, at a cost of £1,886. The interior was covered with silver-and-gold cloth hung with canvas painted with fruits and flowers. The ceiling displayed stars, sunbeams, clouds and the royal arms of England and France. Suspended from the ceiling were baskets full of fruit spangled with gold. At one end of the pavilion, there was a platform with a throne, beneath a silk canopy decorated with roses made of seed-pearls, where Elizabeth welcomed the young Dauphin and his entourage.

A few months earlier, Cecil had taken the extraordinary step of dismissing the Lord Chamberlain, Sussex, from the job of producing the highlight of the festivities. Instead, Cecil had commissioned Dudley's nephew Sidney to write a grand pageant to be staged in the tilt-yard at Whitehall.

Sidney's elaborate pageant featured an enormous fortress which stood at the top of a mount: the Fortress of Perfect Beauty. From there, Elizabeth and Dudley watched the entertainments in the tilt-yard, while music played from a hidden source (there were musicians inside the mount). The Sons of Desire (Sidney and his fellow challengers, including the poet Fulke Greville) rode into the tilt-yard, accompanied by soldiers with wooden cannons firing flowers, perfumes and fireworks at the fortress. The challengers and soldiers then scaled the fortress on ladders, pelting the walls with flowers and love tokens. But it was all in vain: Lady Beauty's (Elizabeth's) stronghold proved impregnable. Sidney's Siege of the Fortress of Perfect Beauty sent a clear message to Alençon that he stood no chance of winning Elizabeth.

As if that were not enough, numerous defenders of the fortress then surged into the tilt-yard. There were knights in classical costumes and in armour painted to look like water, with mirrors as shields, as well as two young Irishmen with long gold hair, riding bareback. A heavily bejewelled knight in armour painted to look like snakeskin came accompanied by a doctor bearing a shield that showed a woman's face. This lovesick knight in snakeskin was defeated by the Unknown Knight, whose face was hidden by his helmet and whose armour and shield bore no heraldic markings: Elizabeth's Champion, Sir Henry Lee, who lived up to his title by breaking six staves in a row. (As for the sinister knight in snakeskin, who else could he have represented but Alençon, seen by Dudley, Cecil and all opponents to the match as a snake in the garden?)

The defenders in the jousts were all friends of Dudley and Sidney, and included Lettice's brothers, who rode as the Sons of

Despair (alongside knights representing Disdain and Despair). On her marriage to Dudley, Lettice's entire family had fallen into disgrace, and her father had compounded the situation by opposing the royal match with Alençon. Her brothers hoped to win back Elizabeth's favour by their performance in the tournament.

Before the jousts, however, they took part in a masque set in the garden of Eden. The stage set was a ruined tower surrounded by fruit trees, with a lantern at its summit, representing a besieged kingdom (England) and the sun (Elizabeth); the knights playing Adam and Eve wore armour pinned with apples, and a large snake crawled out of a hole in the tower towards the fruit on the trees. Behind the tower stood six trumpet-players in eagle costumes.

After a fanfare, an angel stepped forward to rebuke the Sons of Desire for having dared to attack the sun. He then advised Adam and Eve to stay 'in the garden' of the Queen's 'graces'; their reward would be readmission to Paradise. He joked that, on their return, they should try to resist the forbidden fruit and the temptation to argue about who was to blame for the Fall: Elizabeth would decide that at the end of the entertainments.

Sidney's flattery, comparing Elizabeth's England to Eden, was also a private joke. Anyone familiar with Whitehall knew that the staircase leading from the garden gallery to the garden was called 'the Adam and Eve stairs', after a life-size painting of Adam and Eve in the gallery. And, in one way or another, Elizabeth, her 'graces' (her ladies) and her favourites always played at being Adam and Eve in gardens.

Siege warfare had featured in court pageants since the Middle Ages. Its popularity as a subject had been revived during the reign of Henry VIII, who had won glory with his victorious sieges of French towns, culminating in his capture of Boulogne in 1544.

Late Tudor military strategy was, however, mostly defensive. Elizabeth and Cecil preferred to maintain their peace policy until forced to send in troops to defend English strongholds in Europe under attack from France and Spain. This had resulted in the loss of Rouen and Le Havre to the French.

When Elizabeth did nothing to rescue English towns in the Netherlands from the Spanish, William of Orange urged Dudley and Alençon to come to his aid. Dudley's hands were tied, but he encouraged Alençon to take up the governorship of the Netherlands and to try to persuade Elizabeth to provide the necessary finance. Alençon became governor despite Elizabeth's warning that, if he went ahead, she could never marry him, since the Spanish might interpret this as a declaration of war by England.

Alençon remained in England for three months. Officially, his visit was again a secret, and he stayed in a specially made canvas pavilion in the grounds of Richmond Palace. Elizabeth slipped out of the palace to see him there – it was over twenty years since she had met a royal suitor in a garden. During Alençon's stay, Dudley and Cecil pretended to support his marriage plans, knowing that since his acceptance of the governorship, they would come to nothing. Ever the opportunist, Dudley was also taking bribes from Alençon's brother King Henri III of France for supporting the match.

For the first time in the reign, Elizabeth felt isolated. Her two trusted advisers were conspiring to ruin a match which, in other circumstances, might have made her happy. She teased her courtiers by placing a ring on Alençon's finger on the anniversary of the Coronation and called him the 'most deserving and constant of her lovers'. In return, he gave her a little golden flower, on which stood a golden frog, with a delicate pearl pendant.

The outcome of Alençon's second trip to England was mainly financial: Elizabeth agreed to fund his activities in the Netherlands. He made ready to leave in February 1582. Elizabeth arranged for him to be escorted to Sandwich by Dudley, Sidney, her cousin Hunsdon and a hundred gentlemen pensioners, and gave him a parting gift of £25,000 (about £3.7 million today). She also insisted on Dudley, Sidney and Hunsdon travelling with him to the Dutch port of Flushing.

Elizabeth wrote love letters to Alençon, saying that she wished her 'frog' were 'swimming in Thames', rather than in the marshy waterways of the Netherlands. But Alençon proved to be a poor governor. He was jealous of Dudley's friendship with William of Orange, whom he resented, and attempted a coup. When this failed, he retreated to France. With his whereabouts in France unknown, Elizabeth lost touch with him.

10

'[The Earl of] Leicester voluntarily became a prisoner
in his chamber'

Design for a dwarf shrub maze, from Thomas Hill's
Proffitable Arte of Gardening, 1568

The Labyrinth

JUST A FORTNIGHT before Elizabeth's visit to Theobalds, Cecil lay on his couch in his study, writing in his journal:

May 15th 1583. The Queen's Majesty at Theobalds the 27, 28, 29, 30 May. Note, on the 24 May 1575 she was also at Theobalds, on 14 May 1577, and in July 1572.

As he anticipated Elizabeth's four-day stay, he reviewed his earlier successes. He intended to make 1583 another glorious year. It had been several years since she had last come to his palace.

Cecil's apartments were on the north side of the Fountain Court – he kept his best accommodation on the south and west sides for his guests. When he drew up his schedule of accommodation, however, he was full of misgivings. The rooms overlooking the Great Garden, on the south side of the Fountain Court, were reserved for Elizabeth and her inner circle. Dudley's rooms were next to Elizabeth's, as usual. No one openly questioned this arrangement – in the royal palaces, Dudley and Elizabeth had slept in adjoining rooms since the 1560s. Elizabeth's favourite cousin, Lord Hunsdon, and Dudley's family, Lord and Lady Warwick, had suites near by. As always, Elizabeth would be surrounded by the Dudley clan.

On 27 May, Elizabeth arrived at Theobalds, accompanied by an enormous retinue. The day was flooded with sunshine from dawn until dusk. By mid-afternoon, the palace and its grounds glowed in the golden light. But it was still too hot for walking in the wide open spaces of the Great Garden. She had a choice of what to do – she could take a walk in the avenues or, better still, a boat trip in the new waterways. Since her last stay at Theobalds, Cecil had created a maze of canals surrounding the palace on three sides, vying with the great lake that encompassed Kenilworth.

Elizabeth drifted in a barge around the watery labyrinth, accompanied by Dudley and a few of her younger favourites. The banks of the canals were planted with tall shrubs. Turning a corner, they came across a miniature merchant's ship, complete with sails. Friend or foe? The Dutch flags set their minds at rest, and then jets exploded from the ship, transforming it into a fountain.

Dudley was still hoping that Elizabeth would send him to fight the Spanish. But after Alençon's failure as Governor of the Netherlands, she had told the Dutch that she could no longer support them. She had already spent over £60,000 (nearly £9 million today) on the conflict. The peace policy was a victory for Cecil, but how long could it last? Her withdrawal of sponsorship had inevitably led to Spanish advances. Business interests in the Netherlands were surely too lucrative to lose.

Elizabeth felt safe at Theobalds. But the surprise blasts from the fountain brought back memories of another scene on a barge, which had taken place in 1579, at Greenwich.

She had been alone with Jean de Simier, Alençon's flamboyant envoy. They had dined alone together – Dudley hated Simier, so Elizabeth had sent him out hunting with another French diplomat. A trip on the river had seemed the most pleasant way of spending the rest of the afternoon.

Elizabeth and Simier had just sat down in the royal barge when a shot struck one of the rowers. He had been standing just six feet away from them, and the shot passed through both his arms – it had been fired at close range. Elizabeth threw her scarf to the bargemen, who rushed to help him. Simier was in hysterics, claiming someone had tried to kill him, but Elizabeth said that the shot had been aimed at her.

In the subsequent public inquiry, she played down what had happened. The verdict was that the man responsible (a soldier in a nearby boat) had fired his gun by accident. He was pardoned.

But Simier accused Dudley of having made an attempt on his life. In revenge, he leaked the story of Dudley's clandestine marriage to Lettice, little knowing that this was old news at court, although still a secret to the wider world. For Simier's benefit, Elizabeth talked about sending Dudley to the Tower. Lord Sussex jokingly suggested that she should imprison him in the Mirefleur Tower, a banqueting pavilion in the Greenwich park on the Venus Hill. Dudley escaped these punishments and, for a few days, according to Fulke Greville, 'like a wise man . . . voluntarily became a prisoner in his chamber'.

Now the barge was gliding past the fountain, just out of reach of the jets. Elizabeth sank back into the cushions. Herons perched near by, as still as statues. Milk-white swans glided ahead. The water was so clear that Dudley and her other favourites could see the coloured pebbles and glass lining the river-bed. Many different-coloured carp swam just below the surface.

Further along the southernmost edge of the Great Garden, Elizabeth saw an avenue of pyramid-shaped buildings. She asked her bargemen to steer towards the river-bank and stop near by. Dudley helped her to disembark, and they followed the avenue to its end, where a flight of steps led up to a bathing pool with miniature watermills and fountains in the shape of serpents.

Overlooking the pool was a banqueting house, with marble busts of the Roman emperors on a semicircular pillar. Cecil was waiting outside the pavilion, on his little grey mule. He was wearing crimson and held a posy of gillyflowers and honeysuckle. He dismounted and presented the flowers to Elizabeth, then invited her to take a look inside.

Curving staircases led to the first-floor room. The ceiling was covered with frescoes of naked men and women. Cisterns containing fish divided up the room. Elizabeth crossed a little bridge to reach an island where there was a great table made of a solid piece of black touchstone. The design was inspired by the maritime theatre in the Emperor Hadrian's second-century pleasure grounds at Tivoli.

Cecil's complex of banqueting house and pool was a garden within a garden. It was similar to the more elaborate retreat at Gaillon, near Rouen (created by Cardinal de Bourbon in the 1550s), where a classical pavilion overlooked a pool and canal leading to a second pool, in the centre of which stood a rocky island with a Gothic hermitage. Both of these water gardens were modelled on the Emperor Hadrian's enormous outdoor dining room, where guests had lounged on couches, eating from dishes on trays in the shape of ships floating on the pool beneath them.

The banqueting house, with its marble emperors, recalled the glories of ancient Rome, but Elizabeth discovered a new kind of golden age elsewhere at Theobalds. This lay in the Great Garden and inside the palace itself.

11

'I do not think for the knowledge of plants, that he is
inferior to any.'

Detail of the title-page of John Gerard's *Herball*,
engraved by William Rogers, 1597

The Herbalist

CECIL'S SECRETARY and biographer Sir Michael Hicks describes how he 'greatly delighted in making gardens, fountains, and walks', and, in the archives at Hatfield, there survives a plan of the gardens in Cecil's distinctive, spidery handwriting. His sketch for the Great Garden shows nine enormous compartments, which were overlooked by Elizabeth's palatial new bedroom. The garden is surrounded by canals, and centres on a fountain. There is a bowling alley on the left and a 'long alley' on the right, as well as terraces in each of the gardens. The maze garden is shown on the western side of the palace.

The Great Garden was a series of enclosures. Compartments were arranged in an orderly fashion inside hedges surrounded by canals ultimately shielded by walls. The garden offered protection. As long as Elizabeth was at Theobalds, she would be out of danger.

By late afternoon, it was cool enough to take a walk in the gardens. Elizabeth and Dudley left the stone arcade of the Fountain Court and walked through an arch in the whitethorn-and-privet hedge surrounding the Great Garden. The hedges looked as if they had been trimmed with razors.

From the Great Garden, Elizabeth and Dudley admired the three-storey garden façade of the Fountain Court, made up almost entirely of huge windows (with two-storey bay windows in the centre and at the ends). When the sun struck the façade they were dazzled.

They entered the first of the garden's nine gigantic compartments, which were enclosed by herb hedges planted, at intervals, with cherry trees. Seven of the compartments were laid with grass. Only two contained flowers: in the first, there were native flowers inside herb borders cut into the shape of the royal arms and forming a labyrinthine pattern. In the second, simple geometrical shapes enclosed rare flowers, including a Persian lily sent to Cecil by the English ambassador in Constantinople.

If Dudley had the best writers, actors and musicians in the country, Cecil had the best gardener. John Gerard was the leading expert on herbs and rare plants and was in contact with the greatest plantsmen in Europe. He had a house and garden of his own at Holborn, one of the most fashionable areas in London (Cecil had given him the land), and supervised Cecil's gardens at his house on the Strand and at Theobalds. He was also keeper of the physic garden at the Royal College of Physicians.

Today, Gerard is known for his famous *Herbal*, published in 1597 and dedicated to Cecil. Born in Cheshire, Gerard moved to London to train as a barber surgeon. While an apprentice, he travelled in northern Europe and Russia as a ship's surgeon. He brought back plants from these expeditions and, in parallel with his medical career, began to build up a reputation as a herbalist and gardener.

Many of the early plantsmen and botanists began their careers in medicine. Gerard was close friends with the great French botanist Matthias de l'Obel (the lobelia was named after him), who studied medicine at Montpellier. De l'Obel lived in England between 1569 and 1574, and he and Gerard went on plant-hunting expeditions together: both were as interested in native English plants as exotics. In 1570, de l'Obel published his ground-breaking book on English plants, which he dedicated to Elizabeth: the first herbal to classify plants by their leaves, it contains eighty 'first records' of plants in England. About the same time, he also helped Gerard to write the first part of his *Herbal*.

Botany was in its infancy. The sixteenth century saw the creation of the first botanic gardens in Christian Europe: Pisa in 1543 and Padua in 1545. Gerard's garden at Holborn, dating from the mid-1570s, was one of the earliest botanic gardens in England. Gerard made his garden entirely at his own expense, funding it largely by exchanging English natives for rare plants from all over the world.

Cecil hired Gerard in 1577 (two years after Elizabeth's final visit to Kenilworth). Gerard doubled as his gardener and personal herbalist: a winning combination, especially since Elizabeth was, like Cecil, devoted to herbal cures. And sixteenth-century pleasure gardens were, essentially, herb gardens: the geometrical patterns were outlined in herbs (or 'simples', as they were known). Hyssop, thyme and lavender not only produced delightful scents but cloaked foul odours, an important consideration given Elizabeth's notoriously sensitive sense of smell.

One of Elizabeth's chief physicians, George Baker, developed a great admiration for Gerard. In a letter which formed part of the preface to the *Herbal*, Baker told a story about a contest between Gerard and a distinguished French herbalist. He and the French plantsman spent a day 'searching the most rarest simples', as Baker relates, 'but when it came to the trial, my French man did not know one to his four'. Baker had only the highest praise for Gerard:

And if I may speak without partiality of the author of this book, for his great pains, his no less expenses in travelling far and near (for the attaining of his skill) was never contented with the knowledge of those simples which grow in these parts, but upon his proper cost and charges has had out of all parts of the world all the rare simples which by any means he could attain to, not only to have them brought, but has procured by his excellent knowledge to have them growing in his garden, which as the time of year serves may be seen: for there shall you see all manner of strange trees, herbs, roots, plants, flowers, and other such rare things, that it would make a man wonder, how one of his degree, not having the purse of a number, could ever accomplish the same. I protest upon my conscience, I do not think for the knowledge of plants, that he is inferior to any.

It is likely that Elizabeth and Cecil shared this opinion.

When royal astrologer John Dee fell seriously ill in 1594, Elizabeth sent Gerard to treat him. Dee's illness followed a crushing disappointment in his career: Cecil had blocked his promotion to a post which he had long coveted, and which, owing to his financial circumstances, he had desperately needed, the mastership of St John's Cross (a London almshouse). He had enlisted all of his friends and his family to lobby for him, even persuading his wife to accost Elizabeth while she was walking in her private garden at Somerset House. His friend John Whitgift, the Archbishop of Canterbury, however, had told him that at a dinner at Theobalds, Cecil had advised Elizabeth to put off making a decision about the mastership indefinitely. Dee's subsequent illness had grown steadily worse: his doctors and Elizabeth's own herbal remedies had had no effect. Nevertheless, under Gerard's care, Dee made a full recovery and lived for a further fifteen years.

The year 1577 marked a watershed in Elizabethan gardens in more ways than one, with the publication of *The Gardener's Labyrinth* by Thomas Hill. The book appeared posthumously under the mysterious pseudonym 'Didymus Mountain', and was dedicated to Cecil. Whereas earlier books on gardening had been practical manuals, *The Gardener's Labyrinth* presented gardening as a gentleman's occupation, and reflected the shift in gardens from utilitarian plots to pleasure spaces.

Hill was the author of two highly successful gardening manuals: *A Most Brief and Pleasant Treatise, Teaching How to Dress, Sow, and Set a Garden* (1558) and *The Profitable Art of Gardening* (1568), which had been reissued with an additional treatise on 'the Art of Grafting and Planting of Trees' in 1572 (*The Profitable Art of Gardening* would go through ten editions by 1608). A prolific writer, he had also published books on astronomy, astrology, physiognomy, bee-keeping, dreams and palmistry. After his death in 1575, the manuscript of *The Gardener's Labyrinth* had been completed at his request by Henry Dethick, Chancellor of Carlisle.

Dethick's decision to dedicate *The Gardener's Labyrinth* to Cecil reflected both his standing in the kingdom and his well-known love of gardens. The pseudonym 'Didymus Mountain' punned on Hill's name (see John 11:16: 'Thomas, which is called Didymus [Twin]') but also possibly meant 'Twin Peaks' (in Greek myth, Mount Parnassus, the home of the Muses, had two summits). The book's bizarre pseudonym and abstract title were calculated to appeal to Cecil, who loved intellectual puzzles and word games. Gardening had become as much a philosophical as a practical activity.

Gerard built the garden at Theobalds, month by month.

Around the Ides of January, he and his team of gardeners dug, dunged, turned up again and levelled the earth. They used doves' droppings, which were the best because of their strength, strewing it thinly on the ground as if scattering seeds. When this was not available, they used donkey dung, which brought up fewer weeds than cattle dung, throwing it on in heaps. After levelling the earth, they beautified the garden with arbours, either in February, weather permitting, or else in March, before treading out the quarters and beds.

Gerard made his flower beds no more than three feet broad, so that his weeders could reach into the middle without having to tread on them and risk damaging any sprouting seeds and plants. The paths between the beds were about a foot wide, so that they could weed one half first and then easily turn to the opposite one. Whitethorn was laid on them as protection from birds and fowl. When his men had trodden out the flower beds, they had levelled the alleys and walks, measuring them with a line to make them either three or four feet broad, and then cleanly sifted them with river or sea sand. They used the finest sand for the bowling alleys, so that it did not clog up underfoot when it rained.

The phases of the moon and times of year determined the best times for sowing. In February, Gerard sowed cabbages in the vegetable garden, during the waning of the moon. Between February and April, with each new moon, he sowed marjoram, violets, flower-gentles (a type of amaranthus), double marigolds, white poppies, rosemary and lavender. Marigold seeds were sown in well-dressed and well-husbanded soil, on the increase of the moon, and were often replanted in new beds in sunny positions, as near as possible to the time of the moon's increase. Frequent replanting and careful watering made many of Gerard's loveliest flowers, including marigolds, daisies, columbines, primroses, cowslips, Sweet Johns, pinks and carnations, grow bigger, fairer and with more doubles. By planting many seeds together in one hole, during the moon's first quarter, keeping them well watered and removing and clipping the leaves according to the moon's course, his flowers grew bigger, broader and more beautiful than usual, with more flowers at harvest time than in the springtime. He only sowed during temperate weather, and took great care over the quality of his seeds.

In mid-February and in the moon's first quarter, he planted rose trees in short, narrow beds filled with dry, stony earth, but no dung. Wherever possible, he planted old trees, which were better than young ones, and pruned and refreshed them each year by setting new, dry earth around their roots. March and April, when the moon was waning, were the best months for sowing pinks, pansies and wallflowers.

During the springtime, five days before weeding, he and his men dunged and dug the beds again: with frequent, diligent digging, the earth and dung were well mired together. They planted most of the mazes in the compartments with hyssop, thyme or winter savory, which were green all year round, and set some with cotton lavender.

Gerard sowed parsley seeds between mid-May and the summer solstice, keeping them well watered. During the summer months, he protected the beds with a canopy of woollen cloth so that they were not stifled by the heat. This was just one of many remedies against the weather. Droughts usually occurred around the dog star, when his men watered the flower beds twice a day, at dawn and dusk. During heatwaves (as with bitterly cold spells), they covered the beds with thick straw mattresses held up with forked sticks at the corners and sides. There was also a gigantic pump, which sprayed up great fountains, and drip-feed irrigation. The first rule of tending young fruit trees was to keep them watered in dry weather: Gerard and his men bound together wheat straw, which they used to cast water on their saplings every evening, in order to keep them moist. When the ground was clogged with water, they dug deep gutters here and there, leading to deep pits at the end of each garden.

Herbs such as marjoram, thyme, hyssop, basil, savory, sage, bugloss and borage were sown in beds in sunny positions and given frequent raking, weeding and watering. He also grew orange, lemon, pomegranate and myrtle trees and date palms, which were protected on the north side from cold winds. When his lemon trees had grown, he uprooted them and replanted them in chests filled with light earth. His men rolled them here and there, so as to avoid the fierce heat of the sun and the bitter, cold air, or put them under a special cover or glasshouse. Garlic, onions, leeks and mustard seed were sown near the end of the harvest.

Whatever Gerard planted during the moon's increase he cut down during its waning. Most plants were best gathered on the moon's decrease and on a clear day. Between 14 March and 24 June, he took leaves from his medicinal herbs. Towards the end of June, he gathered their stalks and stems and mowed the grass in the meadows. From 14 September onwards, he dug up the roots of his medicinal plants. His men always gathered fruit when the moon was on the wane: it was believed that fruit gathered too early would taste bitter.

During harvest time, he dug and dunged the flower beds again. After All Hallows' Tide (All Saints' Day, November), he dug all over the roots of his biggest trees, uncovering them about four or five feet around the trunk.

Every May, the gardens at Theobalds were full of spring and summer flowers. Orange and lemon trees in tubs lined the paths.

(Since the Middle Ages, Paradise has been depicted as a garden containing plants that flower and fruit at the same time, as well as flowers that usually bloom in different seasons.) In his *Herbal*, Gerard described some of the amazing special effects at Theobalds, such as 'a flourishing show of summer beauties in the midst of winter's force, and a goodly spring of flowers, when abroad a leaf is not to be seen'. This 'summer in winter' effect was achieved by the use of hothouses containing vast numbers of potted plants (pre-dating by a hundred years the extravagances of Louis XIV at Versailles).

Like Kenilworth before it, Theobalds was a place of wonders. It looked like Paradise on earth. But Gerard's horticultural conjuring tricks were made possible by his army of gardeners, who came from the poor of the surrounding areas. As an act of charity, Cecil allotted to them the sum of £10 a week.

Elizabeth's visits (there were thirteen in all) usually took place in May, partly because she liked to begin her progress at Theobalds and partly so that Gerard could achieve his spring-summer effect in the gardens. He had filled the pleasure grounds with the loveliest native plants and the latest, flashiest exotics; native flowers were valued even more highly than exotics, since they included Elizabeth's emblems, the violet, rose, lily and honeysuckle (originally flowers associated with the Virgin Mary, now decorating the Protestant Virgin Queen). In his *Herbal*, he highlighted the rose's royal associations, saying it 'doth deserve the chief and prime place among all flowers whatsoever; being not only esteemed for his beauty, virtues, and his fragrant and odoriferous smell; but also because it is the honour and orna-ment of our English Sceptre, as by the conjunction appeareth in the uniting of those two most royal houses of Lancaster and York'. In his catalogue of plants in his garden at Holborn, he listed sixteen kinds of roses. At Theobalds, he underplanted them with several different varieties of periwinkles: some with blue, some white and some double purple flowers. Although the rose was pre-eminent as the Tudor emblem, he described violets as 'the greatest ornament' of gardens, adding that they were good for the soul:

They admonish and stir up a man to that which is comely and honest; for flowers through their beauty, variety of colour, and exquisite form, do bring to a liberal and gentlemanly mind, the remembrance of honesty, comeliness, and all kinds of virtues. For it would be an unseemly and filthy thing, as a certain wise man saith, for him that doth look upon and handle fair and beautiful things, and who frequents and is conversant in fair and beautiful places, to have his mind not fair, but filthy and deformed.

If that was true, Elizabeth's court must have contained some of the most beautiful minds in the world.

The walkways at Theobalds were lined with pots of carnations, pinks and gillyflowers. Symbols of love and devotion, they came in extraordinary colours, shapes and sizes, and their scents were much stronger and sweeter than usual. There were rose, purple, red and streaked varieties, as well as the scarlet doubles that were fashionable at court. Originally from Central and Eastern Europe, pinks were still exotic and expensive. Gerard's favourite kind were what he called 'feathered' or 'star' pinks, with their delicate, frilled petals and deep pink 'eye'. His great coup was a yellow gillyflower – the first in the country – that a friend had sent him from Poland. ('Gillyflower' derives from 'July flower'; pinks were also known as 'sops-in-wine' since their perfume, reminiscent of cloves, made them a good flavouring for alcohol.)

The most exciting plants at Theobalds were the most rare and expensive. In the Great Garden, Elizabeth was amazed by the glittering purple-and-crimson flowers of the Marvel of Peru, which Gerard said deserved to be called the Marvel of the World. Brought from Peru to Spain in 1568 and from there to England, the Marvel of Peru was also known as the Four O'Clock Flower: in hot weather, its flowers opened in mid-afternoon, stayed open all night and closed at about eight the next morning. But in England on cooler days, as Gerard described, the flowers 'remain open the whole day, and are closed only at night, and so perish, one flower lasting but only one day, like the true Ephemerum or Hemerocallis'. The temperate English climate could be fatal to tropical blooms.

There were hives in the kitchen garden and in holes in the south-facing walls of the Great Garden (the sound and sight of bees enhanced the garden's pleasures). Gerard took diligent care of his bees, all year round. In the second week of April, on a clear, warm day, he cleaned the hives, wiping away the filth – such as spiders' webs – that had gathered during the winter. He then smoked the hives with dried ox dung to destroy the tiny worms, maggots and butterflies that bred in the honeycombs.

From the beginning of May until the end of June, his men watched the hives so that the young swarms did not fly away.

From 10 June until 10 August, they opened the hives every now and then, and smoked them to strengthen them. At midsummer, Gerard drove his bees from their hives in the kitchen garden, setting them in southerly, warm positions. The hives were set on planks not too low to the ground, with herbs and borders surrounding them to protect them from north and north-easterly winds.

From the beginning of the dog days (around 17 July) until 18 September, he kept a close watch on his bees, making sure that they were protected from hornets. Two or three days before the new moon, he cleansed the hives, filling up any chinks and clefts with a mixture of ox dung and clay in order to protect them against butterflies. He cut out the old combs from the hives in October and, during the winter months, kept his bees alive with wine, sweet cream and honey. His technique was to rub two big sticks with fennel or honey and pear-tree leaves or herbs like flowering savory or marjoram, and then sprinkle them with sweet, pleasant wine, setting the sticks in a cross from one side of the hive to the other.

Visitors found at least two more exotics in the kitchen garden: potatoes and tobacco. These star exotics promised untold riches for English merchant-adventurers. To his delight, Gerard's potatoes would 'grow and prosper' at Theobalds 'as in their own native country'. He also described them as 'a food, as also a meat for pleasure, being either roasted in the embers, or boiled and eaten with oil, vinegar and pepper, or dressed some other way by the hand of a skilful cook'.

Gerard had probably been given his potatoes by Thomas Heriot, a botanist who had accompanied Drake on his voyage around the world. It was likely that the potato had been one of the plants collected by Heriot in the aftermath of Drake's raids on Spanish ships anchored in Chilean harbours in 1578. Although potatoes came from South America, Gerard called them Potatoes of Virginia as a way of promoting Raleigh's North American colony, named after Elizabeth, the Virgin Queen.

Cecil served potatoes to Elizabeth as a delicacy. They were objects of desire in more ways than one. Not only were they extremely hard to come by, they were believed to be an aphrodisiac. Surprisingly, potatoes are among the most memorable exotics in Shakespeare. In *The Merry Wives of Windsor*, Falstaff looks forward to spending the night with his beloved and, in the excitement of anticipation, cries out: 'Let the sky rain potatoes!' By the late 1590s, the myth that potatoes were the food of love had become a joke. But they were still news in the botanical world, as shown by Gerard's boast that his *Herbal* contained the first published illustration of a potato.

Tobacco had first been introduced to England in 1564 by Sir John Hawkins, but by 1583 it was still not well known. And, owing to its expense, it was only for the rich. Drake had brought back what he called English tobacco from Virginia. It was unsmokable compared with South American tobacco, and, at first, there had been little commercial interest in the new intoxicant.

But during his months of waiting for Elizabeth to let him set sail on his next expedition to the New World, Drake had shown Sir Walter Raleigh how to smoke South American tobacco.

Raleigh had seen its potential immediately. He had persuaded the Governor of Virginia to teach him how to smoke the long-stemmed clay pipe which he claimed to have invented (in fact, it was a Native American design). Raleigh tried to give the impression that tobacco came from Virginia, but it would be years before seeds brought from South America produced any kind of harvest there. In 1579, Raleigh had staged at Plymouth a double PR coup for tobacco and for Virginia with a demonstration by some of his colonists of the art of 'drinking tobacco': inhaling and swallowing the smoke. The show had been a sensation.

Apart from the pleasure of admiring the plants, what made Theobalds special were its magnificent avenues, where Elizabeth walked with Dudley and Cecil beneath the sycamore tree (or Great Maple), described by Gerard as 'a stranger in England, only it grows in the walks and places of pleasure of noble men, where it especially is planted for the shadow sake'. As they could see, its fruit resembled 'the innermost wings of grasshoppers'. Elizabeth discovered banqueting arbours under the boughs and summer houses in the branches of the tallest trees (probably variations on the two-storey summer house in an ancient lime tree created for Elizabeth by Cecil's close friend Lord Cobham, in the grounds of his house in Kent).

In his first year at Theobalds, Gerard had planted a new avenue of lime trees. The following year, work had begun on several banqueting houses, and Cecil had set about increasing his stock of fish: in a list of improvements to the pleasure grounds, he had noted that his old friend Sir Thomas Gresham (the greatest financier of the age and creator of the Royal Exchange) had sent him some carp.

The bowers were constructed in a similar way to those at Kenilworth: jasmine or willow poles made up frames bound together with willow shoots to form square or arch shapes, which were covered with vines, melons and cucumbers, or rosemary, jasmine and red rose trees. Near the palace, Elizabeth strolled through arched arbours, which had windows facing the garden, to the sound of birds singing in aviaries.

Unlike their contemporaries on the Continent, the Elizabethans did not leave detailed visual records of their most celebrated gardens. Plans of Theobalds date from the seventeenth century and, though impressive, give only the bare outlines of the pleasure grounds. John Thorpe's survey of Cheshunt Park (1611) shows a long, straight drive leading to arched entrance gates and two green courts (the courtyards were laid with grass). The inner court (Fountain Court) has towers bearing flags and a courtyard with a classical-style arcade.

The gardens, which extend on three sides of the palace, are shown simply as green squares. In the garden's western walls, there are two small semicircular projections and one large square-shaped projection with a semicircular recess, which were probably banqueting houses, as at Cecil House in London.

But there is a remarkable painting of an Elizabethan garden by an unknown artist from the Netherlands, which was probably based on Theobalds, dated 1577 (the revolutionary year when Cecil hired Gerard and *The Gardener's Labyrinth* was published, while Dudley temporarily abandoned gardens in favour of exploration, backing Drake's circumnavigation of the globe and Dee's book on empire). The painting was a gift to Cecil from Sir George Delves, who was related to him by marriage. It was a plea for help.

The painting is a life-size portrait of Delves and a mysterious lady, perhaps his late wife, who holds a branch of myrtle (symbol of Venus) in front of her face to represent her recent death, standing on a hill overlooking an elaborate garden. Also shown is a palace with a garden arcade and huge square towers like those of the Fountain Court at Theobalds. The garden is composed of enormous compartments made up of tunnel arbours reminiscent of those in the pattern books of Vredeman de Vries and in Medici gardens. Although at first glance Delves and his companion might seem to be the subjects, this is really the portrait of a great garden and its creator.

As Elizabeth's chief minister, Cecil maintained a secret correspondence with Cosimo I, the first Grand Duke of Tuscany. In 1571, Cosimo wrote to warn him about the threat posed to Elizabeth by Roberto Ridolfi, who had visited the Medici court in Florence on his way to Rome. Cecil used this intelligence to foil Ridolfi's plot to assassinate Elizabeth. Cecil may well have studied plans, drawings and descriptions of the marvellous Medici pleasure grounds in order to trump Dudley in gardens.

In the centre of one of the compartments in the painted garden is a circular maze; in another, we see a candelabra-style fountain. Laurel, symbolising fame, hangs just above Delves's head, while armour lies at his feet. Although Delves's Italian motto, *Altro non mi vaglia, che amor e fama*, translates as 'I value only Love and Fame', his military career had been a failure and, as the double portrait shows, he was mourning the loss of his wife. Underneath the laurel are some verses which convey his difficulties:

> The court whose outward shows
> Set forth a world of joys
> Hath flattered me too long
> That wandered in her toys.
> Where should the thirsty drink
> But where the fountain runs?
> The hope of such relief
> Hath almost me undone.

At the age of forty, Delves was a widower facing hard times, but his commissioning of this portrait marked a turning point in his life. A year later, Cecil gave him a lucrative court sinecure, which helped him rebuild his career.

According to Cecil's secretary Hicks, his 'greatest disport' was 'riding in his garden walks, upon his little mule. For, if he might ride privately in his garden upon his little mule or lie a day or two at his little lodge at Theobalds retired from business or too much company, he thought it his greatest greatness and only happiness'.

In imitation of the pleasure grounds of classical antiquity and Renaissance Italy, Cecil's formal gardens opened out into fields, as revealed by an unusual and delightful painting of Cecil in the park at Theobalds. Most of his portraits show him as a grave statesman, but, in this portrait, he sits on a mule and offers the viewer a posy of gillyflowers (symbols of love) and honeysuckle (Elizabeth's emblem). In the background, there is a tree decorated with his coat of arms and family motto, *Cor unum via una* (One heart, one way). Looking at the beautiful landscape, with its red and white wild flowers beneath leafy trees, it is easy to see why riding in his avenues was his greatest pleasure.

The mule was a gift, either from the French ambassador or from his friend Lady Mason. A well-known symbol of humility, the mule set him apart from Dudley, who rode only the finest Neapolitan and Barbary coursers and prided himself on finding the best horses for Elizabeth. There is further symbolism in the wild flowers: red and white are the colours of the Christian martyrs, appropriated by Tudor propagandists after the War of the Roses. The painting was so popular that several copies were made during Cecil's lifetime.

By Elizabeth's visit of 1583, Gerard had come a long way from his early attempts at managing the gardens at Theobalds. When Cecil had hired him, the orchard had been full of diseased and dying trees, and, in December 1578, Cecil had called in the experts: gardener Thomas Martin and royal fruiterer Harris (probably the son of Henry VIII's fruiterer, Irish-born Richard Harris, who had imported scions of new apple, cherry and pear trees from France and the Netherlands, which he had grown in his orchard at Tenham, in Kent). After their visit to Theobalds,

Martin had reported that many of Cecil's fruit trees were mossy, some were rotting and some sick of gall or worms and other diseases which even 'the very best trees are subject to', and informed him that he had left written remedies with Gerard, as well as notes on techniques for the gardens and ponds.

Until his employment by Cecil, Gerard had specialised in herbs: in his practice as a surgeon, he relied heavily on herbal remedies. Thanks to Cecil's experts, he drew on diverse remedies for his fruit trees. Moss was his worst enemy, since it weakened the fruit and eventually made the trees barren. Flies and other vermin nested in it during the summer and ate the blossoms and tender scions in the spring. As soon as Gerard saw any trees becoming mossy, he uncovered their roots in winter and dunged them with hog's dung mixed with good earth. He also scraped the moss from the bark with a sharp knife.

If the bark of his trees became infected, he cut out the affected area with a chisel. At the end of winter, he put ox's or hog's dung on the infection, bound it with cloths, wrapped it with willow shoots and left it for a long time, until it recovered. He treated rotten cherry trees by making a hole in the trunk about two feet from the ground, so that the infection passed out, and then, before the springtime, he shut up the hole with a branch taken from the same tree. He had also found this to be a useful remedy for trees which did not bear much fruit.

In February, he grafted his apple, pear and plum trees so that no worms or maggots grew in the fruit. He had a set of precision tools for this work: a very thin, thick-toothed saw; a grafting knife (one inch broad); a mallet to drive his knife and wedge into the tree; two sharp knives, one to pare the stock head and the other to cut the graft cleanly; two wedges of hard wood, one for small stocks and a broader one for bigger stocks, used to open the stocks when they had been cut and pared; and good, tough clay and moss.

The process recalled his original occupation of surgeon. First, he chose the best branches for grafting: those with a good 'knot' or 'joint'. He sawed off each graft and pared it with a knife. He split the graft, using a mallet and a knife, and set a wedge in it, then cut open the stock, according to the thickness of the graft. Taking his small, sharp knife, he trimmed the graft on both sides of the joint, making sure that it was thinner underneath. He put the graft into the stock, trimming it until he could not fit the edge of his knife on either side. Finally, he bound the graft with moss and clay, to protect it from the wind.

As a diligent gardener, Gerard was equally careful to destroy pests in his flowers and trees. His men killed pot-herb fleas by sprinkling them with sharp vinegar mixed with henbane. They drove away caterpillars by burning vines, soaking the ashes in water for a few days and sprinkling them on herbs and trees. A water garden like Theobalds required special attention: his men warded off gnats by burning mint and set lanterns at the sides of the canals and pools to prevent frogs from croaking.

In time, Gerard would amaze people with the many varieties of fruit trees in his garden at Holborn (there would be sixteen varieties of cherry tree and sixty kinds of plum tree, 'all strange and rare'). By the end of the century, his list of plants grown from seed included oleander, yucca, abutilon and hibiscus. Expert advice played its part, but his success came mainly through painful trial and error, as shown by his first attempts to grow hibiscus trees:

I had with great industry nourished up some plants from the seed, and kept them unto the midst of May; notwithstanding, one cold night, chancing among many, has destroyed them all.

Some of his introductions were so new to English gardeners that one of his men accidentally pulled up a rare plant, mistaking it for a weed.

The core of the orchard at Theobalds consisted of cherry trees, which, like pear trees, were popular for their blossoms in spring. Cherries were associated with beauty and virginity but also had a practical application. They were a folk remedy for gout, from which Cecil had suffered since the age of thirty-three. In the compartments of his Great Garden, Cecil planted single cherry trees at intervals in the lines of herbs that created the patterns.

A fine orchard was an important status symbol, and high-quality fruit made a luxurious and seductive gift. In the early stages of the marriage negotiations between Elizabeth and Alençon's handsome brother the Duke of Anjou (now the King of France) – which Dudley dared to mock at Kenilworth in his show featuring a country wedding, with a youthful bridegroom and an old and ugly bride – Elizabeth sent Dudley to France to deliver a basket of apricots to Anjou, 'with her commendations, that he might see that England was a country good enough to produce fair fruits'. The French ambassador reported to Anjou that 'these fine apricots showed very well that she had fair and good plants in her realm, where I wished that grafts from France might in time produce fruits even more perfect'. Pleased by the ambassador's flirtatious response, Elizabeth sent Anjou a stag so that he might see the venison of England's forests as well as the fruits of its gardens, adding that she looked forward to hunting with him and to showing him all the beautiful places in her kingdom.

In early 1578, Martin told Cecil that he had left with Gerard a gift of six superb pearmain (pear-shaped apple) trees, to be planted among the cherry trees, adding that Harris had grafted scions from the pearmain on to the rennet (a French dessert apple) trees. Martin also sent a basket of fruit and promised Cecil fruit from his new pearmain and 'pond pear' trees by Easter.

Cecil's interest in fruit trees dated from early in the reign. In the 1560s, he used his contacts in France to procure rare exotics, such as orange, lemon and pomegranate trees. When he sent his eldest son, Thomas, to Paris for a year in order to complete his education, Cecil seized the opportunities that this provided to enhance his gardens.

He first wrote to his son's guardian, Sir Thomas Windebank, with a request to send him any new plants that he came across and to find him a French gardener. In March 1561, on hearing that Sir Francis Carew was buying citrus and other exotic trees in Paris for his garden at Beddington, Cecil urged Windebank to follow suit:

Mr Carew means to send home certain orange, pomegranate, lemon and myrtle trees. I have already an orange tree, and if the price be not much, I pray you procure me a lemon, a pomegranate, and a myrtle tree, and help that they may be sent home to London with Mr Carew's trees, and beforehand send me in writing a perfect declaration how they ought to be used, kept and ordered.

Two weeks later, Windebank reported to Cecil that he had sent the trees and that Carew had helped choose them. Although the arrangement had saved the cost of transportation, Windebank feared that Cecil might still think the exotics too pricey. Windebank added that he was also sending

a lemon tree and two myrtle trees in two pots, which cost me both a crown, and the lemon tree fifteen crowns, wherein, Sir, if I have bestowed more than perhaps you will at the first like, yet it is the best cheap that we could get it. And better cheap than other noble men in France have bought of the same man. You will not think your money lost if it do not prosper, it shall take away your desire of losing any more money in like sort.

Keeping exotics was an expensive and hazardous business which seemed at odds with Cecil's reputation for thrift, but it helped to give his gardens their edge. He has been credited with having built the first orangery in England at his family seat of Burghley, in Lincolnshire, although he probably kept his exotic fruit trees in London, either at his old house at Cannon Row or his new headquarters on the Strand. He would later import fifty varieties of exotic seeds from Florence for the gardens at Theobalds.

His innovations in gardens and architecture in the 1560s also included the arcades which he built at his house on the Strand and at Burghley, with the help of his friend Sir Thomas Gresham. At that time, Gresham was in the Netherlands raising loans as Elizabeth's financier, and from Antwerp he sent Cecil classical-style pillars. In one of his letters, Gresham related that his agent had recommended making the pillars of single stones; his mason had begun a plan for an arcade but needed to know whether Cecil wanted 'antique or modern' design for the pillars and arches.

Cecil's dealings with Dutch stonemasons and architects gave him access to the latest ideas in garden design, published in the highly influential pattern books of Vredeman de Vries. Few English garden designers travelled to Italy, so their knowledge of Italian architecture and gardens was mostly second-hand, based on French and Dutch pattern books and visitors' descriptions. In the early years of the reign, Cecil's diplomatic contacts in Paris, Antwerp and Florence gave him a clear advantage in garden design.

In his plans for his London residence, on the north side of the Strand, he followed the design theory of Renaissance Italy: the house and garden were viewed as inseparable. Structure, geometry and symmetry were the new concerns. Elizabeth paid her first visit in July 1561, even though the house was not finished. Three years later, she made her entrance via a grand approach route along an axial path through elaborate gardens. The broad path was bordered by compartments as well as, on one side, an orchard planted with trees in quincunxes (an arrangement in which five trees are set so that four stand at the corners of a square, with the fifth in the centre, as in the legendary orchards of Cyrus the Great and Cicero) and, on the other, a mount garden (with a cockleshell path to the summit for views over the fields of Covent Garden), and led past banqueting houses and a bowling green to a terrace and classical arcade.

Most of the compartments at Theobalds were centred on cypress trees, symbols of eternity; some had mysterious statues set on alabaster obelisks. Marbled posts with Queen's Beasts lined the paths. In the middle of one compartment stood an obelisk surmounted by a figure of Christ. Was this Christ the gardener, after the Resurrection, or Christ betrayed in the garden of Gethsemane? Elizabeth had been associated with Christ at Kenilworth, where she had been called the 'Prince of Peace'. (Recently, Hatton had remarked that she liked to fish 'for men's souls, and has so sweet a bait that no one can escape her network'.) In the centre of another compartment, there was an alabaster sundial decorated with the royal arms of England, and a solid gold Garter (the emblem of the highest chivalric order in the land).

As they walked towards the heart of the garden on that day in 1583, Elizabeth was in for a surprise, and Dudley for a shock. An octagonal white-marble fountain in the shape of a pillar dominated the central space. Dudley instantly thought of Zuccaro's portrait of Elizabeth, which he had commissioned for her visit to Kenilworth in 1575 and which showed her standing in front of a classical column. He also recalled his own portrait with two pillars in the background, painted ten years earlier, and his emblem of obelisk and vine from the Accession Day tournament held at Whitehall in the first year of the reign.

As in the fountain at Kenilworth, there were surprise jets. Cecil had stolen his best ideas and gone one better. The fountain at Kenilworth, with its bear and ragged staff, was mainly about Dudley, but at Theobalds, the fountain celebrated the Queen.

In the compartments on either side of the fountain, Elizabeth and Dudley discovered the figures of a wild man and woman carved in oak, beneath a columned portico emblazoned with dragons. Theobalds had become a garden of mysteries.

The figures recalled others from inside the palace. On the first floor, overlooking the Great Garden, the Great Chamber contained an artificial cave and fountain. The walls of the cave were coated with shimmering metallic ore, and its craggy roof was studded with crystals, corals and semi-transparent stones. Against a background of tangled trees, a carved wild man and woman held up the basin of the fountain. Wild animals crept through the undergrowth. At the base of the fountain stood a centaur, representing lust and greed.

Italy was the inspiration. The Medicis were obsessed with grottoes. Cecil's was modelled on the famous Grotto of the Animals at Cosimo I's villa at Castello. Caves were believed to be the gateways to the underworld. As the source of life-giving springs, which bubbled up as if from nowhere, they were held sacred. The Castello grotto had three fountain basins full of marble animals, including deer and an elephant with ivory horns and tusks. In the central fountain, a unicorn purified the water by dipping its horn into it, so that the other animals could drink it – the Medicis' way of celebrating their achievement of bringing drinking water to the people of Florence through giant aqueducts. (Cecil's indoor fountain also derived from the Italian Renaissance *sala* – the reception or dining room – which contained a table fountain set against a wall, used for drinking water and for the washing of hands.)

There was one last mystery. When Elizabeth walked with

Dudley to the end of the west-facing garden, they discovered a maze surrounding a small hill. After finding their way through the maze, they followed a cockleshell path lined with rosemary up to the summit, where there was a white marble statue of Venus.

Elizabeth had never seen anything quite like it, although certain elements of the garden must have been familiar. Hampton Court came to mind: the artificial hill reminded her of the riverside entrance to the palace, with its mount crowned by her father's glass pavilion, and inside the palace was a painting dating from the 1550s called *The Labyrinth of Love*, showing lovers in a circular maze.

The maze at Theobalds also recalled a fabulous maze at the palace of Woodstock, where she had been imprisoned as a princess. Woodstock was now the home of her Champion, Sir Henry Lee, and had been one of the last stops on her progress in 1575, after the entertainments at Kenilworth. Elizabeth knew well the legendary story about King Henry II's mistress the Fair Rosamund, who lived at Woodstock at the heart of a maze in a bower which he had created for her, safe from his jealous wife Queen Eleanor. The King used to find his way through the maze to Rosamund by following a silver thread.

Despite being heavily pregnant, Queen Eleanor returned from France to deal with her rival. Outside the maze, Eleanor discovered the silver thread, which had caught on the spur of the knight who guarded Rosamund. In the centre of the maze, she confronted Rosamund and made her take poison. The bower that hid Rosamund also fatally entrapped her.

Cecil's maze, centring on a statue of Venus, drew on the labyrinth of cypresses and roses encircling a Venus fountain at Castello (called the Fountain of the Labyrinth). Goddess of love and gardens, Venus represented Florence to the Medicis. In England, Venus was Elizabeth.

The garden was also thrillingly similar to the pleasure grounds depicted in one of the most popular romances of the day, *The Dream of Poliphilus*, written by a mysterious Italian author. Cecil's garden recalled the novel's maze garden made up of canals in concentric circles centring on a whirlpool, at the top of a hill.

From this new vantage point, Elizabeth and Dudley had a magnificent view of the entire garden. Cecil's labyrinth of canals may also have reminded Dudley of the treacherous waterways of the Netherlands, which he had studied in maps.

Cecil's garden was a synthesis of all that was exotic and exciting in the ancient and modern worlds: the East, the New World, ancient Britain, the hazardous channels of the Netherlands and the Italians' rediscovery of the wonders of ancient Rome.

Elizabeth was impressed, and told Cecil, 'With your head and my purse, I could do anything.'

Soon after her departure, the courtier Roger Manners reported on the success of the royal visit, in a letter to his nephew the Earl of Rutland:

She was never in any place better pleased, and sure the house, garden and walks may compare with any delicate place in Italy.

Over the next two decades, the reputation of Theobalds as Elizabeth's favourite retreat and the equal of the great pleasure grounds of Italy would draw visitors from all over Europe.

❧

The few written accounts of Theobalds by sixteenth-century English writers to have survived are full of praise but lack detail. The historian William Camden, a friend of Dudley's nephew Sidney, described Theobalds in superlative terms as 'a place than which, as to the fabric [building], nothing can be more neat; and as to the gardens, walks and wildernesses about it, nothing can be more pleasant'. In 1598, the cartographer John Norden passed up the opportunity to do justice to Cecil's palace:

To speak of the beauty of this most stately house at large as it deserveth, for curious buildings, delightful walks, and pleasant conceits within and without, and other things very glorious and elegant to be seen, would challenge a great portion of this little treatise, and there-fore . . . I leave it.

In his *Description of England*, William Harrison simply named Theobalds in his list of the greatest gardens of the reign, along with Hampton Court, Nonsuch Palace and Cobham Hall.

Fortunately, towards the end of Elizabeth's reign, Theobalds attracted several tourists from Germany and Austria who wrote about it at length. We owe to them our knowledge of what was really strange and surprising about Cecil's palace and pleasure grounds: the labyrinth of canals and ship fountain; the banqueting house and marble busts of the Roman emperors overlooking the pool with miniature watermills and serpent fountains; the indoor fountain and grotto; the sculptures of wild men and women, Venus and Christ; the octagonal fountain in the shape of a column, with its surprise jets.

The garden's majestic scale was its most striking feature: Cecil's palace and grounds covered about seventeen acres, and his Great Garden was twice the size of Henry VIII's garden at Hampton Court. On his visit to Theobalds with the Duke of Württemberg in 1592, Jacob Rathgeb described the pleasure grounds as 'of immense extent' and, like the palace, 'most magnificent', with 'no expense spared'. Cecil's secretary Hicks would later write that the gardens were divided into compartments by 'quickset hedges' and walls, as well as by gravel walks where 'one might walk two miles before he came to the ends'.

The journal of Paul Hentzner, who toured Theobalds in 1598, reveals that the gardens resembled royal pleasure grounds, with their multitude of beasts on poles, except, at Theobalds, these poles took the form of classical 'columns and pyramids of wood and other materials up and down the garden'. He admired the 'great variety of trees and plants' and 'labyrinths made with a great deal of labour'. In 1600, Baron Waldstein recorded that the gatehouse was painted with 'frescoes showing Brazilians in their native dress'.

A French visitor to Theobalds in 1640, Jean-Albert de Mandelslo, wrote that the garden was 'square-shaped and extremely large', with 'many beautiful walks . . . some with tunnel arbours'. Although his account was written many years after the palace had passed out of the hands of the Cecils, Mandelslo's description evokes the spirit of the original pleasure grounds. He concluded it with a surprise: at the end of one of the avenues, he discovered 'a little hill, called the Venus mountain, in the middle of a labyrinth, which is one of the most beautiful places in the world'.

Since Elizabeth's visit to Kenilworth in 1575, Dudley had been unable to compete with Cecil in buildings and gardens. Theobalds was second to none.

Yet Dudley intended to prove his worth in a domain where Cecil could not challenge him – on the battlefields of the Netherlands.

12

'At the time appointed, a man with a perfect hand attended you three times in your garden, to have slain your Lordship.'

Watering from a pump, from *The Gardener's Labyrinth*

A Second Arthur

IN 1585, DUDLEY sent his nephew Philip Sidney out ahead of him to the key port of Flushing, in Holland. Elizabeth had, at last, granted Dudley's wish to lead her armies in battle. In December, as General of the Forces in the Netherlands, he sailed from the Thames with six thousand foot soldiers and one thousand cavalry. On arrival in Delft, he was given an ecstatic welcome. The festivities cost £5,000. In one of the pageants, there was a crystal-and-pearl castle, with a figure protecting a maiden at the top (a symbol of Elizabeth's reign). At The Hague, he was celebrated as a second Arthur; elsewhere, he was Moses.

He had brought with him his troop of actors and his stepson, the young Earl of Essex, as his General of the Horse. Surgeons William Gooderons and William Clowes, both friends of Gerard, were also part of the expedition.

On New Year's Day, the leaders of the Netherlands offered Dudley the title of Governor. It was equivalent to the crown that Elizabeth had refused ten years earlier for fear of antagonising Spain. Before Dudley had left England, she had forbidden him to accept the title. Although she knew that the governorship might give him the authority he needed in order to prosecute her aims as her deputy, the Spanish might interpret his acceptance as a declaration of war.

With France embroiled in sporadic civil war, rebellions fomenting in Ireland, and hostilities stretching to the New World, England's confrontation with Spain in the European 'cockpit' of the Netherlands threatened to provoke an escalation into all-out war, Catholic against Protestant, that Elizabeth was anxious to avoid.

Dudley wrote for advice to Cecil, who tried to persuade Elizabeth to let him accept the offer, but she refused to commit herself. Cecil reported back to him: 'I am greatly discouraged with her lack of resolutions.'

❧

All through January 1586, Elizabeth refused to give in to Dudley and Cecil. Despite the bitter cold, she took long walks in Richmond Park, trying to work out the best course of action. One day, she was walking with Hatton and her ladies when an assassin approached her. She saw him coming and scrutinised his face until he backed away, unable to go through with the murder. The organiser of this attempt on her life, Anthony Babington (a handsome young supporter of Mary, Queen of Scots), had foolishly arranged for the conspirators to have their portraits painted. Unlikely as it sounds, Walsingham's agents had intercepted the paintings and shown them to Elizabeth, which was how she had recognised her would-be assailant.

In the subsequent trial, one of the conspirators listed the locations where the assassin had planned to strike:

As her Majesty should go into her chapel to hear divine service, he might lurk in her gallery, and stab her with his dagger; or, if she should walk in her garden, he might shoot her with his dag [pistol]; or, if she should walk abroad to take the air, as she often did, accompanied rather with women than men, or with men slenderly weaponed, then might he assault her with his arming sword, and make sure work; and though he might hazard his own life, he would be sure to gain heaven thereby.

This vision of gunshots in gardens and sword thrusts in parks did not, however, deter Elizabeth from taking her daily walks. If anything, she became more determined to move around as freely as she liked.

When Cecil tried to veto her friend the Duchess of Somerset's plans for a new private walk in her garden at Cannon Row, in Westminster, Elizabeth defied him. At St James's Palace, she asked the Duchess why it was not up, promising to come and walk in it when she came to Westminster. Despite his misgivings, Cecil had to let it go ahead, but insisted on the highest security, as in the Duchess's orchard and garden:

Since again all the high places cannot be plucked down that look into the garden, and that many places and houses about the orchard and garden must be trusted to mure or lock up their walks, tiles and windows, let this have some such like grace with like conditions. And yet nothing can be seen nor well discerned in the garden but as one may see from the court overlooking the Thames.

Although Cecil could not guarantee Elizabeth's safety, he did all that he could to protect her.

Whereas, from the beginning, Dudley had encouraged Elizabeth to take risks, Cecil had urged caution. His warnings had gone unheeded. In the early years of the reign, Dudley had wanted her to ride and hunt as much as possible. In September 1560, he had asked Sussex to send over new, swifter 'hobbies' from Ireland:

The Queen's Majesty thanks be to God is in very good health and is now become a great huntress and doth follow it daily from morning till night. She doth mean out of hand to send into that country [Ireland] for some hobbies for her own saddle, specially for strong, good gallopers which are much better than her geldings, whom she spareth not to tire as fast as they can go.

Elizabeth had frequently abandoned state business to watch Dudley compete in sports: jousting, archery, shooting and tennis. In the summer of 1561, she had gone with her ladies, in disguise, to Windsor Park to watch him take part in an archery contest. According to his friend Killigrew, she had joked to Dudley: 'You are beholden to me for that I have passed the pikes for your sake.' The 'pikes' belonged to the guards who stood at the palace gates.

The more Dudley had tempted her to leave the safety of the royal palaces, the more Cecil had acted to minimise the dangers. Between 1565 and 1567, in the wake of the horrific events in Scotland (beginning with the murder of Mary, Queen of Scots's supposed lover Riccio by assassins in league with her husband Darnley), Cecil had ordered a massive increase in security in the royal pleasure grounds. Two elaborate stone gates had been made in St James's Park, as well as forty-two new wooden gates and ten new bridges 'in the fields about London for the Queen's Majesty's walk'. Guards had been stationed at the gates and bridges.

Cecil's fears had peaked in 1575 at Kenilworth. Dudley was supposed to be her bodyguard – her 'Eyes', as she called him – but Kenilworth in 1575 had been swarming with Italians. At the beginning of the year, Dudley had invited to England the Italian painter Zuccaro, on the recommendation of Chiappino Vitelli, Marquis of Cetona. Vitelli had been one of the ringleaders of a plot to assassinate Elizabeth in 1570 (he had personally offered to strike the blow) but had been pardoned, and, at the time of Dudley's last royal entertainments at Kenilworth, he was a general in the Spanish army in the Netherlands: Dudley had been in correspondence with a man who had not only attempted to murder his queen but who was then an enemy commander. It could easily have been a new plot against Elizabeth's life, with the painter, or any one of the many Italian craftsmen and performers employed by Dudley, as hired killer.

Cecil had first-hand experience of the dangers of open spaces. In 1570, two young men from wealthy Norwich families had conspired to murder him in the garden of his house on the Strand. They had blamed him for his part in Norfolk's arrest and had also been in collusion with the Spanish ambassador, who hated Cecil. The plot had been discovered by one of Cecil's spies.

The two conspirators, Berney and Mather, had been tried by Cecil and Dudley. Mather had revealed in his confession that the plot had hinged on Cecil's vulnerability in his garden:

Of late I have, upon discontent, entered into a conspiracy with some others to slay your Lordship. At the time appointed, a man with a perfect

hand [an expert assassin] attended you three times in your garden, to
have slain your Lordship. The which not fallen out, and continuing in
the former mischief, the height of your study window is taken towards
the garden, minding, if they miss these means, to slay you with a shot
upon the terrace, or else, in coming late from the court with a pistol.

After Cecil's non-appearance anywhere near the garden where
he usually spent so much time, in their frustration the conspirators had sent him a death threat, before once more despatching
their assassin to his house on the Strand. But, in the garden, the
assassin had found armed guards waiting for him.

Berney had taken the opportunity in his confession to slander
Elizabeth, Dudley and Hatton, describing Elizabeth as

so vile a woman that desires nothing but to feed her own lewd fantasy,
and to cut off such of her nobility as are not perfumed, and court-like
to please her delicate eye, and place such as are for her turn, meaning
dancers, and meaning you, my Lord of Leicester and one Mr Hatton,
who have more recourse to her Majesty in her privy chamber than reason would suffer, if she were so virtuous and well inclined.

Berney and Mather were hanged, drawn and quartered on Tower
Hill on 10 February 1570, in front of a crowd of thousands,
because that day had originally been fixed for Norfolk's death –
Elizabeth had granted him a temporary reprieve.

Dudley continued to write from the Netherlands to Cecil and
Walsingham about his dilemma, but ill winds delayed their
replies. Since he had heard no news from England for the whole

of January, he decided to accept the governorship. At last, he was the king that he had always wanted to be. On 1 February 1586, six days after the ceremony, he sent Elizabeth's agent William Davison to England to break the news to her. Before Davison's arrival, however, she heard it from one of her women, who had received a letter from a friend living in The Hague.

According to rumour, the letter included the news that Lettice was preparing to leave for the Netherlands 'with such a train of ladies and gentlewomen, and such rich coaches, litters and side-saddles as her Majesty had none such and would establish such a court of ladies as should far pass her Majesty's court'. Shortly before his departure, Elizabeth had been angry with Dudley for taking Lettice with him to Warwickshire. Many now believed that the thought of Lettice becoming Queen of the Netherlands was more than she could take.

Dudley's marriage to Lettice was a success, and Elizabeth was naturally jealous. She refused to allow Lettice to return to court. Elizabeth still preferred not to acknowledge the fact that Dudley was married, although their relationship had changed since his glamorous stepson Essex had caught her eye. As Essex was one of Cecil's wards, she would have first met him at Cecil's palace on the Strand. Cecil encouraged all of his noble wards to develop their talent for field sports, and, like Dudley, Essex excelled in horsemanship and in the jousts (in the Accession Day tournament of 1596, he would challenge all eighteen defenders, running a phenomenal 108 courses and breaking an astonishing 98 lances). Elizabeth would succumb to his charm and gallantry, and, despite the age difference of thirty-two years, she would fall in love with him.

Dudley's love of Lettice is shown by the many gorgeous portraits that he commissioned of her. These include double portraits of the couple, as well as of Lettice with their son Robert, affectionately known as 'the noble imp'. But their happy family life ended in tragedy when, in July 1584, Robert died, at the age of three. Dudley heard the news in the middle of the royal progress, at Nonsuch, and immediately left the court to be with Lettice at Wanstead. Elizabeth asked Hatton to write to advise him not to give in to grief, but Dudley replied in despair that he had now 'run the race of the world'.

Elizabeth took pity on Dudley and gave him compassionate leave. She had herself suffered a loss the previous month, when Alençon had died of fever (in her letter of condolence to Catherine de' Medici, she had described herself as 'a body without a soul'). It had been a double blow for Dudley – when he had heard of his son's death, he had been in mourning for his friend William of Orange, who, eight days earlier, had been assassinated in Delft. Elizabeth arranged for Dudley and Lettice to stay at Theobalds for a few days, as a way of consoling them, while Cecil remained with Elizabeth on the progress. After a day at Theobalds, Dudley had recovered enough to tease Cecil in a letter of thanks for his hospitality, joking that he had made his stags 'afraid, but killed none'.

Initially, Elizabeth was furious with Dudley for accepting the governorship. In a letter delivered to him by her old lover

Heneage (whom she had instructed to ensure that Dudley renounce the title), she accused him of ingratitude and of treating her with contempt. When she froze all payments to his armies, Cecil defended him by threatening to resign. But this had no effect, and so Dudley's sister-in-law Lady Warwick raised a company of soldiers to send to him. Meanwhile, in the Netherlands, there was a disturbing rumour that Elizabeth was secretly seeking peace with Spain. Naturally, this put a strain on Dudley's relationship with his allies.

When Dudley fell ill in March, Elizabeth again forgave him. She asked his young rival Raleigh to write to him with the reassurance that he was still her 'sweet Robin'. But in April, she wrote to him directly, asking why he had not yet relinquished his title. Eventually, as a compromise, he kept the title of Governor but made it clear to the world that his authority was not absolute.

Dudley's first military operation was an attempt to rescue the besieged town of Grave, in Brabant. But he had already given up his dreams of finding glory in the Netherlands and longed for new adventures, as he told Walsingham:

Perhaps if a wiser man had been in my place things had been ill enough, and God knows what a forward and a joyful country here was within this month; God send her Majesty to recover it so again, and to take care of it, on the condition she sends me after Sir Francis Drake to the Indies, my service here being no more acceptable.

There was a new bitterness to Dudley's jokes: in his experience, the people of the Netherlands were anything but joyful and eager to get things done. And the last thing that Elizabeth was likely to do was to send him on a pirate expedition with Drake. Not long before, she had refused to allow Sidney to take his chances in the New World because it was too dangerous.

Although Dudley's men outnumbered the Spanish, there was an acute problem of adequate funds and supplies. Cecil wrote to commiserate with him:

Always I find two obstacles in her Majesty. One is, she is very careful, as a good natural prince, although in such a case as this somewhat too scrupulous, to have her people adventured in fights. The other is, she will not have any more expended on her part than she has yielded to, disliking all extraordinary charges.

Cecil assured him that he was doing all that he could to 'move her Majesty to alter her hard opinion'. As a last resort, Dudley turned to the leaders of the Netherlands for financial aid, but negotiations dragged on into the summer.

Dudley had a formidable adversary in the Duke of Parma, Philip II's nephew. Possessed of an acute military intelligence, Parma was undefeated in battle. But, as his spies informed him, he had a further advantage over Dudley: Cecil was holding back money and troops from Dudley when he most needed them. Thanks to their old feud, the odds were stacked hugely in Parma's favour.

Dudley's expedition to the Netherlands had put Cecil in a position of supreme control: he was now Elizabeth's sole adviser, and as Lord Treasurer he was in charge of military spending. As the Dutch envoys commented, after failing to persuade Elizabeth to release more funds, he held the purse-strings. In Dudley's absence, he secured his friend Whitgift's appointment to the Privy Council and took over some of Dudley's lucrative lieutenantships.

Shortly before Dudley's departure for the Netherlands, he and Cecil had openly fallen out. Dudley had been spreading rumours about Cecil's hostility towards James VI of Scotland: the kind of talk that could have got Cecil killed. Cecil had responded by publicly advising Elizabeth to remain on good terms with James. He had also told his friends that he found himself 'maliciously bitten with the tongues and pens of courtiers' and had reason 'to fear murdering hands or poisoning tricks'. Then his spies had informed him that Dudley had been blaming the fall of Antwerp to the Spanish, that summer of 1585, on what he called the *regnum Cecilianum* (Protestant Europe had been shocked when, in 1576, the Spanish had sacked Antwerp, commercial centre of the Netherlands). Cecil was also under attack for Theobalds: men compared his elaborate buildings to royal palaces.

Cecil had rejected the slur that England had become a *regnum Cecilianum*, suggesting that the names of other courtiers (meaning Dudley, in particular) would fit the 'nickname' better than his. As for Theobalds, he had protested that it was 'begun by me with a mean measure but increased by occasion of her Majesty's often coming, whom to please I never would omit to strain myself to more charges'. He had also pointed out that Elizabeth had forced him to enlarge the Great Chamber in the Fountain Court, adding that it 'need not be envied of any for riches in it, more than the show of old oaks, and such trees with painted leaves and fruit'.

Finally, Cecil had rounded on Dudley, writing to him from Nonsuch: 'No man of my sort has abidden more injuries this way in hearing evil when I have done well.' Dudley had denied everything:

Your Lordship has not found a more ready friend for you and yours than I have ever been. For if you examine all the matters wherein you have at any time employed me, when my credit was somewhat better than since it was, ask yourself whether I dealt not very friendly with you or no.

He had suggested that Cecil should have come to him first, rather than simply believe the rumours. Then, as if Cecil could have forgotten, he had reminded him of his debts to the Dudley family since he had been secretary to his father Northumberland. Lastly, he had challenged Cecil to find proof for the stories that he had heard, provocatively signing himself 'By him that has given you no other cause but to be his friend'.

At first, Dudley's rescue operation at Grave went well. But then, unexpectedly, its governor surrendered. Dudley blamed the governor for this defeat, along with two of his Dutch captains, and later executed them. This shocked the people of the Netherlands, but Dudley was unrepentant.

By July, he had spent over £11,000 (over £1.5 million today) of his private fortune on the conflict. When he wrote to Elizabeth for aid, she taunted him: 'I had supposed my general [Dudley] was another Northumberland but now discover that I was mistaken.' Dudley responded to this humiliating attack by accusing Cecil of withholding funds and calling for his dismissal. The situation was desperate – Dudley called his soldiers 'poor starved wretches', and wrote that 'our old ragged rogues here have so discouraged our new men as, I protest to you, they look like dead men'. Many were deserting and there was the danger of mutiny.

Elizabeth replied cagily, as usual:

And if the treasurer [Cecil] be found untrue or negligent, according to desert he shall be used, though you know my old wont, that love not to discharge from office without desert. God forbid!

Although she did not send Dudley any money, she sent her love:

Now will I end, that do imagine I talk still with you, and therefore loathly say farewell ô ô [shorthand for 'Eyes'], though ever I pray God bless you from all harm, and save you from all foes with my million and legion of thanks for all your pains and cares.

As you know, ever the same, E. R.

(When Drake had sailed into Portsmouth towards the end of April 1586, she had secretly despatched him to the Netherlands to report on the dispiriting performance of her troops.)

In August, Dudley had a narrow escape. Accompanying his friend Sir William Pelham on an inspection of trenches before Doesburg, recently abandoned by enemy troops, they came under sniper attack. Pelham was shot in the stomach (and died the year after of the wound). As Dudley commented in a letter to Walsingham, 'Thus we hourly see in these cases how some be killed, some be hurt, and some narrowly escape.'

Dudley's lack of experience in battle became more and more clear. He had last fought thirty years earlier: in the reign of Queen Mary, he and his remaining brothers, Ambrose and Henry, had gone to fight for Philip II in France, as a way of redeeming the Dudley name. Dudley and Ambrose had paid a terrible price for their pardons, since Henry had been killed at the siege of St Quentin (Dudley had later said that he had died before his eyes).

Dudley now further antagonised his Dutch allies, on whom he depended, not least to help him navigate the treacherous web of their marshes and waterways, calling them 'bakers and brewers' and 'churls and tinkers'. The situation escalated when he forbade the Dutch merchants to trade with the enemy and gaoled one of their foremost politicians, on suspicion of treachery.

Sensing betrayal on all sides, Dudley quarrelled with his younger officers, including his best soldier, Colonel John Norris. He wrote to Walsingham about the 'shame and dishonour' which he endured daily, on account of Elizabeth's lack of support. All the while, Parma's troops were steadily advancing. Dudley's men were in a terrible state: they were desperately short of food, armour and weapons. But the Spanish soldiers were just as destitute. Parma wrote constantly to Philip II for funds – with little success.

Dudley's men began to desert him. One of his secretaries, Bartholomew Clerk, secretly wrote to Cecil, appealing to him as a fellow Cambridge man and begging for permission to return home:

I beseech your good Lordship to consider what a hard case it is for a man . . . who was a public Reader in the University (and therefore cannot be young) to come now among the guns and drums, tumbling up and down, day and night, over water and banks, dykes and ditches . . . hearing many insolences with silence . . . a course most different from my nature and most unmeet for him that hath ever profound learning.

Despite the appalling conditions, Dudley captured the town of Doesburg and laid siege to the main Spanish garrison at Zutphen, before going on to take several forts in the area. At Zutphen, his soldiers fought like heroes. He proudly described how Lieutenant Edward Stanley fought alone 'first with his pike, then with the stumps of his pike, and afterward his sword'. Dudley knighted many of his soldiers in the trenches, singling out Sir William Stanley and Captain Reade, whom he described as 'worth their weight in pearl'. Eyewitnesses said that Dudley behaved like a father towards his men.

On 22 September, there was heavy fog on the battlefield at Zutphen. On discovering that Pelham was not wearing his cuisses (leg-armour), Sidney removed his own. But, shortly afterwards, he was hit in the leg by a musket-ball. Seeing it happen, Sir William Russell broke down in tears.

There had been few casualties on their side, but Dudley was devastated, as he told Heneage:

Albeit I must say it is too much loss for me, for this young man was my greatest comfort, next to her Majesty, of all the world, and if I could buy his life with all I have to my shirt, I would give it.

While waiting to be taken to hospital, Sidney is famously supposed to have given his last few drops of water to a dying soldier, saying, 'Thy necessity is yet greater than mine.' Sidney died on 17 October, at the age of thirty-one.

Soldier, poet, courtier and scholar, Sidney was the flower of his age. Plans were made for a state funeral at Westminster

Abbey in February. (But months later, the funeral would still be unpaid for. Sidney had died 'in debt to value of £20,000 more than his goods and chattels' were worth, according to the official auditor. His father-in-law, Walsingham, would eventually settle the bill, having failed to get Dudley, who was by then virtually bankrupt, to contribute.)

Between October and November, Dudley's army deteriorated even further. He wrote to Walsingham about the indignities suffered by his 'poor soldiers':

There was no soldier yet able to buy himself a pair of hose and it is great shame to see how they go, and it kills the hearts to show themselves among men.

Pelham wrote to Dudley about the pitiful state of his men, saying that such were their 'miseries as I know not how to turn me to satisfy them, for some wanting wherewith to feed them, others almost naked, many falling daily sick, and all in general barefoot wanting hose or shoes, do by hundreds flock about me if I stir abroad amongst them, crying for relief of these extremities'.

Meanwhile, in England, Cecil was fighting a different kind of battle. He was waiting for Elizabeth to return to Whitehall so that he could confront her with damning new evidence against Mary, Queen of Scots. His men had intercepted letters which proved her treachery. But Elizabeth prolonged her stay at Richmond indefinitely and, when he sent delegates from Parliament to beg her to ratify Mary's death sentence, she refused.

In Cecil's view, Mary presented the most dangerous of the current threats to the kingdom. He had persuaded Dudley that her death was the only option and had foiled Dudley's secret plans to marry her. Though jealous and fearful of Mary, Elizabeth still refused to contemplate killing her cousin, an anointed queen.

There was one thing that might galvanise Elizabeth into action: Dudley's return. So Cecil wrote to him, saying that Elizabeth missed him and was concerned about his health. If he returned, Cecil hoped that she would finally leave Richmond for London, as she usually did, where it would be easier to persuade her to proceed with Mary's execution. At the same time, the leaders of the Netherlands wrote to ask Elizabeth to recall Dudley, saying that he was so unpopular that he could not govern them.

Dudley's return seemed inevitable. But Sir Edward Stafford (husband of Dudley's ex-lover Lady Douglas) advised Cecil to keep Dudley in the Netherlands for as long as possible:

If I might be bold to tell you what I think: if I had as much credit as your Lordship hath and he born to do me no more good than he is, I would keep him where he is and he should drink that which he hath brewed. Her Majesty is not for his tarrying there but I would keep him there to undo himself and sure enough from coming home to undo others.

It was a tempting proposition, but Cecil put his long-term project of Mary's execution before his feud with Dudley. Both Dudley and Cecil were, for reasons of politics, determined to bring about Mary's death, and Elizabeth would eventually agree to it.

*

Dudley set sail for England towards the end of November, vowing never to return to the Netherlands. Elizabeth stayed on at Richmond until 20 December, when she left not for Whitehall, as was her custom at Christmas, but Greenwich. She travelled via Clapham and Lambeth, and, on the way, made a secret detour to Dudley's mansion on the south side of the Strand, Leicester House, arriving at the watergate so that she could arrive unnoticed.

Although Elizabeth had not returned to Kenilworth since 1575, she often visited Dudley at Leicester House and at Wanstead, where he kept up his interest in gardens and plants.

During the 1580s, he made major changes to his London and Essex pleasure grounds. In 1582, he paid four gardeners to design and lay out a knot at Wanstead. The months before Elizabeth finally sent him to the Netherlands were particularly busy. In February 1585, he laid out a new lawn at Leicester House. In the spring, he bought four stone pots for violets and paid for a basketful of violets to be gathered at Blackwall and brought to Wanstead, where workmen were repairing and improving the ponds. He then commissioned a pot-maker to make hundreds of pots to line the paths in the garden at Wanstead (a hundred of the pots were for pinks).

Dudley's accounts record payments of twenty shillings to a gardener called White for filbert trees and pink seeds, and ten shillings to an Irish gardener for seeds from the royal gardens at Greenwich. In the summer, the paths and knots in the garden at

Wanstead were newly gravelled, and his workmen constructed a glasshouse (one of the first in the country). Throughout the decade, Dudley also gave numerous rewards to people for presenting him with herbs, rosewater, oranges, apples, lemons, grapes and preserved quinces, and bought great quantities of artichokes and roses.

Dudley met Elizabeth at the watergate and brought her into the garden, where he had a surprise waiting for her. They walked through the garden into the orchard, where she saw a group of strawberry trees ablaze with blossoms and ripe fruit, even though it was winter. It was a vision of Paradise.

Earlier that year, Dudley had heard about these extraordinary trees from one of his Irish agents. The trees grew only in Munster, and he had arranged for them to be shipped to England. Outside Ireland, only he and Walsingham had them in their gardens, as shown by a letter from Dudley's agent in Ireland to the gardener at Leicester House, describing the techniques needed for their care:

You shall receive herewith a bundle of trees called the woolaghan tree, whereof my Lord of Leicester and Mr Secretary Walsingham are both very desirous to have some, as well for the fruit as the rareness of the manner of bearing, which is after the kind of the orange to have blossoms and fruit green or ripe all the year long, and the same of a very pleasant taste, and growing nowhere else but in one part of Munster, from whence I have caused them to be transported immediately unto you, praying you to see them safely delivered and divided between

them my said Lord and Mr Secretary, directing that they may be planted near some ponds or with a great deal of black moory earth, which
kind of soil I take will best suit them, for that they grow best in
Munster about loughs and prove to the bigness of cherry trees or more
and continue long.

The strawberry trees were a novel kind of exotic, especially
prized for their rareness.

Elizabeth celebrated Christmas 1586 with Dudley, at Greenwich.
On 26 and 27 December, New Year's Day and Twelfth Night,
there were plays performed by their companies of actors. Over
the holiday, they talked about her plans to commission a French
gardener to redesign the gardens and orchards at Hampton
Court. In the springtime, the royal gardeners would bring great
quantities of lavender, double primroses and daisies for the new
gardens at Hampton Court. And work would resume on the
Great Fountain with its figure of Justice, begun nearly three
years before.

13

'The world is never so dangerous, nor so full of treasons and treacheries as at this day.'

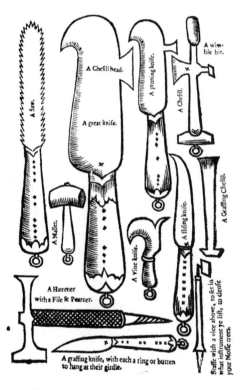

Instruments for grafting, from Leonard Mascall's *Booke of the Arte and Maner, Howe to Plant and Graffe all Sortes of Trees*, 1572

A Sharp Stroke

IT WAS TWO YEARS since Elizabeth had come to Theobalds. Cecil had spent the entire spring and early summer of 1587 hoping and praying for this visit. Four months earlier, Elizabeth had banished him from court as punishment for his part in the execution of Mary, Queen of Scots in February. It had been the longest estrangement in the history of their forty-year relationship.

At last, in late June, while Dudley was back in the Netherlands, Elizabeth was returning to Theobalds to be reconciled with her most trusted adviser. Against all the evidence, Cecil had been proved right. No one had risen to avenge her cousin Mary's death. Her fears had been unfounded. But she had not come simply to make the peace. As she approached the palace, she was looking forward to sharing the news of Drake's return just the day before, with a captured merchant's ship belonging to the King of Spain. According to rumour, the ship held more treasure than she could ever dream of.

Dudley had long been one of Drake's main backers. Although, officially, Cecil had distanced himself from Drake's adventures, that year he had kept close watch over his movements, especially his raid on Cadiz in April, which had delayed the departure of the Armada. At that moment, Drake was still on board the King of Spain's ship in Plymouth harbour, guarding the treasure until he heard word from his queen. In case this took a while, Drake had had his wife and servants brought to live with him on the ship. But this time, there would be no delay. Elizabeth could hardly wait to see the Spanish royal jewels and had summoned Drake to bring them to her.

For Cecil, the waiting was nearly over. He still felt some trepidation, however, remembering his latest encounters with Elizabeth. In February, although officially still banned from court, he had been summoned to Whitehall for advice about the war in the Netherlands. As soon as he had been admitted to her presence, she had commanded him to justify his actions in the execution of Mary, Queen of Scots. He had hardly said a word when she had attacked him, calling him a traitor, false dissembler and wicked wretch, and had ordered him from her sight. Soon afterwards, he had fallen into a sickness that had confined him to his house. At the end of May, she had summoned him to court at Greenwich for another blistering attack because of Mary's death and had then banished him again.

He was paler than usual but, dressed in Elizabeth's colours, black and white, still an imposing figure. His steady gaze was compelling. But, at sixty-six, he felt old and longed to retire. As he left the garden by the southern arcade, he repeated the verses that had strengthened him during his exile: 'Whom the Lord loves He chastens', 'It is better to do well and suffer than to do evil', 'Charity is nowhere more becoming than in a prince'. In a last attempt to steel himself for the royal visit, he even murmured, 'Death brings an end to all woes.'

It was only in the last few weeks that things had changed. Earlier that month, Elizabeth had sent her top privy councillors to ask about his health. Just a week earlier, she had again commanded him to come to Greenwich, where she had told him to expect her at Theobalds that day for a visit of two or, perhaps, three weeks. He still did not know if this meant that he was forgiven.

His spies had told him what brought her here. The gamble on the maverick Drake had paid off. She had found piracy to be a much more attractive option than warfare: minimum outlay and maximum rewards. But whereas pirates like Drake came and went, Cecil hoped that he could depend on her loyalty. There was more in this for them than just Spanish booty. Drake's adventures had made him the terror of the seas, the embodiment of English naval supremacy. The Spanish called him 'El Draque' (the dragon) and feared that he was invincible.

The porter's boy met him at the end of the arcade. The outriders were at the gates. Elizabeth and her retinue drew nearer and nearer. After his four-month exile from court and her two-year absence from Theobalds, her return was like manna from heaven. More than anything, Cecil reflected, he owed his good fortune to Theobalds. The palace was one of the most magnificent in the kingdom, but for Elizabeth the real attraction was the garden. Thanks to the unusually warm weather, she would be able to spend all day, and night, if she liked, outside.

After nearly thirty years on the throne, Elizabeth still only listened to Cecil and Dudley. With Dudley out of the country, she had no one else to turn to. This was Cecil's chance to put Dudley to sleep. One by one the towns of the Netherlands were falling to the Spanish. Dudley's weakness as a commander would do the rest. A second disastrous campaign would force Elizabeth to withdraw all military support.

꽃

With just a week's notice, preparations for the visit had been intense. New rails and balusters had been ordered for the Fountain Court. Cecil had despatched servants to London to buy poles for the frame and rushes to line the Queen's Arbour in the Great Garden, which was hung with a state canopy. As for the catering, there was just one item on Cecil's 'urgent' list: 'more beer to be brewed'.

So much had changed at Theobalds, even since the previous year. The old palace gates now stood at the entrance to the estate and led to a newly levelled, straight drive, replacing the old, dog-legged approach. An expansive fifteen yards wide, this majestic avenue was planted with young elm and ash trees. On the south side ran a parallel avenue, the Satyrs' Walk, backed by orchards full of rare fruit trees.

The palace was virtually complete. At first sight, Elizabeth's courtiers were struck by the numerous turrets, with their forest of brightly coloured flags held by gilded beasts, and the four monumental square towers of the Fountain Court. Cecil had created a fairy-tale castle to rival the royal palaces of Richmond and Nonsuch.

From the outer gate, at the beginning of the new avenue, Elizabeth could see straight through the Middle Court to the black-and-white marble fountain of Venus and Cupid in the centre of the Fountain Court. The magnificent new gates which Dudley had seen during his visit in 1584, after the death of his son, slowly came into view. They had been designed by her own architect, John Symons.

As she arrived at the gatehouse, Elizabeth paused for a moment to perform a minor miracle. Set into the elaborate stone gateway before her was a vessel in the shape of a huge bunch of grapes: on her approach, one side began to pour white wine and the other red. It was good to see that at Theobalds she still had the goddess touch.

During her last visit, the lavish decorations at Theobalds had only made her want more. As she entered the Great Chamber in 1587, she saw that it was much bigger, as she had requested (Cecil had demolished and rebuilt a wall, making the next-door room smaller). The Chamber had been completely redecorated, so that the fountain competed for her attention with several new attractions.

She had already heard about the columns in the shape of oak trees, with coats of arms hanging from their branches, and was delighted to see how lifelike they were, covered with real bark, leaves, fruit and birds' nests. While she and her courtiers were admiring the trees, birds flew in through the windows, perched on the branches and started to sing.

Above her, a glistening mechanical sun travelled across a sky painted with the twelve signs of the zodiac. As it grew dark, the constellations would appear on the ceiling. A staircase of sixty steps led up to the roof and the Astronomer's Walk, where she and her favourites could stargaze, while enjoying the spectacular panorama of the Great Garden and park, illuminated by torches.

The roofs of all four sides of the Fountain Court were accessible, and there were three specially designed walks, with the latest in rooftop architecture. As well as the Astronomer's Walk, guests had a choice of the walk on the west side of the court, overlooking the maze garden, and the walk on the east side, next to the Middle Court, where they would be seen, with delight, by people travelling on the London road.

Cecil had finally finished Elizabeth's spacious new bedroom, just along the corridor from the Great Chamber. But she would not sleep there that first night, saying that she preferred her old room in the Middle Court. The servants had to race against time to get this smaller, plainer room ready. As it turned out, she would never stay in her palatial suite.

❧

After the success of the canals during the last royal visit, Cecil had turned to creating new 'rivers' and a 'sea' at Theobalds. Gerard's head gardener, Mountain Jennings, doubled as an expert on hydraulics: in 1585, he had fixed the underground pipes that conveyed water from one river to another and had clayed the ground for Cecil's 'great sea'.

When Elizabeth climbed to the statue of Venus at the top of the mount in the maze garden, she saw a second peak, beyond the formal gardens – had Cecil created a modern Parnassus? This new mount was enclosed by green-and-white wooden fences and stood in the middle of a pool. There was a swan's nest at its summit.

A painting of Elizabeth with the goddesses Juno, Pallas and Venus shows Venus' chariot in the background, drawn by swans on the Thames. As a beauty icon, Elizabeth was associated with Venus, so the swans at Theobalds were a nice touch. And Elizabeth loved to sail along the Thames, with its great colonies of swans, past the gorgeous palaces lining its banks. The rivers and lake at Theobalds, with their exotic pavilions, offered a scaled-down, private version of one of her favourite experiences. As at Whitehall, her barge at Theobalds was covered with white satin and decorated with feathers, pearls and honeysuckle. Cecil had come a long way since his early days, when he had felt that he could not compete against Dudley's expertise as a courtier.

Gerard had new wonders for Elizabeth. From the host of new introductions, he singled out the Flower of the Sun, or the Marigold of Peru, which he had grown from seed in April and which now stood fourteen feet tall. He was fascinated by its extraordinary flowers, some of which were sixteen inches in width and weighed over three pounds:

This great flower is in shape like to a camomile flower, beset round about with a pale or border of goodly yellow leaves [petals], in shape like the leaves of the flowers of white lilies: the middle part whereof is made as it were of unshorn velvet, or some curious cloth wrought with a needle, which brave work, if you do thoroughly view and mark well, it seemeth to be an innumerable sort of small flowers, resembling the nose or nozzle of a candlestick, broken from the foot thereof.

As Elizabeth could see, said Gerard, the sunflower's stalk was the size 'of a strong man's arm'. Perhaps strangest of all, the flowers smelt of turpentine, but as for the story that they turned with the sun, he had never seen it.

There was also the crown imperial from Constantinople. The back of each bell-like flower was 'streaked with purplish lines' and, inside, as he described in his *Herbal*, lay 'six drops of most clear shining sweet water, in taste like sugar', resembling 'fair orient pearls'. Pearls were Elizabeth's favourite jewels, and she was notorious for her sweet tooth.

Many of the flowers at Theobalds were used to make confectionery and cordials. Gerard talked to Elizabeth about how violets and sugar made 'sugar violet, violet tables, or plate, which is most pleasant and wholesome, especially it comforts the heart and the other inward parts'. He especially rated gillyflowers as confectionery:

The conserve made of the flowers of the clove gillyflower and sugar is exceeding cordial, and wonderfully above measure doth comfort the heart, being eaten now and then.

In the wake of Drake's triumphant return from South America, Gerard's highlight for this year was the ginger growing in the kitchen garden. As he showed Elizabeth, his plants were fresh, green and full of juice. While he dug up some roots for her supper, she asked where they came from. Although, as he admitted, he had been sent this particular ginger from Spain, he delighted her with the news that his first plants had come from Santo Domingo, a Spanish town on an island near Cuba raided by Drake two years earlier. In his *Herbal*, Gerard reported: 'Ginger groweth in Spain, Barbary, in the Canary Islands, and the Azores. Our men who sacked Domingo in the Indies, digged it up there in sundry places wild.' But those original plants had not survived the English winter. As Gerard had discovered, although ginger 'sprouted and budded forth in the heat of summer, as soon as it hath been but touched with the first sharp blast of winter, it presently perished both blade and root'.

As usual, Elizabeth took long walks with her favourites in the gardens' great avenues, and thanks to Cecil's expansion of the palace, she could also walk in safety through courtyards, galleries and arcades.

In the next century, Cromwell's surveyors would contemplate demolishing the palace for its materials and fittings, but would be seduced by the walk 'through the several courts' from the inner gates up to the fountain of Venus and Cupid in the centre of the Fountain Court:

This walk is so delightful and pleasant, facing the middle of the house, and the several towers, turrets, windows, chimneys, walks and balconies, that the like walk for length, pleasantness, and delight is rare to be seen in England.

After a year's indecision, however, the Parliamentarians would destroy the palace for its materials, estimated at £8,275 (nearly £1.2 million today).

The interiors reflected Cecil's love of genealogy, topography and the ancient world. The Green Gallery above the gatehouse was painted with fifty-two trees, each representing one county, with the coats of arms of the nobility on the branches, and, between the trees, the towns, mountains, river, livestock and fruit of each region. On the west side of the Fountain Court, the walls of the first-floor Great Gallery were painted with the Knights of the Golden Fleece, the greatest cities in the world, with their inhabitants, showing their typical fashions and customs, and colour portraits of the Roman emperors. There were also busts of the emperors, an enormous globe, and portraits of the kings of England and internationally famous statesmen, including Don John of Austria, the Admiral of France, the Prince of Condé, the Duke of Saxony and, remarkably, the Duke of Parma, Dudley's enemy in the Netherlands. Two more galleries showed all of the arms of the English nobility, as well as portraits of Cecil's family, with accompanying notes about their achievements. The south-facing garden arcade was painted with the kings and queens of England and Cecil's family tree, along with the family trees of ancient aristocratic families, and paintings of famous castles and battles.

The magnificent staircase leading to the Great Chamber was carved with musical instruments (lutes and horns, as well as sheets of music), carpenters' and gardeners' tools, military trophies, classical herms and wild men and women (the staircase still survives, at Herstmonceux Castle, in Sussex). In addition to the new staircase which led from the Great Chamber to the roof, there were now thirty-two stone steps at the south-west corner of the Great Gallery, which took guests down to the beginning of the Long Avenue in the Great Garden.

Cecil blamed his four-month exile from court on Dudley. On his return from the Netherlands in November, Dudley had agreed to work with Cecil to bring about the execution of Mary, Queen of Scots. But, knowing Elizabeth's superstitious fears about killing Mary, an anointed queen, Dudley had been careful not to implicate himself in the case.

Elizabeth had been horrified when she had heard about Mary's death. Cecil had persuaded her to do the thing that she had most dreaded: to kill a queen, her own cousin Mary. In October 1586, Cecil had accelerated events by conducting a show trial at Fotheringhay Castle, in Northamptonshire, in which Mary had been found guilty of treason. Elizabeth had, at first, refused to ratify the verdict and had returned to him what she called her 'answer answerless'. After months of delay, however, she had at last signed the death warrant and had given it to her agent Sir William Davison, but, according to her version of events, she had told him not to despatch it without her permission.

After signing the warrant, she had wanted to revoke her decision, but it had been too late: Davison had given the warrant to Cecil, who had taken the matter out of her hands. Mary was executed on 8 February.

When Elizabeth had sought a scapegoat for having put to death her rival monarch, Dudley had told her that those responsible should face a traitor's death. Elizabeth had responded by sending Davison to the Tower and banishing Cecil from court. Dudley must have made a convincing case against Cecil: many years later, in the presence of her courtiers, Elizabeth would still berate Cecil for Mary's death.

Dudley's advantage over Cecil had not lasted. In April, Dudley had fallen ill, suffering from shortness of breath. He had visited the spas of Bath and Buxton, though it had seemed unlikely that he would be fit enough to return to the Netherlands, and Walsingham had thought that Norris would replace him. But Dudley had been keen to return, on condition that he was given enough money and troops. In May, he had begged Elizabeth to release him from his debt to five mort-gagees who had loaned him £5,800 and to allow him to resume his command. Finally, she had agreed to all of his requests, even recalling from the Netherlands his enemies (and best soldiers) Norris, Buckhurst and Wilkes.

After his triumphant advance through the southern Netherlands, the Duke of Parma had assembled half of his troops (six thousand infantry, two thousand cavalry and thirty heavy guns) in Bruges for an attack on the port of Sluys. The siege had begun on 12 June. In preparation for his departure, Dudley had recruited 4,500 soldiers as reinforcements for Sir Roger Williams's army, which was stationed in a fort outside Sluys.

Dudley had set sail on 25 June 1587 – just two days before Elizabeth's arrival at Theobalds. For the first time ever, Elizabeth had come to the palace without him. Her younger favourites Raleigh and Hatton were there, but they had none of Dudley's power over her. Theobalds would cast its spell, while Cecil wait-ed for her to turn to matters of state and, in particular, the astro-nomical expense of the war in the Netherlands.

Elizabeth ruled England from the garden at Theobalds. She summoned Cecil to her bower several times, and instructed him to write letters to Philip II and to Parma, who had captured the English army's fort outside Sluys, from which he was bombard-ing the town. (On his arrival, Dudley had discovered that there was no armour or food for his troops, despite the fact that he had written in advance to the leaders of the Netherlands – a setback from which he struggled to recover.)

On 16 July, Cecil wrote to Walsingham, expressing his unease:

I am unfit to be an executor of these sudden directions, especially where the effects are so large and dangerous. But lords and ladies command and servants obey.

He signed off: 'From my garden at Theobalds where her Majesty is and chargeth me to write in haste'. Elizabeth had decided in favour of peace with Spain. She was determined to bring the campaign in the Netherlands to an end before the autumn, even if that meant humiliating Dudley and double-crossing her allies.

After her last meeting with Cecil, Elizabeth sat alone in her bower for a while. Surrounded by rosemary, jasmine and sweet briar, beneath a sunshade of silver and silk, the battlefields of the Netherlands seemed a world away. She let the delights of the garden sink into her senses.

On 13 August 1587, Elizabeth left Theobalds for Windsor. It had been her longest stay ever – over six weeks.

Cecil remained at Theobalds to conduct an inquiry into Drake's conduct during his latest expedition. He cautioned Drake for his harsh treatment of his crew but could not persuade him to reveal what had happened to all of the treasure from the King of Spain's ship.

Meanwhile, in the Netherlands, Dudley was planning his final assault on the besieging Spanish army at Sluys, a deep-water port situated within a maze of inland waterways and fortifications. First, he would send a fireship to destroy the temporary floating bridge spanning the channel that led to the Spanish camp. Then he and his Dutch allies would sail through the gap in their warships, followed by a flotilla of smaller boats.

But when his fireship approached, Parma swung the bridge out of the way. Dudley sailed at full speed to try to get through the gap, though his allies did not follow him. As Parma closed the bridge, the wind changed direction, leaving Dudley stranded. Shots were exchanged, but somehow Dudley got himself and his ship back to safety. It was a humiliating defeat; nevertheless, within a year, fireships would be used to devastating effect against the Armada.

Sluys fell to the Spanish on 26 July. The leaders of the Netherlands urged Dudley to keep fighting for them and promised new aid. But, like his army, he was now completely demoralised, as he told Walsingham on 16 August:

For my own part I am even heartily weary of my generalship, for there is no comfort in taking charge where the poor soldier is not more certainly provided for.

On the 22nd, he heard reports that his troops were deserting to the enemy. Less than a week later, he again wrote to Walsingham, this time in despair, confiding that 'this place has almost brought me into sickness'.

When Cecil returned to court at Richmond in September, he drafted the instructions for Dudley's recall.

Before he left the Netherlands, Dudley wrote to Elizabeth, warning her to be on her guard:

The world is never so dangerous, nor so full of treasons and treacheries as at this day.

Although things had never looked worse, he still hoped for the future because, after her 'presence', his 'one great part of comfort coming home' would be his attempt to serve her.

But Dudley returned to England a broken man. Within days, he confirmed the transfer of his office of Master of the Horse, which he had held for nearly thirty years, to his stepson and heir, Essex. Dudley then retired to Wanstead. A month later, still at Wanstead, he described himself as 'wretched and depressed'. When he wrote to ask Elizabeth for a favour (a grant of Church land valued at £2,000 per annum), she turned him down, and he lost a battle for the wardship of the late Earl of Rutland's children to Cecil. Dudley's one satisfaction was seeing Essex made a Knight of the Garter, in April.

In July 1588, Elizabeth made Dudley her 'Lieutenant General'. He described his new duties as having to 'cook, cart and hunt' for the army. (In August, his stepson, Essex, took over his lodgings at court.) Although he joked that his new appointment was a demotion, Elizabeth felt so threatened by the prospect of an imminent Spanish invasion that she tried, for the second time, to make him her deputy, even going as far as to have patents drawn up to make him 'Lieutenant in the Government of England and Ireland'. But Cecil again vetoed the plans, supported by Hatton.

Dudley took charge of the army stationed at Tilbury, guarding the approach routes to London. It was his idea that Elizabeth visit his troops to boost morale. In a matter of weeks, he transformed the camp into a fairy-tale scene of brightly coloured tents and pavilions decked with heraldic flags.

On 8 August, the royal bodyguards, dressed in scarlet, entered the camp at Tilbury. With Dudley on her right and Essex on her left, Elizabeth rode out on a silver-white horse to meet her troops, who looked like medieval knights in their full battle armour, mounted on horses with rich trappings and colourful plumes. Her speech at Tilbury has become famous, in particular, for her memorable words: 'I know I have the body but of a weak and feeble woman, but I have the heart and stomach of a king and of a king of England too.' It is usually forgotten, however, that she concluded by entrusting her troops to her 'Lieutenant General' Dudley, 'than whom never prince commanded a more noble or worthy subject'.

Afterwards, Dudley wrote to the Earl of Shrewsbury about the great day:

Our gracious Mistress has been here with me to see her camp and people which so inflamed the hearts of her good subjects, as I think the weakest person amongst them is able to match the proudest Spaniard.

On hearing rumours that the Spanish had landed at Dungeness, Dudley had urged Elizabeth to retreat upriver: she had returned to London in her barge on the evening of the 9th.

When news reached Dudley of the defeat of the Armada, he disbanded the army. He then went to Wanstead, where he rested for a few days, before making a triumphant entry into London, accompanied by a select band of soldiers and courtiers. But, for the previous few weeks, he had been suffering from severe stomach pains, and, a few days into the celebrations (which included a review of the troops by Essex), Elizabeth granted him permission to visit the spa at Buxton.

Dudley and Lettice left Wanstead on 26 August. They planned to break the long journey into stages, taking in Kenilworth before going on to Buxton. Their first stop was at Rycote, on the 28th, where they stayed with Lady Norris, in the room usually reserved for Elizabeth. From there, Dudley wrote to Elizabeth to thank her for the medicine which she had given him before he had left – in a postscript, he also thanked her for the 'token' which arrived just as he was finishing his letter, brought by her messenger.

Although he was in great pain, Dudley and Lettice travelled a further twenty-five miles to his lodge at Cornbury, in the heart of Wychwood Forest in Oxfordshire (the keeper of the forest was one of Lettice's cousins). Dudley took to his bed, where, over several days and nights, his condition rapidly worsened and he developed a burning fever. On 4 September, within a month of his triumph at Tilbury, he died. When Elizabeth heard the news, she locked herself in her bedroom for days and refused to speak to anyone, until Cecil had the door broken open.

Dudley's death at the age of fifty-five shocked the entire court. There was talk of murder. According to rumour, his page

William Haynes, who was said to be Lettice's secret lover, had given him a cup of poisoned wine. The Privy Council investigated claims that Edward Croft, the eldest son of one of Dudley's most bitter enemies, had hired a conjuror to cast a deadly spell on him. Eventually, the Council reached a verdict of death by natural causes. (Modern historians have suggested that Dudley's symptoms might indicate malaria, which was common at the time, or stomach cancer.)

Dudley's death was forgotten in the mood of national celebration following the defeat of the Armada. There was no state funeral or public memorial. He was buried in the Dudley family chapel at St Mary's Church in Warwick, as he had requested in his will. Slanderous verses were published about him, including a mock-epitaph supposedly by Raleigh:

> Here lies the noble warrior that never blunted sword:
> Here lies the noble courtier that never kept his word.

Few of Dudley's friends defended his memory. But, eight years later, when Elizabeth's godson John Harington published a book which included criticism of Dudley, she banished him from court until he had 'grown sober'.

In his will, Dudley admitted that he had always lived 'above any living I had (for which I am heartily sorry) lest that through my many debts, from time to time, some men have taken loss of me'. It is hard not to detect a sense of humour in what seems to be a massive understatement: Dudley's debts were enormous. Despite his bankruptcy, he bequeathed two final gifts to Elizabeth: a brooch made of emeralds and diamonds and a rope of six hundred pearls.

In his last letter to her, written at Rycote, he assured her that 'the chiefest thing in this world' for which he prayed was for her to 'have good health and long life'. She kept this final communication from him in a small casket labelled 'His last letter', and in the Armada portrait, she wore his pearls. But, after his death, she never spoke about him. It was said that the reason was that, like her father, she hated mourning. This was borne out in her reply to a letter of condolence from Lord Shrewsbury:

As for other matter contained in your said letters, although we do therein accept and acknowledge your careful mind and good will, yet we rather desire to forbear the remembrance thereof as a thing whereof we can admit no comfort otherwise than by submitting our will to God's inevitable appointment, who notwithstanding his goodness by the former prosperous news [the defeat of the Armada], has nevertheless been pleased to keep us in exercise by the loss of such a personage so dear to us; which though it be a most sharp stroke to us in particular, yet we account it the greater in respect of the public.

It was the last thing that her senior courtiers expected to hear – that Dudley's death was more England's loss than hers.

Within a month of Dudley's death, Elizabeth seized almost all of his lands, houses and possessions in an effort to recoup what he owed her. Many courtiers saw this as her revenge on Lettice.

After nearly a year of mourning, Lettice married Sir Christopher Blount, who had been Dudley's Master of the Horse. Blount was more than ten years younger than her. Lettice was happy in her third marriage and came to court, once more, in the hope of a reconciliation. But Elizabeth refused to see her.

The fate of Kenilworth Castle still hung in the balance. In his will, Dudley had left it to Warwick and, after his death, to his illegitimate son Robert. Elizabeth honoured Dudley's wish, allowing Warwick to take possession of the castle. But, after his death in 1590, Lettice's husband Blount entered it by force and took up residence until he was removed by soldiers acting on the orders of the Privy Council (now dominated by Cecil). Although Dudley's son Robert was the rightful heir, the Council ruled that he had to prove his legitimacy before claiming his inheritance. He began a long and ultimately futile battle to prove that his parents had been legally married. Frustrated by his failure at court, he would eventually leave England for Italy to achieve success in the service of the Medici as an engineer and inventor of navigational instruments.

Cecil's favourite son, Robert, and Dudley's stepson, Essex, continued the feud between their families. As in the case of Dudley, however, Essex's limitless ambition was to be his downfall. His military ability would be no match for Robert Cecil's cunning.

14

'For green grass are come grey hairs.'

Gardeners surrounded by their instruments,
from *The Gardener's Labyrinth*

'Paradise Is Grown Wilderness'

BY THE SUMMER of 1597, everyone was worried about Cecil's health. But he still kept working and entertaining distinguished guests, giving a dinner at Theobalds at which Sir Jerome Bowes, ex-ambassador to Russia, was the guest of honour (early in the reign, Bowes had been banished from court for slandering Dudley). Cecil's other guests were his nephew Francis Bacon and John Hare, Clerk of the Court of Wards. Tactfully, they did not stay long, as Cecil's secretary Michael Hicks told Robert Cecil:

They be all gone since dinner and now we be alone, my Lord under a tree in the walks with a book in his hand to keep him from sleeping, and we ready to take bowls into our hands but that the weather is somewhat too warm yet.

But in August, another of Cecil's secretaries, Henry Maynard, heard a rumour that Elizabeth was planning a surprise visit to Theobalds, towards the end of her progress. It had been a few years since her last stay. The palace, gardens and park had been neglected. Although Cecil had tried to delegate their upkeep to his secretaries and his son Robert, no one had kept up the standards that Elizabeth expected. There had been trouble with trespassers and poachers. Cecil's deer stock, in particular, had suffered: not long ago, Hicks had written to Robert Cecil to ask him to send him a buck because the 'chase is very poor'.

Maynard wrote to Hicks three times in five days, with increasing panic. But Hicks had more immediate worries. Elizabeth had told him that she was coming to see him at his house at Ruckholt in Essex, even though there was no adequate accommodation. On 10 August, Maynard told Hicks that it was almost certain that she would be at Theobalds the following week 'if the gites [royal lodges] hold, which after many alterations is so set down this day'. He added that he would let Hicks know if there was any change of plan 'for we are greatly afeared of Theobalds'.

Two days later, Maynard confirmed that the odds were on for a visit 'but as yet it is not set down'. He was in an agony of doubt, confiding to Hicks, 'This progress much troubles me, for that we know not what course the Queen will take.' The highways to the palace were in a terrible state. Maynard employed a way-maker to repair them, but time was short. By the 15th, since there had been no more news, it seemed nearly definite that she would come. Maynard added that he had relayed Hicks's concerns about entertaining her at Ruckholt to the Lord Chamberlain, who had replied that 'you were unwise to be at any such charge: but only to leave the house to the Queen: and wished that there might be presented to her Majesty from your wife some fine waistcoat, or fine ruff, or like thing, which he said will be acceptably taken as if it were of great price'.

Towards the end of the month, Cecil was well enough to invite his entire family to dinner at Theobalds. According to Hicks, he was rarely happier than when sitting around the table surrounded by his children and grandchildren. As feared, however, Elizabeth came to Theobalds for three days in September.

During her visit, Cecil presented her with a copy of Gerard's *Herbal*. There were over 1,800 hand-painted colour illustrations, and the print quality was superb: this was the first time that Roman typeface had been used in a herbal. The cover showed a lady being shown around a garden. On the first page, there was a portrait of Gerard brandishing a branch of a flowering potato plant. His *Herbal* contained not only the first published illustration of the potato but the first 'true figure' of ginger, sent to him by de l'Obel. In the afternoons, Elizabeth went hunting in Waltham Forest. She also gave an audience to the Danish envoys and called on Robert Cecil at Enfield Chase.

Edmund Spenser was the only poet to defend Dudley after his death. In *The Ruins of Time*, published in 1591, Spenser reflected on how easily Dudley had been forgotten:

> He now is dead, and all his glory gone,
> And all his greatness vapouréd to nought,
> That as a glass upon the water shone,
> Which vanished quite, as soon as it was sought.
> His name is worn already out of thought,
> Nor any poet seeks him to revive;
> Yet many poets honoured him alive.

Spenser wrote that, in stark contrast with Dudley's generosity to poets, 'he that now wields all things at his will' – Cecil – 'scorns' poetry 'in his deeper skill'. There was also a repeat attack on Cecil as a crafty 'fox' and usurper. (More affectionately, Essex would call his former guardian Cecil 'the old fox' on account of his manoeuvrings to ensure that his son Robert took his place as Secretary.)

In his *Prothalamion*, published five years later, Spenser again remembered Dudley in a description of Leicester House, as part of his musings by the banks of the 'sweet Thames':

> there stands a stately place,
> Where oft I gainéd gifts and goodly grace
> Of that great Lord, which therein wont to dwell,
> Whose want too well now feels my friendless case.

Although he missed Dudley, Spenser turned to his successor, celebrating Essex as

> a noble peer
> Great England's glory and the world's wide wonder.

But Spenser's hopes of finding a new patron in Essex were not realised.

Spenser celebrated Dudley as King Arthur in *The Faerie Queene*, published between 1590 and 1596 and dedicated to Elizabeth (Arthur was in love with the Fairy Queen, Elizabeth). In his guise of the Red Cross Knight, Spenser paid tribute to Dudley both as his patron and as the only man worthy of marrying Elizabeth:

> And you, my Lord, the patron of my life,
> Of that great Queen may well gain worthy grace,
> For only worthy you through prowess prief [proved],
> If living man might worthy be to be her lief [darling].

The poem was full of gardens which brought out the best and the worst in people. Spenser's favourite garden resembled a botanic garden. In the Garden of Adonis, souls grew like plants in orderly rows, as in a medicinal herb garden. Here, it was always spring, and there was no need for a gardener because everything grew by itself. The only threat to universal contentment was 'Time', which took the form of a mower.

Most of the gardens in the poem were, however, dangerous locations which bore striking resemblances to courtly pleasure grounds. The Bower of Bliss recalled both Theobalds and Kenilworth. (There were also reminders of Elizabeth's banqueting pavilion at Whitehall, created in 1572, where she welcomed the Duke of Montmorency.) At the entrances to Dudley's and Cecil's greatest gardens, Elizabeth had been welcomed with wine, which had magically appeared in her presence. The same thing happens at the gates to Spenser's diabolical garden. His hero Guyon is twice offered wine: first, by 'pleasure's porter', who gives him a full bowl which he overturns, and, secondly, by a temptress called Excess, beneath a porch covered with vines, some of which are

> of burnished gold,
> So made by art, to beautify the rest.

In Elizabeth's second – and more sumptuous – banqueting pavilion at Whitehall, built in 1581 to welcome the French delegation, baskets full of fruit spangled with gold had hung from the ceiling. Despite the beguiling setting, Guyon casts the golden cup to the ground, as if it were poison. (Later on, he tears down all of the Bower's pavilions and gardens.)

In the centre of the Bower stands a fountain from which 'infinite streams' fall into a jasper basin, creating the impression of 'a little lake', so that the structure appears to 'sail' in a 'sea'. It is decorated with little statues of

> naked boys,
> Of which some seemed with lively jollity,
> To fly about, playing their wanton toys,
> Whilst others did themselves embay [bathe] in liquid joys.

The description called to mind Dudley's Italianate fountain at Kenilworth, with its carvings designed to inflame the mind, as Patten put it, but Spenser may also have been inspired by Cecil's ship fountain in the canals at Theobalds. Nude damsels wrestle in the fountain of the Bower in an effort to tempt the chaste hero. The scene brought to mind the fresco of naked men and women on the ceiling of the waterside banqueting house at Theobalds. Was this just a fashionable backdrop or something more? At the heart of the Bower, a sorceress sucks the souls out of her victims on a bed of roses, before turning them into beasts. In Elizabeth's banqueting pavilions at Whitehall, rose petals steeped in perfume lined the ground, and, at Kenilworth in 1575, Dudley had entertained Elizabeth with his pageant about the enchantress Zabeta, who had transformed her suitors into arbours.

Spenser also described a garden that bore a close likeness to Cecil's maze at Theobalds. The garden consists of a mount with a maze at its summit. At the heart of the maze, Venus conceals her beloved Adonis from the jealous gods. As far as the gods know, Adonis has bled to death from a wound in his thigh, inflicted by a wild boar, but secretly Venus has stolen him away. The high walls of her labyrinth garden screen them.

The most unusual garden in the poem was a poison garden. This was the Garden of Proserpina, goddess of the Underworld, planted with trees and herbs with black leaves, fruits and flowers, including cypress, poppy and hellebore. A fiend tempts Guyon to sit in a shady arbour with a silver seat and eat some golden apples, but he resists. Spenser mentions that the fiend would have torn Guyon into a thousand pieces if he had succumbed.

Some of the most elaborate arbours in the country could be found in the garden at Theobalds, from where Elizabeth had ruled England during the summer of 1587 (Cecil's most ornate banqueting house was called the Queen's Arbour). In his descriptions of gorgeous pleasure grounds, and especially arbours, Spenser issued coded warnings about the dangers lying in wait there.

> Art, striving to compare
> With nature, did an arbour green dispread,
> Framed of wanton ivy, flowering fair,
> Through which the fragrant eglantine [sweet briar] did spread
> His pricking arms, entrailed with roses red.

Spenser's image of Elizabeth's emblematic flowers locked in an embrace with wanton ivy was potentially slanderous.

Spenser's ambivalent portraits of elaborate gardens such as Theobalds coincided with a sharp decline in Cecil's health. By 1591, he was longing to retire. But when Elizabeth arrived at Theobalds in May of that year, she presented him with a letter addressed to the 'hermit' of Theobalds 'and to all other disaffected souls'. The letter resembled a royal charter.

Since Cecil had been spending so much time at Theobalds lately, and her last visit had taken place nearly four years earlier, she accused him of having '(for the space of two years and two months) possessed yourself of fair Tybolts [Theobalds], with his sweet rosary [rose-garden]'. She then blamed him for bringing 'desolation and mourning' to the palace and for neglecting the gardens:

Paradise is grown wilderness, and for green grass are come grey hairs.

Her meaning was clear: Cecil had to forget all thoughts of retirement and become his old self again. He could not keep Theobalds and its lovely rose-garden to himself.

During the royal visit, Cecil staged pageants which recommended his son Robert as his successor. Cecil had expanded the pleasure grounds at Theobalds to include meadows (with bridges for security) and a hermitage (a rustic-style pavilion – the latest fashion in courtly gardens). While Elizabeth was walking through the Great Garden, on her way back to the palace, a hermit appeared, blocking her way. He asked her to restore his hermitage to him, complaining that, after ten years of peace and quiet, Cecil had evicted him. Cecil's bereavements (in the space of six years, he had lost both his daughters, his mother and his wife) had led him to take up residence in the hermitage himself, putting the hermit in charge of the palace. The hermit begged Elizabeth to

> call my founder home to his house,
> That he may entertain your Majesty,
> And see these walks, wherein he little joys,
> Delightful for your Highness and your train;

Wherein likewise his two sons that be present
Will be both dutiful and diligent.

He then presented her with a hermit's bell which Cecil had
given him.

Next in line was a gardener 'whose art', as he told Elizabeth,
was 'to make walks pleasant for princes, to set flowers, cast knots,
graft trees, to do all things that may bring pleasure and profit'. He
then told her about a new garden laid out in her honour, at nearby Pymmes, which belonged to Cecil's son Robert, the man, of
course, in the hermit's costume. In one of the four compartments,
the gardener had created an unusual maze, made not of mere 'pot-
herbs', like hyssop and thyme, but flowers: the 'virtues were done
in roses', 'the graces of pansies part-coloured', and the Muses in
nine different kinds of flowers, all 'winding and wreathing' around
a statue of 'your Majesty'. His master, Lord Robert, had commanded him to make an arbour planted entirely with eglantine
because 'Eglantine,' he said, 'I most honour, and it has been told
me that the deeper it is rooted in the ground, the sweeter it
smelleth in the flower, making it so green that the sun of Spain at
the hottest cannot parch it.' With this joke about the invincibility
of eglantine, even in the heat of the hottest Spanish sun, Robert
Cecil neatly credited her with the defeat of the Armada.

Robert Cecil's maze garden at Pymmes was more than a
miniature Theobalds. Composed entirely of Elizabeth's
emblematic flowers and statuary devoted to her, it brought
courtly gardens into a new era. Whereas Dudley had teased and
complimented her at Kenilworth, in their gardens at Theobalds
and Pymms, the Cecils turned flattery into a cult.

Cecil noted the official highlight of her stay in his diary: 'Her Majesty dined abroad in the chamber called the Queen's Arbour in the company of the French Ambassador.' There was also a recitation of 'Italian verses' by the Lord Admiral.

Cecil had changed his tune about the value of Italian. In the early 1590s, the Venetian ambassador reported that, on one occasion, Cecil gave a dinner for the Privy Council at his house on the Strand, at which almost the entire conversation was in Italian. Astonishingly, every councillor could speak or understand it. Thirty years earlier, Elizabeth and Dudley had used the language to speak in code. As the century drew to a close, trading opportunities with Venice made a knowledge of Italian essential for a courtier.

In his Italian textbook, published in 1591, John Florio wrote that 'the best speak it best, and her Majesty none better'. The title of his book combined the fashion for Italian with the vogue for gardens and, specifically, rare varieties of fruit trees: *Florio's Second Fruits, to be Gathered of Twelve Trees, of Divers but Delightsome Tastes to the Tongues of Italian and English Men, to which is Annexed his Garden of Recreation Yielding Six Thousand Italian Proverbs*. In his preface, he gallantly defended his late patron Dudley, calling him 'a noble Maecenas' and 'the honour of England', whom 'like Hector, every miscreant myrmidon dare strike, being dead, yet . . . that Hector must have his desert: the general of his prince, the paragon of his peers, the watchman of our peace . . . the supporter of his friends, the terror of his foes, and the . . . patron of the muses'.

*

Officially, the total cost of the royal visit in 1591 was £1,000 (less than half the rumoured amount), of which £100 was spent on a dress for Elizabeth. Before her departure, she knighted Robert Cecil and proposed his appointment to the Privy Council. But she said nothing about making him Secretary.

Elizabeth had never liked Cecil's son Robert. Whereas Cecil was her 'spirit', she taunted Robert, calling him 'elf' and 'pygmy' (he was hunchbacked). In her view, he would make a poor substitute for his father.

That summer, the entertainments on the royal progress were more lavish than ever. At Cowdray in Sussex, Lord Montague staged a sea battle, as well as pageants starring a nymph, a pilgrim and a wild man covered in ivy. There were also musicians hidden in bushes and a royal bower. According to one contemporary account, while Elizabeth was on her way 'to take the pleasure of the walks', she heard beautiful music, which she followed and so arrived at a pond where an angler caught a great number of fish in a huge net (a compliment associating her with Christ and referring to Hatton's remark about her pleasure in fishing 'for men's souls'). Afterwards, she and her courtiers feasted 'most sumptuously' at a table twenty-four yards long 'in the walks' in the forest. The next day, there was more alfresco hospitality, this time in one of the garden avenues, where they dined at a table forty-eight yards long. On her last day, as she walked through a garden arbour which led to where her horse stood ready, Elizabeth discovered six men (presumably courtiers), whom she knighted.

In August, the Earl of Hertford found out that, as one of the last stops on her progress, Elizabeth was planning to drop in on him, unannounced. The worst thing was that she was coming not to one of his great houses but to tiny Elvetham, in Hampshire. Hertford had been out of favour ever since his marriage to her cousin Katherine Grey, the younger sister of Lady Jane Grey. He was also the son of the late Lord Somerset, with whom Elizabeth had fallen out as a princess. With the odds stacked against him, Hertford had needed to come up with something to eclipse all that had gone before.

In just a few weeks, Hertford's army of labourers extended the house and dug an enormous crescent-shaped lake in the centre of the pleasure grounds at Elvetham. This was a tribute to Elizabeth as Diana, the moon goddess (as goddess of chastity and the hunt, Diana was associated with Elizabeth, and the moon was linked with women because of its changeability). The lake lay between the house and a hill where Hertford built a set of wooden-and-canvas banqueting houses decked with boughs and 'clusters of ripe hazel nuts', according to an official account of the entertainments. Inside the banqueting houses, the ceilings were hung with ivy and the floors strewn with herbs and rushes.

On 12 September, accompanied by two hundred men wearing gold chains, Hertford rode out to meet Elizabeth. When they were about halfway between the park gates and the house, a poet dressed in green appeared from nowhere and praised Elizabeth for her learning, her wealth, her beauty and for being 'more worthy than the gods'. As she rode on, girls crowned with flowers and dressed as the Hours and Graces (the handmaids of Venus) strewed flowers in her path, calling her 'O beauteous Queen of second Troy'. During her four-day stay, she was also addressed as 'Beauty's Queen', 'the fairest queen, / That ever trod upon this green', 'fair Cynthia' (the moon goddess, again), 'sweet lively sun', 'world's star-bright eye' and 'world's chief delight', as well as 'dread Eliza'. The entertainments starred two of her favourite characters from Dudley's pageants at Kenilworth and Wanstead: the wild god of the woods Sylvanus scared the life out of the local people when he ran towards them, beside the lake, and there was a song about the Lady of May, which Elizabeth liked so much that she asked to hear it again.

The highlight of Hertford's festivities took place on the second day, after dinner, by the lake. Elizabeth sat enthroned on a platform at the water's edge, in a pavilion made of four silver pillars covered by a silk-and-silver canopy topped with four white plumes spangled with silver. Here, she watched battles between floating islands: Neptune's Fort and an English fleet in the shape of an island with ship's masts clashed with the Spanish Monster Mount, which they defeated by transforming it into an enormous snail. No one had staged the defeat of the Armada more winningly. Neptune's fort was planted with willows and the English fleet's masts were young oak trees. The snail mount was planted with a maze (spiralling circles of twenty-foot-high privet hedges) and had horns 'full of wild-fire, continually burning'. There were boats carrying musicians, which floated dangerously here and there in the midst of the action. At the end of the show, a fully rigged miniature galleon decked with flags and streamers of every colour glided over to Elizabeth. Hertford's men stepped ashore and presented her with two exquisite jewels.

On the last morning of her stay, no sooner was Elizabeth at her gallery window overlooking the garden than three cornets began to play 'fantastic dances'. Immediately afterwards, the

Fairy Queen came into the garden, dancing with her maids. They sang a song in six parts, accompanied by 'the music of an exquisite consort, wherein was the lute, bandora, base viol, cithern, treble viol and flute'. According to the official reporter, this spectacle 'so delighted her Majesty that she caused to hear it sung and to be danced three times over, and called for divers lords and ladies to behold it'. Before the actors, singers and musicians left, she thanked them and gave them 'a gracious largesse'.

Although it was pouring with rain when Elizabeth left Elvetham by coach, the entire cast of the previous four days' pageants assembled near the lake to mourn her departure. They pleaded with her to stay or else to return soon. As she passed through the park gates, a group of musicians and singers hidden in a bower performed a song called 'Come Again'. She took off her mask (a playful piece of artifice) and thanked them wholeheartedly.

Elvetham went down in history as the greatest entertainment of the age. Engravings of the lake theatre became best-sellers. Kenilworth was forgotten. Elizabeth pardoned Hertford and promised that he would find his reward in her 'especial favour'. But although he was welcomed at court, he gained no further reward. Elizabeth did not feel obliged to keep all of her promises. As she had once said, 'Words are no better than leaves.'

Over the course of a few decades, inordinate sums of money had been spent in Elizabeth's honour, on buildings, gardens and festivities sometimes designed to last just a day or a few weeks. The average cost of entertaining her and her retinue was £1–2,000 a day, at a time when, according to Penry Williams, labourers earned between 8d and 10d a day (£11 14s a year). Officially, these extra outlays were paid for by her courtiers and her townspeople; given her generosity to her favourites, however, most of the money may be said to have come from the Exchequer.

Elizabeth's conspicuous consumption throughout her reign demonstrates the closeness of the relationship between majesty and display. It would also seem to reflect the prosperity of the age. Williams observes that 'deficient though the fiscal system was, it enabled the Crown to build up an accumulated surplus of nearly £300,000 by 1584'. Between 1547 and 1603, the Crown's total revenue rose from £170,000 to about £300,000. Customs revenues increased from £26,000 in 1547 to about £90,000 between 1558 and 1598, and, although, as Williams points out, rents from the Crown's landed estates 'rose slowly, from £86,000 in 1558–9 to only £111,000 in 1601–2', taxation, 'in the form of parliamentary subsidies, yielded an average of £20,000 a year in times of peace, about £140,000 in the later years of war'. Between 1588 and 1603, 'the total cost of war to the Exchequer, including the cost of defeating the Armada, came to £4,500,000, of which nearly £2,000,000 were spent on Ireland', with a result that in 'the last years of the reign the Crown was hard pressed to pay its bills'.

15

'You will enter a tortuous path and fall into the
hazardous wiles of the labyrinth.'

Cabbages, from *Paradisi in Sole Paradisus Terrestris*

Alpha and Omega

WHEN ELIZABETH RETURNED to Theobalds in 1594, she was again welcomed by Robert Cecil in the guise of a hermit, who pleaded with her to let his father retire. Although, as he admitted, 'Sons are not always of their fathers' condition', he suggested that when Cecil's son gained possession of Theobalds, he would 'use it for a place of recreation than of meditation; and then of a beadsman shall I become a pilgrim'. If Elizabeth would only appoint him Secretary, he would devote Theobalds entirely to her entertainment, returning it to a shrine to her (since her last visit in 1591, he had helped his father to create a new garden and orchard at Cheshunt Park, supplying him with cherry trees and, as Cecil had requested, causing 'the fruiterer at Westminster to be spoken unto for thirty or forty young trees'). Robert then presented her with a gold bell and gold-plated prayer book, as well as a 'candle of virgin's wax, meet for a Virgin Queen'. But although she accepted his gifts, she ignored his plea.

The prospect of a Theobalds run by Robert Cecil did not appeal. In any case, she had no need of more courtly pleasure grounds. There was already a host of great gardens designed in her honour. And new gardens were being created each year.

Her progresses were much shorter than before, and many of her favourite destinations now lay south of the river, close to London. Theobalds had long since lost its usefulness as a stopping-point – and courtiers who lavished great sums on distant gardens in the hope of a royal visit were usually disappointed.

In 1579, Cecil paid a visit to Sir Christopher Hatton's new 'prodigy house' at Holdenby, in Northamptonshire, while Hatton was away. Cecil wrote to congratulate Hatton on his work in progress, paying him the greatest compliment by likening Holdenby to Theobalds. He then expressed their joint devotion to Elizabeth with the wish, 'God send us both long life to enjoy her, for whom we both meant to exceed our purses in these.'

Directly modelled on Theobalds, Holdenby was bigger and considerably more expensive. The 410-foot south-facing garden façade was made up almost entirely of enormous windows and resembled an immense sheet of glass. The grounds were still more ambitious. The house stood at the top of a hill, and the garden had been carved into vast terraces with pools and mounts crowned by banqueting houses. Hatton's gardener was a mysterious priest who had worked for Cecil at Burghley House and had trained the gardeners at several other great houses: since the Middle Ages, priests and monks had been recognised for their horticultural expertise.

Unlike Cecil, Hatton really did bankrupt himself with his improvements to Holdenby. As Receiver of Tenths and First Fruits, he contracted enormous debts to his own office. Elizabeth never visited Holdenby because it was not finished in time, and Ben Jonson made it a symbol of the extravagance and corruption of her reign, while joking about Hatton's reputation as 'the dancing chancellor' (he had first caught Elizabeth's eye while dancing in one of Dudley's Christmas masques at the Inner Temple):

> They come to see, and to be seen,
> And though they dance afore the Queen,
> There's none of these doth hope to come by
> Wealth to build another Holmby [Holdenby].

In Derbyshire, Bess, Countess of Shrewsbury, commissioned elaborate tapestries of Elizabeth as Diana and Venus for Hardwick Hall, preparations for a state visit that never happened – Elizabeth had a lifelong distrust of Bess because of her ambition. Bess had never given up hope that one day her granddaughter Arabella Stuart might become queen.

The improvements in the grounds included a new formal garden and orchard, with elaborate banqueting houses, and pools in the hunting park. Built by Robert Smythson between 1591 and 1597, the house took the fashion for huge windows further than ever, as reflected by the mocking rhyme 'Hardwick Hall, more glass than wall'.

Long journeys to the north were things of the past, and the now ageing Elizabeth preferred to call on loyal courtiers who lived close to her palaces at Richmond and Greenwich. Two gardens in Surrey were particular favourites: Nonsuch and Beddington Park. When Theobalds had begun to fall into neglect, Nonsuch had taken its place.

Henry VIII had prized Nonsuch for its deer park. He had transformed what was originally a royal hunting lodge into a palace, calling it 'Nonsuch' because it had no equal. It resembled a fairy-tale castle, with numerous turrets bearing a forest of flags.

Elizabeth's half-sister, Mary, had sold Nonsuch to the Earl of Arundel, as a reward for his support on her accession. The Arundels were the most powerful Catholic family in the country – and Cecil's bitter enemies. In 1569, Arundel and his son-in-law Lord Lumley had been involved in the Northern Uprising; although convicted of treason, they had subsequently been pardoned (they had been of more use to Elizabeth alive and in her debt).

After Arundel's death in 1580, Lumley had inherited Nonsuch and devoted it to Elizabeth, as a way of showing his gratitude. But the palace had only become one of Elizabeth's favourite residences after his dramatic improvements to the gardens.

Lumley's father-in-law Arundel had travelled in Italy, and, at Nonsuch, there were wonderful Italianate fountains: one had a statue of Diana with a crescent moon in her hair. A path lined by pyramids, as at Theobalds, led to a grove adorned with fountains of Diana and her nymphs spraying the voyeur Actaeon as he changed into a stag. The moral of Ovid's story was underscored by inscriptions exhorting visitors to scorn the example of lustful Actaeon and to lay low the fires of the passions. Elsewhere, visitors encountered a pyramid fountain with jets issuing from the mouths of thirsty-looking heads.

In the 1590s, Lumley emerged as Cecil's new rival in gardens by creating a spectacular maze with hedges so high that it was impossible to see over them. The design was based on the maze at Theobalds and was one of the first of its kind. Until then, Tudor mazes had been only about two feet high and similar to the two-dimensional labyrinths on the floors of medieval cathedrals (representing the journey of the soul through the dangers of the world).

A contemporary visitor to Nonsuch, Anthony Watson, warned future guests that there was a 'snake in the grass': Lumley's maze.

You will enter a tortuous path and fall into the hazardous wiles of the labyrinth.

The best Elizabethan mazes were amazing in the modern sense of the word. In his poem *The Garden Plot*, Harry Goldingham (Dudley's star performer at Kenilworth) described one of the thrills of his imaginary garden as 'the maze that mazed me'. He added that it would take him too long to describe all of the fabulous things in the garden (the maze, as well as the knot gardens, bowers of birds and pleasant walks and ways), probably as a joke about the excesses of fashionable gardens.

The love of mazes was linked to the contemporary delight in puzzles. In December 1593, Cecil wrote to his son Robert about a joking letter he had sent him, which Elizabeth had also read. Cecil complimented her on her skill in solving the letter's puzzles:

I must confess that my cunning therein was not sufficient to hide the sense from her Majesty, though I think never a lady besides her, nor a decipherer in the Court, would have dissolved the figure [puzzle] to have found the sense as her Majesty has done. And where her Majesty allows of me that I made myself merry, in very truth I did it rather to make her some sport, myself therein not altered, no otherwise than her Majesty's lute is in her hand, that makes others merry and continues itself as it was.

While a maze could represent confusion and bewilderment, it was also a symbol of order, as shown by a later version of a painting given by Elizabeth to Walsingham in celebration of the peace treaty with France which he had negotiated in 1572. The painting shows Elizabeth's entrance into a luxurious garden pavilion from a formal garden laid out in circular mazes. Accompanied by Peace and Plenty, she joins Henry VIII, her half-brother Edward and the rest of her family. On the left-hand side of the painting, her half-sister Mary stands next to Philip II and Mars, God of War; behind them, there is a view of what appears to be Whitehall Palace set against a fiery sky. England under Elizabeth was like a beautiful garden, a place of order and calm, in contrast with the chaos of Mary's reign.

Many years earlier, Dudley had drawn on similar imagery in devising the entertainments for Elizabeth's procession through the City, on the eve of her coronation. His most elaborate pageant showed two hills on either side of a cave. The southernmost hill was green and covered with flowers, with a well-dressed boy standing beneath a lovely tree; the northern hill was stony and barren, with a sad and dishevelled-looking boy sitting beneath a dead tree. Two figures were locked inside the cave: a girl in a white silk dress (Truth) and an old man with wings attached to his back, carrying a scythe (Father Time).

There had been a considerable build-up to this pageant. Earlier, Elizabeth had asked what it was about. On being told that the pageant showed Time, she had replied, 'Time hath brought me hither.' When she arrived at the set, the old man, Time, unlocked the gate of the cave from the inside and led his daughter, Truth, up to the top of the beautiful hill, on the south side of the stage.

Now that Elizabeth (Truth) was free, the future looked bright, as represented by the fertile hill. The past – the barren hill, representing Mary's reign – could be forgotten. As a finale, Truth lowered into Elizabeth's chariot a copy of the English Bible on a silken string; she kissed it, to a great cheer from the crowd.

By the 1570s, a labyrinthine garden had replaced a lovely landscape as the symbol of a well-governed kingdom.

At Nonsuch, Watson marvelled at the delicacy of the planting in the gardens:

Plants and shrubs mingle in intricate circles as by the needle of Semiramis [the Assyrian queen said to have created the Hanging Gardens of Babylon].

The topiary was equally ingenious, taking the shapes of deer, horses, rabbits and dogs, which 'give chase with unhindered feet and effortlessly pass over the green'. From a distance, they were said to have been mistaken for real ones.

Beddington Park belonged to Sir Francis Carew, a well-connected courtier. He was the brother-in-law of the late Sir Nicholas Throckmorton, who had been the English ambassador to Paris and Scotland. Carew loved France and lived there for several years, spending his time very differently, however, from his brother-in-law. When Throckmorton had nominated Carew as his successor as ambassador to Paris, Cecil had objected on the grounds that he was given 'chiefly to pleasure' (although he had happily capitalised on Carew's love of gardens when purchasing exotic fruit trees).

Carew's father had been a favourite of Henry VIII and Master of the Horse, but his implication in a plot by the Marquess of Exeter had led to his execution for treason. His feats in the tilt-yard had nevertheless passed into legend: he had jousted blindfold on a blindfolded horse and had run the length of the tilt-yard balancing a twenty-foot beam on his head. Carew proudly displayed this beam in his Great Hall. He had inherited his father's exceptional ability to please, but, a generation on, he knew that gardens rather than jousts were a better way of entertaining the Queen.

Carew had used his lifetime of leisure to create a water garden inspired by the most innovative French pleasure grounds, which derived from Italian gardens. A stream diverted from the River Wandle ran through his garden at Beddington. Close to the house, two gardens opened out into a fantastic designed landscape. In the first garden stood a fountain adorned with marvellously lifelike sculptures of fish and frogs (inspired by the faience sculptures of the great ceramicist Bernard Palissy for Catherine de' Medici at the Tuileries; recent excavations at Beddington have revealed that the fish were made of moving parts skewered on poles so as to appear to swim in the fountain). The second garden was planted with rare orange, lemon and fig trees. Near by, the stream emerged from a little hill decorated with lifelike statues of little people and animals. Small boats and a ship sailed on the stream and miniature corn mills lined its banks, as at Theobalds. These mills linked the garden with the wider landscape since the Wandle powered numerous mills, thanks to its fall of 124 feet within nine miles.

Further on, in the middle of the stream, stood a shell pavilion built on a rock. Inside the pavilion, guests discovered a hydra fountain, with water spouting from its heads. Not far away was a two-storey pavilion made of brass. The ground-floor room had a ceiling from which artificial rain fell. In the first-floor room, there was a mirror inlaid with different kinds of marble, and the ceiling was painted with a map of the Netherlands. Elsewhere in the grounds, there was an oval fish pond encircled by hedges. Towards the end of the reign, Carew's pleasure grounds at Beddington would be described by a French visitor as 'the most curious garden in England'. Elizabeth would visit Beddington thirteen times during her reign – a total equalled only by Theobalds.

Although Elizabeth finally made Robert Cecil her Secretary of State in 1596, she still relied on his father as her chief counsellor. In September of that year, she made Robert Chancellor of the Duchy of Lancaster, a post which Cecil had sought for him. In reply to Cecil's letter of thanks, Elizabeth directed her Lord Chancellor, Admiral Howard, to express her gratitude to him for his faithful service:

Yet are you to her in all things and shall be Alpha and Omega. Wheresoever your Lordship is, your service to her giveth hourly thanks; and prayeth your Lordship to use all the rest possible you may, that you may be able to serve her at the time that cometh.

Cecil must have been delighted with this extraordinary tribute, though he was probably equally troubled by her relentless dependency.

A month earlier, he had used the phrase 'Alpha and Omega' in a letter to his son Robert, regretting her reluctance to go to war with Spain. Cecil had written that his loyalty to her had its limits: he preferred 'in policy, her Majesty afore all others on the earth and in divinity the King of Heaven above all betwixt Alpha and Omega'. But while he could oppose her in matters of principle, he could not persuade her to let him retire.

The previous year, he had, however, resigned himself to the fact that he could not escape from public life by retreating to Theobalds. In April, he had gone there to recover from illness, but, by the summer, he had returned to court, where he had written to Robert that he was 'well weaned from Theobalds and without desire to see it for any contentment'. Granted leave to take a holiday in August, instead of retiring to Theobalds, he had gone to stay with his old friend Cobham, in Kent. They had spent their time riding and hunting. Cobham Hall made a good substitute for Theobalds. Apart from the famous tiered tree house, there was a 'rare garden', according to the antiquarian Francis Thynne (writing in 1587), 'in which no variety of strange flowers and trees do want, which praise or price may obtain from the further part of Europe or from other strange countries'.

At the age of seventy-seven, Cecil lay on his deathbed at his house on the Strand, where Elizabeth sent him cordials, with the message: 'I do entreat Heaven daily for your longer life, else will my people, nay, myself, stand in need of cordial too. My comfort hath been in my people's happiness, and their happiness in thy discretion.' In his last days, she came to his bedroom and spoon-fed him, giving him more cordials. But when she left, he refused all medicine. He longed for death, crying out, 'Oh, what a heart have I that will not die.' On 4 August 1598, in his final hours, he lay motionless, saying nothing.

He was buried in his family chapel at Stamford, in Lincolnshire, but Elizabeth honoured him with a ceremonial service in Westminster Abbey. Sir William Knollys wrote to Dudley's stepson, Essex, about Cecil's death, telling him that Elizabeth was taking it 'very grievously, shedding of tears, and separating herself from all company. Yet doubt I not but she in her wisdom will cast this behind her, as she hath done many other before time of like nature'.

Elizabeth is said to have paid a state visit to Theobalds either just before or just after Cecil's death. She never visited Theobalds again, but, years later, she still shed tears at the mention of his name. He had been like a father to her, and she probably never recovered from her loss.

❧

Robert Cecil inherited Theobalds and lands that brought in around £1,800 a year. He retained his father's head gardener, Jennings, and his team. In December, Jennings asked for a raise of £4 a year. He was supported by the keeper of the park at Theobalds, who described him as 'very needy'. But Robert Cecil's steward argued that there was no reason for an increase in Jennings's wages since Cecil (Robert Cecil's father) had 'given him the benefit of the garden' (meaning the produce). Robert

Cecil would later entrust the care of his gardens to the great plantsman John Tradescant.

Now that Theobalds would never be the same again, Elizabeth made Greenwich her new summer headquarters. Out of all of the royal palaces, after Whitehall, she had spent the most money on Greenwich. Her love of its gardens is reflected in Sir John Davies's acrostic poem addressed to Flora (representing the Queen – 'Elisa').

> Empress of Flowers! Tell, where away
> Lies your sweet Court, this merry May?
> In Greenwich garden alleys!
> Since there the Heavenly Powers do play,
> And haunt no other valleys.

Between 1567 and 1569, works carried out in the palace and gardens, including several new fountains and a terrace, cost nearly £3,000. By the 1580s, the gardens and park were among Elizabeth's favourite places for walking. Elizabeth maintained Henry VIII's banqueting house, the Mirefleur Tower on the Venus Hill, as well as a temporary banqueting house made of fir poles and decked with birch branches and flowers created in the first summer of her reign. In the palace, there was a 'field room' made up almost entirely of an enormous bay window overlooking the formal gardens, meadows and river, where she sat on silk cushions beneath a canopy decorated with feather plumes.

As the century drew to a close, Greenwich became her favourite royal residence: it was where she had been born and, as such, provided a link with her mother. (There is a rare mention of a garden in connection with Anne Boleyn, in a report that she once complained to Henry VIII about the noise made by the peacocks in the pleasure grounds at Greenwich; as a result, they were removed.)

In the late 1580s, Elizabeth commissioned Richard Dixon to carve four six-foot-long seats for the gardens at Greenwich. According to the Office of Works accounts, the seats were 'turned with rails and baluster with a lion and a dragon supporting the queen's badges, with two arches under the seats and two elbows to lean, one carved with pediments crested for the weather carved with the rose and crown with the Queen's letters, with an ostrich, a tassel and an eagle crowned holding a sceptre crowned'. Numerous new seats were added to the gardens and orchard. There were long seats for the garden, one in 'a jasper colour', which gave the appearance of marble and symbolised chastity. In the orchard, three seats, seven benches and several arbours were repainted in jasper, and a canopy was added to the Queen's seat. Four seats in the orchard were painted the colour of brick, and a 'back board for her Majesty to sit against' was painted in diverse colours and gilded.

Towards the end of the century, Portington, the Master Carpenter, made 'a fair standing seat in the mulberry tree garden and new seat with four pillars under the same tree for her Majesty'. The seat was eight feet long and six feet wide, 'standing upon terms arched and carved'. It was painted 'with ash-colour and jasper like rance [a kind of marble, of a red colour varied with veins and spots of blue and white] in water colour'. The four pillars made a pavilion, built around the mulberry tree. Joiners added six five-foot-long and five-foot-high seats with balusters and 'a carved pediment on top' painted jasper and gilded. In 1600, nineteen seats in the orchard and garden were given a new coat of paint. The following year, one last seat was made for the garden: it had a brick base painted a stone colour and a blue lead-covered roof.

The impression is that Elizabeth built a suite of outdoor meeting rooms in her gardens at Greenwich. We might imagine her conducting state business there, recalling her meetings with Cecil in the garden at Theobalds concerning the war in the Netherlands, during the fateful summer of 1587.

Robert Cecil took his father's place as the most powerful politician in the country, but Essex, Dudley's stepson, was a thorn in his flesh. They vied with each other for lucrative appointments for their supporters. Elizabeth favoured Robert Cecil's candidates; Francis Bacon, Cecil's nephew, headed Essex's growing band of spurned supporters. Essex took every disappointment as a rejection and, ultimately, a dishonour.

Essex was sent to Ireland to suppress the rebellion by the Earl of Tyrone in March 1599, but his military campaign was a miserable failure. Unilaterally negotiating a truce, Essex returned to England in September without the Queen's permission, and then barged into her chambers, for all of which he was banished from court and placed under house arrest, though his scheduled Star Chamber trial was later cancelled. Meanwhile, Robert Cecil quietly courted James VI of Scotland (the future King James I), promising to ensure his smooth transition to power after Elizabeth's death in return for being allowed to keep his position, and probably also fulminated Essex's alleged treason.

When Essex fell ill, Elizabeth visited him at York House on the Strand. She later arranged for him to be moved into the grandest bedroom, sent him cordials and gave him permission to walk in the garden, where his friends saluted him.

In the spring of 1600, Elizabeth took long walks in the park at Greenwich, trying to decide Essex's fate. As before, this made her a target. A would-be assassin, Anthony Sparke, approached her in the park but dropped one of his pistols, which fired. In the confusion that followed, her courtiers disarmed him.

Despite this latest attempt on her life, Elizabeth planned a long summer progress to Wiltshire. When her courtiers tried to persuade her against it, she told them, 'Let the old stay behind, and the young and able go with me.' But even some of her most loyal friends begged to be spared a visit: Sir Henry Lee wrote to Robert Cecil that he had heard that 'Her Majesty threatens a progress' and planned to come 'to my house, of which I would be most proud' but 'my estate without my undoing cannot bear it'. When Lord Lincoln heard that she was planning to visit him in Chelsea, he left for the country. On arriving to find the house empty, Elizabeth sent him a message that she would return the following week. In the end, she travelled with a small retinue to Nonsuch and Oatlands, in Surrey, making a few day excursions to the houses of courtiers who lived near by, including Whitgift's Croydon Palace and Carew's Beddington Park.

Fortunately, she could still count on Carew to astonish her. For her twelfth visit to Beddington, he came up with a horticultural conjuring trick to rival Gerard's. As they walked in his orchard of exotic fruit trees, Carew steered her over to a cherry tree bearing huge cherries 'at the least one month after all cherries had taken their farewell of England' (as garden writer Hugh Platt later put it in his *Garden of Eden*). While Elizabeth ate one of the cherries, Carew revealed the secret behind the magic: he had kept the fruit back by covering the tree with canvas, and, when he had been certain that she was coming, he had removed the canvas and a few sunny days had done the rest.

By artificially delaying the ripening process, he had created the flattering illusion that she had the power to prolong the spring. Since cherries represented youth and virginity, this was a doubly flattering and seductive gesture. By the end of the century, skills in arboriculture could do a lot for a courtier.

In comparison with Dudley's and Cecil's pleasure grounds, Carew's garden won him a more lasting fame. In the seventeenth century, Platt admiringly gave details of Carew's technique of holding back the fruit of the cherry tree. Carew's garden outlasted Kenilworth and Theobalds by more than a century. John Evelyn described Beddington as 'the first orange garden of England'. In 1691, J. Gibson called it 'the best orangery [orange garden] in England. The orange and lemon trees grow in the ground, and have done so near one hundred years, as the gardener, an aged man, said he believed.' On Gibson's visit to the garden, the gardener told him that the previous year, his men had picked ten thousand oranges.

In 1600, the seventh bad harvest in a row created the conditions for rebellion. Despite her misgivings, Elizabeth released Essex, on Bacon's advice, on condition that he stayed away from court. Seriously in debt and facing bankruptcy, he begged her to renew his monopoly on sweet wines. When she failed to reply, he pleaded with her to see him: 'Say you come, from pining, languishing, despairing SX.' She sent him a message that 'thankfulness is ever welcome' but called him an 'ungovernable beast' in public. In October, she finally refused to grant his suit.

At Essex House on the Strand (formerly Dudley's Leicester House), Essex brought his plans for rebellion to a head. But in November, he wrote wistfully to Elizabeth about the Accession Day jousts:

I sometimes think of running [in the tilt-yard] and then remember what it will be to come into that presence, out of which both by your own voice I was commanded, and by your own hands thrust out.

His appeal might have brought back for her memories of the masque set in the Garden of Eden, which Dudley had commissioned for the great tournament at Whitehall in 1581. Sidney's angel had then advised her knights dressed as Adam and Eve to stay 'in the garden' of her 'graces' so as to regain Paradise.

In February, Essex was panicked into putting his plans into action when Elizabeth summoned him to appear before the Privy Council. When he led his army through London, he was arrested with eighty-five conspirators, including his stepfather, Sir Christopher Blount, and Shakespeare's patron, the Earl of Southampton.

At first, Essex pleaded not guilty to treason but later confessed that 'the Queen could never be safe as long as I live'. In his speech on the scaffold, he said, 'My sins are more in number

265

than the hairs on my head. I have bestowed my youth in wantonness, lust and uncleanness; I have been puffed up with pride, vanity and love of this wicked world's pleasures.' Calling his rebellion his last 'infectious' sin, he asked God to preserve Elizabeth 'whose death I protest I never meant, nor violence to her person'. His stepfather, Blount, was also executed. Within a few days Lettice, Countess of Essex, had lost both her son and her husband. But Essex's death also left Elizabeth bereft. She had lost her last friend and – perhaps – lover.

That summer, Elizabeth set out on what turned out to be one of the most lavish progresses of her reign. Her extravagance amazed even the most jaded of her courtiers when she entertained the French ambassador at Basing, in Hampshire, the home of the Marquess and Marchioness of Winchester, and at The Vine, a nearby mansion belonging to Lord Sandy. The ambassador stayed at The Vine, which Elizabeth had equipped with furnishings and gold-and-silver plate from Hampton Court and the Tower. At just two days' notice, the people of Southampton had supplied extra beds. Elizabeth invited the ambassador to dine with her at Basing, and he returned the compliment. On her departure, she knighted ten men (a record number) and declared her pride in the entertainments:

I have done more than any of my ancestors have ever done, or any other prince in Christendom has been able to do – namely, in my Hampshire progress this year, entertained a royal ambassador royally in my subjects' houses.

266

Her love of exercise also continued unabated. The following spring, she went walking on Richmond Green every day. The French ambassador remarked on her amazing energy despite her years. At the end of April, she threw a banquet for the Duke of Nevers at Richmond and danced the first dance with him: a galliard. Afterwards, he kissed her hand, and, when she lifted her skirt, he also kissed her foot. She went a-Maying in the fields at Lewisham. During the summer progress, she was extravagantly entertained at Harefield Place, near Uxbridge, by her Lord Keeper, Egerton, and his wife, the Countess of Derby. In August, Elizabeth rode ten miles in one day, before hunting, and the next day took a long walk. That September, at court, according to one observer, there was 'much dancing' of 'country dances before the Queen's Majesty, who is exceedingly pleased therewith', to 'Irish tunes', which were then particularly fashionable.

Although she seems increasingly to have used her gardens for business, Elizabeth continued to the end to see them as places of pleasure, as shown by the story of her rendezvous with a young German aristocrat in the garden of her palace at Oatlands, in 1602. The anecdote is told by F. Gershow, the personal assistant of the Duke of Stettin-Pomerania who was in England on his European tour. On his arrival at Oatlands, the Duke was invited to meet the Queen in the garden. When Elizabeth appeared, she was wearing a mask and, as Gershow records in his journal, teased and flirted with the Duke:

Her Royal Majesty passed us several times, walking as freely as if she had been only eighteen years old, always taking off her mask and bowing deeply to his princely Grace, who, however, not willing to make himself known, stood almost behind.

The story reveals the kind of garden games that Elizabeth played with favourites, as well as her undiminished appetite for fun. She was sixty-nine.

In December, Robert Cecil entertained Elizabeth at his house on the Strand with a masque about Astraea (Virgil's wise maiden, whose appearance signalled the return of the golden age, represented Elizabeth). Seven years earlier, at Theobalds, he had donned a hermit's costume in an attempt to persuade her to make him his father's successor: in return, he had promised to return Theobalds to a shrine to her and to become a 'pilgrim'. At his town house, the set for the masque was an altar ('Astraea's shrine'), with tapers devoted to a 'saint' whose picture hung above it: here was Elizabeth, in the most gorgeous painting ever painted of her, commissioned by Robert Cecil especially for her visit.

The fantastical painting of Elizabeth in Robert Cecil's 'shrine' has become known as the Rainbow Portrait (now at Hatfield Palace). As a sign of the peace that follows a storm (representing harmony after chaos: Elizabeth's reign after that of Mary and England's survival despite the threats of armadas), the rainbow was now part of the royal iconography. One of Essex's gifts to Elizabeth in 1587 was a gold jewel in the shape of a rainbow, set with rubies and showing two pillars, one of which was broken; ten years later, another courtier, whose identity is unknown, gave her a golden rainbow jewel with the sun above it 'garnished with sparks of diamonds'. Rainbows were especially fashionable in

1602: at Harefield, during the summer progress, the Countess of Derby had given Elizabeth a heart-shaped diamond and a 'rainbow' dress.

Elizabeth's phantasmagorical costume in the Rainbow Portrait had probably been made for a masque held earlier in the year. She wears a low-cut white dress in the Spanish style, with a mantle resembling those worn in Ireland, but golden and edged with pearls. Her bodice is embroidered with wild flowers – honeysuckle, gillyflowers, pansies and cowslips – and the mantle is covered with eyes and ears, references to her universal fame, her royalty (in a masque performed during her 1591 visit to Theobalds, an usher compared her servants to her eyes and ears) and her all-seeing, all-knowing semi-divine status, thanks to her network of spies created by Cecil and Walsingham.

In 1587, Harrison reported that he had seen about four hundred exotic plants in English gardens 'of the half of whose names within forty years past we had no manner of knowledge', commenting, 'It is a world also to see how many strange herbs, plants and unusual fruits are daily brought unto us, from the Indies, Americas, Taprobane [Ceylon], Canary Isles and all parts of the world.' As spring flowers, the English meadow flowers on her bodice represented eternal youth, while showing her love of native flowers and, of course, her country. At a time when exotic new flowers from far-off lands were arriving every day, transforming English gardens, it is striking that Elizabeth chose only flowers of the field as adornments.

The painting presents further puzzles. The large snake (wisdom) embroidered on her left sleeve, knotted into a figure of eight (eternity) with a heart-shaped ruby hanging from its mouth, has been interpreted as meaning 'my head always rules my heart'. A miniature gauntlet pinned to her ruff signals her love of chivalry. Her goddess-like status is reinforced by the jewel in the shape of a crescent moon, symbol of Diana, at the top of her elaborate headdress.

She holds a rainbow in her right hand, next to the motto 'No rainbow without the sun'. In conversation with Hilliard, she said that she liked to be painted in bright sunlight. Here, she literally lights up the painting – there is no other source of light.

A week after her visit to Robert Cecil on the Strand, she dined with Lord Nottingham at Arundel House – he had fought alongside Drake against the Armada, and his wife Catherine Carey was the daughter of Elizabeth's favourite cousin, the late Lord Hunsdon, and a favourite herself. According to commentator John Chamberlain, the feast 'had nothing extraordinary, neither were [Nottingham's] presents so precious as was expected, being only a whole suit of apparel, whereas it was thought he would have bestowed his rich hangings of all the fights with the Armada in 1588'.

Elizabeth spent Christmas at Whitehall, as usual, and, afterwards, planned to go to Richmond, her 'warm winter box'. But Robert Cecil tried to persuade her to stay in London, in case her health suddenly failed. As well as dancing and plays, there was 'great golden play [gambling]' at court, according to one observer. Robert Cecil lost £800 'in one night, and as much more at other times'. Another courtier wrote, 'All is to entertain the time, and win her to stay here if may be.' Nevertheless, Elizabeth made ready to leave London, sending her carts and carriages ahead of her, as usual. When Robert Cecil turned them back, she summoned her old friend and astrologer Dee to cast her horoscope. He warned her to leave Whitehall as soon as possible.

On her journey to Richmond, she wore 'summer-like garments' despite the extreme cold. In February, she received the Venetian ambassador, telling him, in Italian, 'It is high time that the Republic sent to visit a queen who has always honoured it on every possible occasion.' After forty years of estrangement, the Venetians were keen to do business with England, in defiance of Rome.

When Catherine Carey, Nottingham's wife, died later that month, Elizabeth's grief was so intense that she temporarily withdrew from public life, postponing a meeting with the French ambassador. The Venetian ambassador commented on the remarkable change:

She has suddenly withdrawn into herself, she who was wont to live so gaily, especially in these last years of her life.

This latest bereavement brought on her fatal illness. When Hunsdon's youngest son, Robert Carey, told her, 'My chiefest happiness is to see you in safety and in health, which I wish may long continue', she took him by the hand and replied, 'No, Robin, I am not well,' confiding, 'My heart has been sad and heavy for ten or twelve days.' Carey described how 'in her discourse she fetched not so few as forty or fifty great sighs. I grieved at the first to see her in such plight, for in all my lifetime before I never knew her fetch a sigh but when the Queen of Scots was beheaded.'

In the last few weeks of her life, Elizabeth was haunted by nightmares. In the end, she refused to go to her bed, sleeping on cushions on the floor. There was no one to comfort her as she had comforted Cecil and Dudley. Carey said that nothing could be done since she had lost the will to live. But she did not forget who she was. When Robert Cecil tried to persuade her to go to her bedroom, saying that 'to content the people, she must go to bed', she rebuked him: 'The word "must" was not to be used to princes', adding, 'Little man, little man, if your father had lived, you would not have dared to have said so much, but you know I must die, and that makes you so presumptuous.'

When Nottingham returned to court from mourning, he tried to persuade her to go to her bed, but she told him, 'If you were in the habit of seeing such things in your bed as I do when in mine, you would not persuade me to go there.' Then she revealed her greatest fear: 'I had a premonition that, if I once lie down, I will never rise.' But finally she gave in and took to her bed. At first, she felt better and asked for a cordial of rosewater. True to herself, with her belief in herbal remedies, she refused all physic.

On Elizabeth's death, everyone looked to the rising sun, King James I, but no one could forget her. In her grand funeral procession to Westminster Abbey, her Master of the Horse led her white palfrey behind her hearse, upon which stood a life-size waxwork of her beneath a royal canopy carried by six earls. During her life, Elizabeth had defied old age, sanctioning only youthful portraits of herself. In a strange reversal, her marble effigy in the Abbey, designed by Maximilian Colt and painted by Hilliard, shows her as an old woman (it may have been modelled on her death mask). Beneath this unflattering image, however, a Latin inscription pays tribute to her as 'the mother of her country, the nurse of religion and learning; for perfect skill of very many languages, for glorious endowments, as well as mind as of body, a prince incomparable'.

Elizabeth and her world lived on in the pre-coronation entertainments for James I. Robert Cecil celebrated James's entry into London with a pageant in which Sylvanus, god of the woods, told him to 'walk into yonder garden', where there stood an arbour covered with artificial fruit and flowers called Plenty's Bower. James was praised as the sun which created the spring. Dressed like a gardener, Vertumnus (god of the seasons, change and gardens) then greeted him on behalf of Peace and the Governors of the City 'who carefully prune this garden [the kingdom], weeding out all hurtful and idle branches that hinder the growth of the good'.

16

'Of the ruinous castles of England Kenilworth is
undoubtedly one of the grandest.'

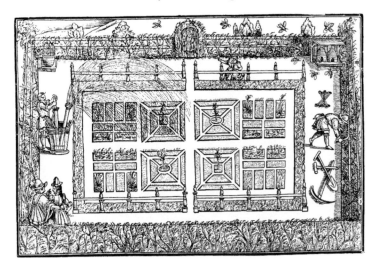

Watering the garden from a pump in a tub,
from *The Gardener's Labyrinth*

Paradises Lost – and Remembered

FOR NEARLY A QUARTER of a century, Theobalds was the model for palaces and courtly gardens. In May 1603, Robert Cecil welcomed King James to the palace. During the day, James took refuge from the heat in the shade, as John Savile reported:

The King went into the labyrinth-like gardens to walk, where he recreated himself in the meanders, compact of bays, rosemary, and the like overshadowing his walk, to defend him from the heat of the sun, till supper time.

On his second visit to Theobalds, in July 1606, during which he entertained the King of Denmark, there was a performance of a masque by Jonson: *Solomon and the Queen of Sheba*.

But, according to Sir John Harington, the show was a fiasco because the actors and James's guest, the King of Denmark, were drunk – the masque took place after what must have been a particularly convivial feast:

The Lady who did play the Queen's part, did carry most precious gifts to both their Majesties; but, forgetting the steps arising to the canopy, overset her caskets into his Danish Majesty's lap, and fell at his feet, though I rather think it was in his face. Much was the hurry and confusion; cloths and napkins were at hand, to make all clean. His Majesty then got up and would dance with the Queen of Sheba; but he fell down and humbled himself before her, and not a little defiled with the presents of the Queen which had been bestowed on his garments; such as wine, cream, jelly, beverage, cakes, spices, and other good matters.

The entertainment and show went forward, and most of the presenters went backward, or fell down; wine did so occupy their upper chambers.

Harington's satirical description would seem to support the view that Elizabeth's entertainments were restrained compared with the excesses of James's court.

The chaos described by Harington did not lessen the appeal of Theobalds for James, and after that second visit, he persuaded Robert Cecil to exchange it for Hatfield. He celebrated his acquisition of the palace the following May, commissioning a new masque by Jonson for the occasion. Gerard was appointed royal gardener and herbalist – and the new queen, Anne of Denmark, gave him an additional garden next to Somerset House, where he grew plants for the palaces.

Continuing the family tradition, Robert Cecil commissioned top designer-engineer Salomon de Caus to lay out a lavish new French- and Italian-inspired garden at Hatfield, and Thomas Cecil, his eldest son, created Italianate gardens with grand terraces at Wimbledon. Francis Bacon's water garden at Gorhambury was inspired by his uncle's much larger one at Theobalds.

Kenilworth also continued to be an atmospheric setting for court festivities: in August 1624, Jonson's *The Masque of Owls* was performed there. Jonson celebrated James's arrival at the castle by recalling Dudley's entertainments for Elizabeth in 1575:

> Room! room! for my horse will wince
> If he come within so many yards of a prince;
> For to tell you true, and in rhyme,
> He was foal'd in Queen Elizabeth's time;
> When the great Earl of Lester
> In this castle did feast her.

James formed a menagerie at Theobalds which included an elephant, flying squirrels, a white hind, a sable, and five camels sent by the King of Spain with strict instructions that they were to be exercised daily with 'every precaution taken to screen them from the vulgar gaze'. By 1620, the park covered 2,500 acres.

Theobalds was also part of James's great plan to promote English silk. The Long Walk in the Great Garden was planted with red mulberry trees: at Hatfield, he had already planted 500 mulberries. But it was all a terrible mistake. Red mulberry trees were suited for the English climate; unfortunately, silkworms only thrive on white mulberries, such as were grown in France. Although the venture was a catastrophe, it shows how much Theobalds and Hatfield were places of experimentation.

When James died in the park at Theobalds in 1625, Charles I was proclaimed king at its gates. Theobalds was even more of a retreat for Charles than it had been for Elizabeth. At Holdenby, there is a painting entitled 'Charles I at Theobalds', attributed to Hendrick van Steinwyck, which appears to offer a rare view of the palace interior and garden (some historians have suggested that the scene derives from images in Vredeman de Vries's architectural copybooks). Charles stands in front of the first of four arches forming a tunnel through to the garden beyond. He is wearing black and white, the colours of the Parliamentarians. Two large landscape paintings hang near by. In the background, the last archway is green, leading to a column surmounted by an urn.

As the century unfolded, garden designers fell more heavily under the influence of Italy. By the outbreak of the Civil War, the Italian designs first seen at Kenilworth and Theobalds were everywhere – terraces, fountains and statues were especially fashionable. The most expensive gardens had grottoes with animated statues, which were powered by hydraulics. With the Restoration, Charles II's enthusiasm for the great landscapes of Le Nôtre created a new obsession with long clean lines, unified design and increasingly elaborate topiary and parterres, although plain lawns and grass-filled compartments remained popular in England.

Today, there are no surviving sixteenth-century gardens or designed landscapes in England. Formal gardens were difficult to maintain. Any that lasted into the eighteenth century were replaced by easier-to-manage, naturalistic layouts – this was the fate of Theobalds. After the Parliamentarians' destruction of the palace, the estate fell into neglect, and, in the eighteenth century, the grounds were remodelled to form a park.

The landscape at Kenilworth was another casualty of the Civil War. The Parliamentarians dug a protective ditch in front of the keep, which involved cutting through the garden terrace. Gunpowder was later used to demolish the keep's northern wall so that the castle could not be used in warfare again, obliterating what was left of the original garden. The great lake was drained to create land for farming: the soldiers had not yet been paid, so this was the reward for their service.

Although the garden and lake were lost, the castle ruins are still haunting, as Nikolaus Pevsner wrote:

Of the ruinous castles of England Kenilworth is undoubtedly one of the grandest. It has superb Norman, 14th-century, and Elizabethan work, and where, as on the way back from the Plaisaunce, one sees all three together and all three in the strong yet mellow red of their sandstone, the view could not be bettered.

Kenilworth's present-day obscurity is comparatively recent. In 1821, Sir Walter Scott published *Kenilworth*, a murder mystery about the death of Dudley's first wife Amy, which takes as its backdrop the entertainments of 1575. Scott was inspired to write his novel by a contemporary celebration of royalty: the elaborate plans for the Coronation of July 1821.

Although *Kenilworth* is full of anachronisms – Amy had been dead for fifteen years by the time of the Kenilworth pageants, and Shakespeare has a walk-on part as 'wild Will', as Dudley calls him in the novel, while promising to obtain for him a licence for his company of actors – this did not detract for Scott's readers from the magic of Elizabeth and Dudley's romance in the garden at Kenilworth. There are some marvellous set-pieces, such as the scene where Raleigh lays down his cloak in the mud for Elizabeth to walk on. In another memorable scene, Amy secretly spies on Dudley in the garden at Kenilworth, by pretending to be one of the living statues in a grotto. But there she is interviewed by Elizabeth herself, on her evening stroll around the garden. Fortunately, Elizabeth believes her to be one of the entertainers. It was, however, the royal romance between Elizabeth and Dudley that made *Kenilworth* a best-seller and helped to create the Victorian mania for Elizabethan matters.

At the time of the publication of Scott's novel, Kenilworth was little more than a ruin. When he returned to the castle in 1823, he described how, since his last visit eight years earlier, 'these trophies of time' had become 'preserved and protected': so much for novels, he reflected. Visitors came from all over the world. Arthur Sullivan (later, of Gilbert and Sullivan) wrote *The Masque at Kenilworth*, which featured songs by the Lady of the Lake, Arion and a Chorus of Sylvans, for the Birmingham Festival of 1864, winning popular and critical acclaim. By that time, the American consular agent in Birmingham estimated that Scott's novel had added £10,000 a year to the Kenilworth tourist trade – the castle had become one of England's greatest attractions.

In the summer of 1878, Henry James toured Warwickshire, which he described as 'the core and centre of the English world', staying with friends whose house had a fine view of the castle. He had long been a great fan of Scott's tales of adventure and bravery, but, in his opinion, Kenilworth was best seen from a distance. He deplored the 'cockneyfication' of the castle, now besieged by hawkers, paupers and pamphlet-sellers, its paths lined with beer-shops:

I remember perfectly my first visit to this romantic spot; how I chanced upon a picnic; how I stumbled over beer-bottles; how the very echoes of the beautiful ruin seemed to have dropped all their *h*'s.

Despite all this, he concluded that there was 'still a good deal of old England in the scene'.

Epilogue

WHEN I BEGAN to investigate the story of Dudley and Cecil's rivalry, there were no real plans to develop the sites of their most celebrated gardens. John Watkins of English Heritage is now overseeing the re-creation of Dudley's garden at Kenilworth, and Broxbourne Council has received funding from the Big Lottery Fund and the Heritage Lottery Fund to develop a conservation plan for the site of Theobalds, opening up the possibility of re-forming the Elizabethan maze garden and boating lake.

August 2006. I am walking through the intersecting arches of Dudley's Italianate arcade at Kenilworth towards what was once the beginning of the garden terrace. Beyond the last archway, there is a sheer drop. Nothing remains of the ten-foot-high grass-covered terrace with its obelisks, stone spheres and statues of bears.

Looking down on a bare archaeological site, I try to imagine what Elizabeth would have seen – something new and astonishing. I find myself projecting images of Italian gardens designed to be viewed from above, the dizzying terraced water gardens of the Villa d'Este and the Villa Lante and the simpler geometrical patterns of Cecil Pinsent's re-creation of a Renaissance garden at the Villa Medici in Fiesole. Other possibilities come to mind, in the shape of the romantic paintings of the garden celebrating

Elizabeth's visit of 1575 – most vividly, Gheeraerts's painting of the lakeside pleasure grounds.

When I return to the castle, the scene will look very different. After two years of excavations, work is set to begin on re-forming Dudley's garden, as described by 'Langham'. There will be arched arbours entwined with roses at each end of the terrace, overlooking geometrical patterns of flower beds interplanted with pear trees, holly cones and sweet bay standards centred on obelisks. At the heart of the garden will stand a new version of Dudley's marvellous fountain of a pair of Atlases each bearing a globe surmounted by a ragged staff, and the terrace will face the bejewelled aviary.

The palaces and gardens of Theobalds, Holdenby and Nonsuch survive only in magnificent fragments. Theobalds Palace does not even exist on modern maps. The site is now a public park called The Cedars, near Cheshunt, laid out in the eighteenth century in the landscape style and named after the large cedars which once grew there.

At The Cedars, in 2006, the gardens are, at first, hidden from view, as they were in the sixteenth century. The approach routes have gone. Nevertheless, as Neil Robbins, curator of nearby Lowewood Museum, shows me, it is possible to envisage where the grand avenue once was, by standing sideways to the outbuildings and looking past them. In the sixteenth century, a line of sight would have stretched from the grand entrance gates along the great avenue flanked by orchards to the second set of palace gates, through the gatehouse with its magical bunch of grapes and frescoes of people from the New World, and on through the Middle Court to the black-and-white statue of Venus and Cupid in the centre of the Fountain Court.

We walk past the outbuildings to the park, and it is a great surprise to come upon an open landscape enhanced by fragments of the Elizabethan palace and gardens. The site of Theobalds remains a place of tranquillity and charm. The air is refreshing and mild, reminding me of how much Cecil valued his garden as a place to escape from the incessant demands of life at court.

As we explore the grounds, I see little that resembles Cecil's Middle and Fountain Courts – almost all that was left of the palace buildings was demolished after the Second World War. But the garden's original red-brick walls with bee boles (recesses for hives) still stretch into the distance, recalling Cecil's secretary's claim that visitors could walk for miles in the avenues before coming to an end. These beautiful walls seem to be all that remains to give a visitor a sense of the scale of Cecil's ambition in creating his pleasure grounds, which covered eighteen acres, compared with Dudley's one-acre castle garden at Kenilworth.

There is more to the ruins of Theobalds than meets the eye. Parts of the western side of the Fountain Court survive, thanks to the labours of eighteenth-century property developer George Prescott. He incorporated stone taken from the palace into a beautiful mansion, Old Palace House, which formed part of a square (this involved transporting sections of the Fountain Court's western side to a site a little further west). The centrepiece of Old Palace House was a magnificent stone three-light window (a mullioned window with three perpendicular divisions) from the original palace. When Old Palace House burnt down in 1970, most of this window survived – its stone mullions remain in safe keeping.

Sections of the eastern side of the Fountain Court have been incorporated into the park's twentieth-century buildings. Most of these fragments have been absorbed by the modern material, but then we come across the solitary remains of the south-facing garden arcade: a massive red-brick structure, decorated with bold geometric patterns carved in stone and with smooth stone facing at its base. This was the pier that once supported the most south-westerly arch of the covered walk.

Only the beginning of the stone arch survives, but there is enough of it to enable you to trace the continuation of its arc, as it soared upwards and curved round to form the last bow of Cecil's arcade. This mighty arch and pier conjure up the splendour of Theobalds. Critically, the pier stands in its original location – making it possible to determine the layout and immense size of the rest of the lost palace and gardens.

The pier marks where the stone outdoor staircase would have brought Elizabeth down from the Great Chamber to the terrace and the start of the long avenue, planted with tall elm trees. Whereas the garden which she loved resembled a labyrinth, today's park is entirely open, reflecting its former life as an eighteenth-century square. There are no signs of the artificial hills described by sixteenth-century visitors and mentioned in Cecil's papers: the mount at the centre of the maze garden and the small hill crowned by a swan's nest. Although we walk as far west as possible, there is no higher ground.

It is staggering to think how much once was here and how almost all of it has been lost – as if the palace and gardens never existed. Was this flat parkland in front of me really filled with dense tunnel arbours forming interlocking square-shaped compartments, as shown in the portrait of Sir George Delves and as described by contemporary visitors? Yet here, by all accounts, Elizabeth and her courtiers could have explored nine green rooms containing mysterious statues.

The Great Garden has been divided in two by what is probably a seventeenth-century brick wall. At first, this makes it difficult to grasp the scale of the garden, and then, as I try to see through the wall, I am even more impressed by its extent. When we reach this wall, standing about halfway between the Elizabethan stone pier and the end of the park, I realise that the Great Garden's central pillar fountain would have stood close by. Continuing towards the park's southern limits, I visualise beneath my feet not grass seared by the summer sun, but a wide gravel path leading to a canal and banqueting houses, where Elizabeth and Dudley might have taken a boat to explore the maze of canals. Disembarking, they would have followed the winding path lined by pyramids to arrive at the banqueting house with its statues of the Caesars, overlooking a pool with fountains in the shapes of serpents and miniature watermills.

It is possible that on the banks of one of the canals stood the banqueting house called the Queen's Arbour, where Elizabeth might have made the fateful decision to recall Dudley from the Netherlands and to declare a peace with Spain – a peace which proved short-lived. There is no sign of water at the southern perimeter wall, nor at the Great Garden's western boundary.

But in the eastern section of the park, we see that the modern pond with its central fountain feeds an overgrown watercourse which could have its origins in Cecil's labyrinthine canals lined with tall reeds.

On our walk back through this leafy part of the park, we come upon the surviving mulberry tree planted by King James in his doomed attempt to create a silk industry in England. The mulberry still appears rare and exotic with its slender branches, gnarled trunk, glossy, heart-shaped leaves and bright-red fruits. I pick one, and, at first bite, it bursts in an explosion of lurid crimson dye. The experience brings to mind Sir Francis Carew's present to Elizabeth in his orchard at Beddington, a cherry tree bearing out-of-season cherries.

Although the original gardens of Kenilworth and Theobalds have long since disappeared, they have left a lasting legacy. It is possible, for example, to trace a direct line from Gerard's achievements to the bold plant-hunting expeditions of the Tradescants and, in the eighteenth century, the diverse collecting campaigns of Sir Joseph Banks, which helped to establish the Royal Botanic Gardens at Kew as a centre of scientific research.

In the modern garden room, the architecture of the house extends into the garden, as in the Renaissance. The twenty-first-century garden façade constructed of folding glass panels opening out on to a terrace dissolves the boundaries between interior and exterior space – an effect achieved by means of arcades and terraces at Kenilworth and Theobalds. The approach to a garden was a vital element in Elizabethan design; the sense of arrival is highlighted at the new garden at Portland Castle, in Dorset, reached by visitors via a metal bridge flanked by pine trees. There has also been a revival of interest in gardens designed with an underlying story or philosophy.

The sixteenth-century garden is often imagined purely as a highly controlled space, with sharp-edged topiary, paths and geometrical flower beds. The cottage garden, with its informal planting and carefree layout, seems a world away from this. Like the Roman gardens which inspired them, however, the grounds of Elizabethan palaces were made up of formal and informal areas. Structure was important, but much of their appeal lay in the frisson created by the juxtaposition of the cultivated and the wild.

At Kenilworth, Dudley's garden encompassed an orchard and strawberry beds, and the terrace and banqueting house gave views of the magnificent forest, lake, park and fields. Cecil expanded his domain at Theobalds by planting meadows and groves beyond the formal gardens. With the vogue for wild-flower meadow gardens, English gardeners have come full circle. In gardens such as those at Loseley Park and Petersham House, in Surrey, meadow gardens and borders planted in the style of hedgerows complement more formal gardens – a boon for the environment and wildlife, these wild spaces fulfil the Renaissance ideal of being both beautiful and useful.

In the last decade, herb gardens have become one of the most popular kinds of gardens and, in terms of design and planting, hark back to their zenith in the sixteenth and seventeenth centuries. The widespread interest in herbal remedies has its origins in the sixteenth century, and we may also trace our enduring love of rose-gardens and garden mazes to this era.

I discovered this story of a horticultural rivalry while teaching garden history at the Centre for Extra-Mural Studies at Birkbeck in London. I came to garden history by chance. Six months earlier, I had completed a PhD on eighteenth-century literature. My subject was Alexander Pope's friendships with Lord Burlington, the 'Architect Earl', and the statesman and financial expert Lord Bathurst: I was investigating how Pope's dealings with these and other powerful patrons enabled him to become one of the few poets to have made a fortune from writing poetry.

As I searched their works and papers for evidence of their friendship, it emerged that all three men were passionate about landscape design and collaborated with each other in their innovative projects: Burlington's garden at Chiswick, Bathurst's Cirencester Park in Gloucestershire, and Pope's garden and grotto at Twickenham. While a love of nature played its part, their gardens were also a form of resistance. In the eighteenth century, a garden could be a political campaign, as shown most strikingly by Viscount Cobham's Stowe. In its diverse collection of buildings, cascades, fountains, lawns and vales created by garden design luminaries Charles Bridgeman, Sir John Vanbrugh, William Kent and Capability Brown, the landscape park at Stowe set the nobility of the ancient world against the corruption of modern times and the government of Sir Robert Walpole.

At Birkbeck, I taught courses which charted the evolution of gardens from the plots of ancient Egypt to the landscape parks of eighteenth-century Europe. I found Renaissance gardens to be the most intriguing, as much for the vibrancy of their creators and the extraordinary stories attached to them as for their beauty of design. Like the designed landscapes of the eighteenth century, gardens in Renaissance England seem to have meant much more than gardens do today.

I completed my initial research on Elizabethan gardens and their creators in the British Library and with visits to the London Library, University of London Library, Birkbeck Library and the RHS Lindley Library. To a large extent, the appeal of garden history lies in its visual impact, and I drew inspiration from the prints, engravings and photographs in Birkbeck's slide library, as well as from those shown in seminars and lectures on Renaissance gardens.

During the second phase of my research, I consulted the archives. Dudley's papers are kept at Longleat House in Wiltshire, and Cecil's at Hatfield House in Hertfordshire. When I contacted the librarian at Longleat, it appeared that the British Library contained all of the printed material that I needed about Kenilworth. But Theobalds was more elusive. While Cecil's letters and papers are published in calendars of manuscripts, the transcriptions often miss out what was most interesting to me: the details of his gardens.

I had originally planned to go to Hatfield to see Cecil's drawing of his Great Garden at Theobalds, amongst other things, such as a design for a fountain at Hampton Court. When I mentioned the ellipses in the calendars of Cecil's works to Robin Harcourt Williams, Archivist to the Marquess of Salisbury at Hatfield House, he reflected that details of plants and gardens were not considered important when the papers were transcribed. Mr Harcourt Williams was invaluable in helping me to decipher Elizabethan script, and, with his assistance, I discovered Cecil's planting lists and inspiring, previously unknown features of his garden at Theobalds, including his swan's nest at the top of a mount and the designs for the murals of family trees that decorated his garden arcade, made up of figurative trees with delicate branches and leaves.

There are no Elizabethan gardens in England, only ruins and reconstructions, some more authentic than others. At the beginning of my investigations, I imagined that there would be little to see at these sites, in contrast to eighteenth-century grounds such as Kent's timeless landscape at Rousham in Oxfordshire, and the lakeside idylls of Stourhead in Wiltshire, and Painshill and Claremont in Surrey. It would not be easy to find places that resembled the sumptuous pleasure grounds described by contemporary visitors.

Before seeing the ruins of Kenilworth and Theobalds, I was familiar with re-creations of sixteenth-century gardens, such as the knot garden at Hampton Court laid out in the 1920s by Ernest Law on the site of gardens created successively by Cardinal Wolsey and Elizabeth. In the original gardens, herbs such as thyme, hyssop and lavender would have formed interlacing bands enclosing flower beds. Modern planting – box and annuals – now replaces the less hardy Elizabethan herbs and native flowers.

Until recently, the Elizabethan garden has been imagined as a small, private space, with the knot garden as its archetypal design – there are striking examples at Hatfield and at the Tudor House Museum in Southampton. But the princely gardens visited by Elizabeth and her court consisted of many gardens within a garden, as described by Sir Francis Bacon in his essay *Of Gardens*. A knot garden, like a low-level maze, was just one of many compartments in a larger garden, which opened out to wider expanses, leading to pools, tall mazes, mounts topped with banqueting houses, meadows and parkland – and the entire landscape was integrated with the house.

After return visits to Kenilworth and Theobalds, I toured Elizabethan houses such as Knole and Sissinghurst in Kent, and Loseley Park in Surrey, and their gardens, which evoke the spirit of the past, embracing Tudor and modern planting. My field-work progressed to ruins, including Nonsuch Palace in Surrey, and Holdenby and Lyveden in Northamptonshire, where my reading of guidebooks and monographs was supplemented by archaeological reports and articles published in journals such as *Garden History*.

At Sir Christopher Hatton's Holdenby, two monumental sixteenth-century gates survive, together with the garden's original great terraces (planted in the nineteenth century with yew hedges) and a huge boating lake now covered with reeds. Hidden away among the modern gardens, I found a small, enclosed 'Elizabethan garden' designed by Rosemary Verey. Circular in form and medieval in structure, with two paths meeting at a central fountain, geometrical compartments and a romantic arbour, this overgrown but still charming haven seemed to embody the image of a garden of that era.

Arriving at the water gardens of Lyveden New Bield was something entirely different. Currently undergoing major conservation work, with its expanse of meadows and parkland leading to a banqueting house and moated orchard, Lyveden came closest for me to recreating sixteenth-century pleasure grounds. Laid out by Sir Thomas Tresham, a landowner and courtier, in the 1590s, the gardens were probably modelled on Theobalds. But with Lyveden still a work in progress, my search for an authentically Elizabethan garden continued – and would take me out of England.

In *Orlando*, Virginia Woolf describes the Elizabethan world as a place where colours were brighter and life was lived more intensely:

The age was the Elizabethan; their morals were not ours; nor their poets; nor their climate; nor their vegetables even. Everything was different. The weather itself, the heat and cold of summer and winter, was, we may believe, of another temper altogether. The brilliant amorous day was divided as sheerly from the night as land from water. Sunsets were redder and more intense; dawns were whiter . . . The rain fell vehemently, or not at all. The sun blazed or there was darkness.

Woolf goes on to suggest that in the subsequent age of King James, the 'very landscape outside was less stuck about with garlands and the briars themselves were less thorned and intricate. Perhaps the senses were a little duller and honey and cream less seductive to the palate.' These descriptions evoke elaborate gardens bathed in a Mediterranean light and heat.

Elizabeth and her courtiers spent so much time in gardens and parks that some historians have speculated that the climate in England was warmer than it is today – and perhaps resembled that of mainland Europe. Experts on climate change advise that temperatures in England have not changed much since the sixteenth century. Nevertheless, when I visited the National Meteorological Office's archives in Exeter, I discovered intriguing descriptions in Elizabethan chronicles, diaries and registers of heatwaves and droughts lasting up to five months, which brought to mind Thomas Hill's strategies for protecting his exotic fruit trees and vines from the 'sun's great heat'. Piecing this evidence together, it would seem that summers in the 1560s and 1570s could be unusually hot.

Although there are no surviving Renaissance gardens in northern Europe, Italy is full of intact and, in some cases, beautifully preserved and maintained pleasure grounds dating from the fifteenth to the seventeenth centuries. The sense of scale and complexity of these sites is still astonishing.

Gardens such as those belonging to the Villa d'Este, the Villa Lante and the Villa Farnese, in Lazio, made famous by Montaigne, Evelyn and countless visitors on the Grand Tour, and the Villa Medici on the Pincian Hill, described by Henry James as 'perhaps on the whole the most enchanting place in Rome', gave me a glimpse of what Theobalds and Kenilworth might have looked like. Here were architectural gardens laid out on many different levels, with buildings, statues and unforgettable fountains unlike anything I had seen in England. A further revelation was the Sacro Bosco ('Sacred Wood') at Bomarzo created by Count Vicino Orsini and celebrated in film four hundred years later by Salvador Dalí. A sinuous path through the wood charts the story of Ludovico Ariosto's *Orlando Furioso*, one of the most popular romances of the time, in fantastical sculptures and buildings, including a banqueting house known as 'Hell's Mask', which has as its entrance a grimacing mouth. This frightening but refreshingly cool pavilion, with its built-in dining table and seats, also acts as an echo chamber.

After the gardens of Rome and Lazio, I visited the Medici gardens in Tuscany; I had first been dazzled by these gardens in reproductions of the brilliantly coloured lunettes of Flemish painter Giusto Utens, which now hang in the Topographical Museum in Florence. I revisited the Boboli Gardens and then took day trips to the Medici villas of Castello, Poggio, La Petraia, Fiesole and Pratolino, where I discovered architectural planting, sculptures and feats of engineering which rivalled and often surpassed what I had seen in the south. Most memorably, there were the dense tunnel arbours and eastern-style pool of La Petraia, the copies of Michelangelo's unfinished 'slaves' in the four corners of artist-engineer Bernardo Buontalenti's grotto in the Boboli Gardens, and, in the vast palace grounds of Pratolino ('Little Meadow'), laid out by Buontalenti at the foot of the Apennines, Giambologna's Man Mountain, pressing the ground so as to bring springs to the surface. This giant once contained several grottoes studded with corals and pearl, and jets spouted from the pool in front of him and from his head, as the snow and icicles on his long hair and beard melted. Among the many restoration projects at Pratolino was the re-creation of an enchanting water pergola, with delicate jets forming a tunnel of water above a shady path.

Neither Elizabeth, Dudley nor Cecil travelled to Italy, and so they would have relied on prints and their agents' descriptions for their knowledge of the exciting new gardens – as Elizabeth's chief envoy, Dudley would also have seen imitations of Italian pleasure grounds in France and the Netherlands. The Italians were the leaders in garden design, as in so many of the arts, and, despite her country's troubled relationship with Rome, Elizabeth wanted to see their work in English gardens.

When I picture Elizabeth, I see her not crowned on a throne in a palace, as she is so often represented, but in a garden. An Elizabethan garden was a place of pleasure, a multi-sensory experience. As well as the beautiful sights of flowers, fountains, statues and pavilions, there were exquisite scents, the delightful sounds of hidden music and birds singing in aviaries, and the thrilling touch and taste of rare fruits and plants. Within its boundaries, Elizabeth could catch a glimpse of places she would never visit, from Italy to the Indies.

The pleasure grounds of Kenilworth and Theobalds were made – at enormous cost – to be lived in by Elizabeth. Here, she walked every morning and evening for exercise and, in the afternoons, strolled with her courtiers, admiring the plants and buildings and enjoying the entertainments staged in her honour. Her love of gardens made gardeners of courtiers, statesmen and soldiers. She encouraged Dudley and Cecil to lead the way. In their lifelong rivalry and devotion to their queen, they created the most sensational gardens ever seen in England. The lost world of the Elizabethan garden holds an enduring fascination.

Sources and Acknowledgements

QUEEN ELIZABETH IN THE GARDEN has been inspired by my reading of original journals, memorials, diaries, letters, poetry and prose. The Cecil manuscripts at Hatfield are the main source of William Cecil's diverse writings, which include his memorials for royal visits, schedules of accommodation, diary and handwritten plan for the Great Garden at Theobalds; I also drew on the Lansdowne, Harleian and Cotton manuscripts in the British Library for Cecil's and Dudley's writings.

In the British Library, I read papers relating to Elizabeth I, Cecil and Dudley published in calendars of manuscripts for the Dudley and Salisbury papers, the calendars of state papers, domestic and foreign, and the two-volume collection of state papers left by Cecil transcribed by Samuel Haynes and William Murdin, 1740 and 1759. Dudley's letters written during his time in the Netherlands are published in *The Correspondence of Robert Dudley, Earl of Leicester*, ed. John Bruce, London, 1844. Elizabeth's letters and writings are published in *The Word of a Prince*, ed. Maria Perry, London, 1990, and *Collected Works*, ed. Leah S. Marcus, Janel Mueller and Mary Beth Rose, Chicago, 2000.

The two major works on sixteenth-century English gardens are Sir Roy Strong's *The Renaissance Garden in England*, London, 1979, and Paula Henderson's *The Tudor House and Garden*, New Haven and London, 2005. Also, in 1999, *Garden History* published a volume on Tudor Gardens, 27/1, which contains detailed studies of particular gardens. The main sources for Kenilworth are the 'Langham' letter, probably written by William Patten, London, 1575, and George Gascoigne's *Princely Pleasures at the Court at Kenilworth*, London, 1576, William Dugdale's *The Antiquities of Warwickshire*, London, 1730, E. H. Knowles's *The Castle of Kenilworth*, Warwick, 1872, the report on the

Elizabethan garden and Dudley's stables at Kenilworth published in 1995 in *Transactions of the Birmingham and Warwickshire Archaeological Society* and Northamptonshire Archaeology's assessment report on the Elizabethan garden, 2007; for Theobalds, see the sixteenth- and seventeenth-century visitors' accounts listed in the Select Bibliography which follows, as well as John Gerard's *Herball*, London, 1597, John Nichols's 'Theobalds Palace', *Gentleman's Magazine*, 106/1, 1836, John Summerson's 'The Building of Theobalds 1564–1585', *Archaeologia*, 97, 1959, and Martin Andrews's 'Theobalds Palace: The Gardens and Park', *Garden History*, 21/2, 1993. Elizabeth's progresses are documented in John Nichols's *The Progresses and Public Processions of Queen Elizabeth*, London, 1823.

I have given modern equivalents (in terms of spending power) for some of the sums of money mentioned in the book, using the National Archives online currency convertor: www.nationalarchives.gov.uk/currency/

I would like to thank all those who have helped me with this book, especially my editor Julian Loose for his encouragement, vision and creativity, Kate Ward and Kate Murray Browne, my copy-editor Neil Titman, Henry Volans, Angus Cargill, Becky Fincham and all at Faber. I am indebted to Karl Miller for his great support from the beginning. I am very grateful to the following people for their advice and encouragement: to Michael Symes, who established the MA in Garden History at Birkbeck; to Nick de Somogyi for his scholarly reading of the proofs; to Neil Robbins, John Watkins, the Marquess of Salisbury, Robin Harcourt Williams, Sir Roy Strong, Paula Henderson, Elizabeth Goldring, Brian Dix, Brian Kerr, Tony Fleming, Martin Andrews, Jane Miller, René Weis, Susanne Groom, John Mullan, Mark Ford, Kate Bomford, Michael Newton, Caroline Dakers, James Lowther, Caroline Rhind, Mark Bradshaw, Tom Rutter, Karen Hearn, Phil Jones, John Kington, Alexander Marr, René Burrough, Kate Harris, Jon Culverhouse, Patrick McGuinness, Catherine Hilliard, Anne Townsend, Jane Badrock,

SOURCES AND ACKNOWLEDGEMENTS

Kate Tyrer, Katy Boswell, Jennifer Fraser-Smith and Liam Liddy; to the staff of the British Library, the London Library, the University of London Library, University of Sussex Library, the RHS Lindley and Wisley Libraries, Brighton and Hove City Libraries and the National Meteorological Office; to Nicola and Declan Liddy, Neil Fraser-Smith, Duncan Stewart, Madalena and Paul Borg, Tania Spooner, Chris Pattison, Bee Keskin, Robin Begley, Sean Hennessy and Matt Willis.

Latest developments at Kenilworth and Theobalds can be found at: www.treamartyn.com

SELECT BIBLIOGRAPHY

Ackroyd, Peter, *London: The Biography*, London, 2000
— *Shakespeare: The Biography*, London, 2005
Adams, Simon, 'The Dudley Clientèle, 1553–1453', in G. W. Bernard, ed., *The Tudor Nobility*, Manchester, 1992
— ed., *Household Accounts and Disbursement Books of Robert Dudley, Earl of Leicester, 1558–1561, 1584–1586*, Cambridge, 1995
— *Leicester and the Court: Essays on Elizabethan Politics*, Manchester, 2002
Adams, William Howard, *The French Garden, 1500–1800*, London, 1979
Alford, Stephen, 'Reassessing William Cecil in the 1560s', in John Guy, ed., *The Tudor Monarchy*, London, 1997
— *The Early Elizabethan Polity: William Cecil and the British Succession Crisis, 1558–1569*, Cambridge, 2002
Andrews, Martin, 'Theobalds Palace: The Gardens and Park', *Garden History*, 21/2, 1993
Anglo, Sydney, *Spectacle, Pageantry and Early Tudor Policy*, Oxford, 1969
Anon., *Secret Memoirs of Robert Dudley, Earl of Leicester* [*Leicester's Commonwealth*], ed. Drake, London, 1706
Arber, Agnes, *Herbals: Their Origin and Evolution. A Chapter in the History of Botany 1470–1670*, Cambridge, 1938
— 'Edmund Spenser and Lyte's "Nievve Herball"', *Notes and Queries*, 160, 1931
Archer, Jayne Elisabeth, Elizabeth Goldring and Sarah Knight, *The Progresses, Pageants, and Entertainments of Queen Elizabeth I*, Oxford and New York, 2007
Archer, Percy Charles, *Historic Cheshunt*, Cheshunt, 1923

Arnold, Janet, *Queen Elizabeth's Wardrobe Unlock'd*, Leeds, 1988

Atlee, Helena, *Italian Gardens*, London, 2006

Axton, Marie, 'Robert Dudley and the Inner Temple Revels', *Historical Journal*, 13, 1970

— 'The Tudor Mask and Elizabethan Court Drama', in *English Drama: Forms and Development*, ed. Marie Axton and Raymond Williams, Cambridge, 1977

Biddle, Martin, 'The Gardens of Nonsuch: Sources and Dating', *Garden History*, 27/1, 1999

Binney, Marcus, 'Northamptonshire's Lost Gardens', *Country Life*, December 1979

Bird, Sarah, et al., 'A Late Sixteenth-Century Garden: Fact or Fantasy. The Portrait of Sir George Delves in the Walker Art Gallery, Liverpool', *Garden History*, 24/2, 1996

Bradbrook, M., 'Princely Pleasures at Kenilworth', Rice Institute pamphlet, 46, 1959–60

Bradley-Hole, Christopher, *The Minimalist Garden*, London, 1999

— and Mark Griffiths, *Making the Modern Garden*, New York, 2007

Brears, Peter, *All the King's Cooks*, London, 1999

Breight, Curtis C., 'Realpolitik and Elizabethan Ceremony: The Earl of Hertford's Entertainment of Elizabeth at Elvetham, 1591', *Renaissance Quarterly*, 45, 1992

Brock, Alan Francis Clutton, *A History of Fireworks*, London, 1949

Brown, A. E., and C. C. Taylor, 'The Garden of Lyveden, Northamptonshire', *Archaeological Journal*, 139, 1972

Bülow, Gottfried von, and Wilfred Powell, 'Diary of the Journey of Philip Julius, Duke of Stettin-Pomerania, through England in the Year 1602', *Transactions of the Royal Historical Society*, 6, 1892

Bushnell, Rebecca, *Green Desire: Imagining Early Modern English Gardens*, Ithaca, 2003

Campbell-Culver, Maggie, *The Origin of Plants*, London, 2001

Cecil, William, Lord Burghley, *A Collection of State Papers Relating to the Affairs . . . from the Year 1542 to 1570 . . . Left by William Cecill, Lord Burghley*, transcr. Samuel Haynes, London, 1740

— *A Collection of State Papers Relating to the Affairs in the Reign of Queen Elizabeth from the Year 1571 to 1596*, transcr. William Murdin, London, 1759

Chambers, E. K., *The Elizabethan Stage*, 4 vols, Oxford, 1923–51

Cole, Mary Hill, *The Portable Queen: Elizabeth I and the Politics of Ceremony*, Amherst, 1999

Colonna, Francesco, attrib., *Hypnerotomachia Poliphili*, Venice, 1499

Colvin, Howard, ed., *The History of the King's Works*, 5 vols, 1963–82

Creighton, Mandell, *Queen Elizabeth*, London, 1899

Croft, Pauline, ed., *Patronage, Culture and Power: The Early Cecils*, New Haven and London, 2002

Dent, John, *The Quest for Nonsuch*, 2nd rev. edn, London, 1970

Dictionary of National Biography, ed. Sir Leslie Stephens and Sir Sidney Lee, 63 vols, 1st edn, Oxford, 1885–1912

Dictionary of National Biography, ed. H. G. G. Matthews and Brian Harrison, 60 vols, new edn, Oxford, 2004

Dobson, Michael, and Nicola J. Watson, *England's Elizabeth: An Afterlife in Fame and Fantasy*, Oxford, 2002

Doran, Susan, *Monarchy and Matrimony: The Courtships of Elizabeth*, London and New York, 1996

— ed., *Elizabeth*, exhibition catalogue, 2003

Dudley, Robert, Earl of Leicester, *Correspondence of Robert Dudley, Earl of Leicester, during his Government of the Low Countries in the Years 1585 and 1586*, ed. John Bruce, London, 1844

Dugdale, William, *The Antiquities of Warwickshire*, 2 vols, 2nd edn, London, 1730

Duncan-Jones, Katherine, *Sir Philip Sidney: Courtier Poet*, London, 1991

Dunlop, Ian, *Palaces and Progresses of Elizabeth I*, London, 1962

Earle, John Charles, *The Palace of Theobalds in the Olden Time: A Lecture*, London, 1869

Elizabeth I, *Letters of Queen Elizabeth*, ed. G. B. Harrison, London, 1968

— *The Word of a Prince*, ed. Maria Perry, London, 1990

— *Collected Works*, ed. Leah S. Marcus, Janel Mueller and Mary Beth Rose, Chicago, 2000

Feuillerat, Albert, ed., *Documents Relating to the Office of the Revels in the Time of Queen Elizabeth*, Louvain, 1908

Fraser, Antonia, *Mary Queen of Scots*, London, 1994

Frommel, C. L., 'Poggioreale: Problemi di Ricostruzione e di Tipologia', in Daniela Lamberini, Marcello Lotti and Roberto Lunardi, eds, *Giuliano e la Bottega dei da Maiano*, Florence, 1994

Frye, Susan, *Elizabeth I: The Competition for Representation*, Oxford, 1993

Gascoigne, George, *Princely Pleasures at the Court at Kenilworth* (1576), London, 1821

— *The Complete Works of George Gascoigne*, 2 vols, ed. J. W. Cunliffe, London, 1907–10

Gerard, John, *Catalogus Arborum, Fruticum ac Plantarum . . . in Horto Johannis Gerardi*, London, 1596

— *The Herball*, London, 1597

Girouard, Mark, *Life in the English Country House: A Social and Architectural History*, New Haven and London, 1978

— 'Elizabethan Holdenby', *Country Life*, 166, 25 October 1979

— 'Burghley House – I', *Country Life*, 186, 23 April 1992

— 'Burghley House, Lincolnshire – II', *Country Life*, 186, 30 April 1992

Goldingham, Henry, *The Garden Plot: An Allegorical Poem, Inscribed to Queen Elizabeth, from an unpublished manuscript in the Harleian Collection in the British Museum*, London, 1825

Goldring, Elizabeth, 'Portraits of Queen Elizabeth I and the Earl of Leicester for Kenilworth Castle', *Burlington Magazine*, 147, 2005

Googe, Barnaby, trans., Conrad Heresbach of Cleves, *Foure Bookes of Husbandry . . . Conteyning the Whole Arte and Trade of Husbandry, Gardening, Graffing and Planting*, London, 1577

Graves, Michael A. R., *Burghley: William Cecil, Lord Burghley*, London, 1998

Gravett, Christopher, *Knights at Tournament*, London, 1998

Greenlaw, E. A., 'Spenser and the Earl of Leicester', *Publications of the Modern Language Association*, 25/3, 1910

Griffin, Benjamin, 'The Breaking of the Giants: Historical Drama in Coventry and London', *English Literary Renaissance*, 22, 1999

Gristwood, Sarah, *Elizabeth and Leicester*, London, 2007

Griswold, Mac, *Pleasures of the Garden: Images from the Metropolitan Museum of Art*, New York, 1987

Hackett, Helen, *Virgin Mother, Maiden Queen: Elizabeth I and the Cult of the Virgin Mary*, Basingstoke, 1995

[William Harrison] *Harrison's Description of England in Shakespeare's Youth* (1577), ed. F. J. Furnivall, 3 vols, London, 1877–1908

Haynes, Alan, *The White Bear: Robert Dudley, The Elizabethan Earl of Leicester*, London, 1987

Hearn, Karen, ed., *Dynasties: Painting in Tudor and Jacobean England 1530–1630*, exhibition catalogue, London, 1995

Hellerstedt, Kahren Jones, *Gardens of Earthly Delight: Sixteenth- and Seventeenth-Century Netherlandish Gardens*, Pittsburgh, 1986

Henderson, Paula, 'Sir Francis Bacon's Water Gardens at Gorhambury', *Garden History*, 20/2, 1992

— and Jill Husselby, 'England's Earliest Garden Plan?' *Country Life*, 194, 23 March 2000

— *The Tudor House and Garden*, New Haven and London, 2005

Henrey, Blanche, *British Botanical and Horticultural Literature before 1800*, London, 1975

Hentzner, Paul, *A Journey into England in the Year 1598*, ed. Horace Walpole, Strawberry Hill, 1757

Hersey, G. L., 'Poggioreale: Notes on a Reconstruction, and an Early Replication', *Architectura*, I, 1973

Hill, Thomas, *A Most Briefe and Pleasaunt Treatyse, Teachynge How to Dresse, Sowe, and Set a Garden*, London, 1558

— *The Profittable Arte of Gardening, now the Third Tyme Set Fourth*, London, 1568

— [another ed.] *Wherunto is Newly Added a Treatise, of the Arte of Graffing and Planting of Trees*, London, 1572

— *The Gardeners Labyrinth* [by Didymus Mountain], London, 1577

Hilliard, Nicholas, *A Treatise concerning the Arte of Limning*, ed. R. K. R. Thornton and T. G. S. Cain, Ashington, 1981

Hintz, E. W., 'The Elizabethan Entertainment and "The Faerie Queene"', *Philological Quarterly*, 14, 1935

Howell, Roger, *Sir Philip Sidney: The Shepherd Knight*, London, 1968

Hoyles, Martin, *Gardening Books from 1560 to 1960*, 2 vols, *Gardeners' Delight*, London, 1994, and *Bread and Roses*, London, 1995

Hume, Martin A. S., *The Courtships of Queen Elizabeth*, London, 1896

Hunt, John Dixon, *Garden and Grove: The Italian Renaissance Garden in the English Imagination, 1600–1750*, Princeton, 1986

— ed., *The Italian Garden: Art, Design and Culture*, Cambridge, 1996

— *Greater Perfections: The Practice of Garden Theory*, London, 2000

Hurstfield, Joel, 'Burghley: William Cecil, 1520–1598', *History Today*, 6, 1956

— *The Queen's Wards: Wardship and Marriage under Elizabeth I*, London, 1958

Husselby, Jill, and Paula Henderson, 'Location, Location, Location! Cecil House in the Strand', *Architectural History*, 45, 2002

Huxley, Anthony, *An Illustrated History of Gardening*, New York and London, 1978

Isham, Sir Giles, 'Sir Thomas Tresham and his Buildings', *Reports and Papers of the Northamptonshire Antiquarian Society*, 65/2, 1966

Islip, Adams, *The Orchard and the Garden*, London, 1594

Ives, E. W., *Anne Boleyn*, Oxford, 1986

Jacques, David, 'The Compartment System in Tudor England', *Garden History*, 27/1, 1999

James, Henry, *Collected Travel Writings: The Continent*, New York and London, 1993

Jeffery, R. W., *Was It Wet or Fine? Being an Account of English Weather from Chronicles, Diaries and Registers*, Oxford, 1933

Jenkins, Elizabeth, *Elizabeth and Leicester*, London, 1972

Johnson, F. R., 'Thomas Hill: An Elizabethan Huxley', *Huntington Library Quarterly*, 7/4, 1944

Judson, A. C., *The Life of Edmund Spenser*, Baltimore, 1945

Kelsey, Harry, *Sir Francis Drake: The Queen's Pirate*, New Haven and London, 2000

Kemeys, Brenda, and Joyce Raggatt, *The Queen Who Survived: The Life of Katherine Parr*, London, 1993

Kendall, Alan, *Robert Dudley, Earl of Leicester*, London, 1980

Kermode, Frank, *The Age of Shakespeare*, London, 2004

Klarwill, Victor von, *Queen Elizabeth and Some Foreigners*, London, 1928

Knowles, E. H., *The Castle of Kenilworth*, Warwick, 1872

Kuin, R. J. P., 'Robert Langham and his "Letter"', *Notes and Queries*, 25, 1978

— 'The Purloined *Letter*: Evidence and Probability Regarding Robert Langham's Authorship', *The Library*, 7, 1985

Lamb, Keith, and Patrick Bowe, *A History of Gardening in Ireland*, Dublin, 1995

Langham, Robert [William Patten], *Laneham's Letter* (1575), ed. F. J. Furnivall, London, 1907

— *Robert Langham, A Letter*, ed. R. J. P. Kuin, Leiden, 1983

Law, Ernest, *The History of Hampton Court*, London, 1885

Lawson, William, *A New Orchard and Garden . . . with the Country House-wifes Garden* (1618), ed. Eleanour Sinclair Rohde, London, 1927

Lazzaro, Claudia, *The Italian Renaissance Garden: From the Conventions of Planting, Design, and Ornament to the Grand Gardens of Sixteenth-Century Central Italy*, New Haven, 1990

Leahy, William, *Elizabethan Triumphal Processions*, Ashgate, 2005

Leslie, Michael, 'Gardens', in *The Spenser Encyclopedia*, ed. Michael Leslie and John Dixon Hunt, Toronto, 1990

— 'Spenser, Sidney and the Renaissance Garden', *English Literary Renaissance*, 22/1, 1992

'Something Nasty in the Wilderness: Entertaining Queen Elizabeth on her Progresses', in *Medieval and Renaissance Drama in England*, vol. 10, ed. John Pitcher, Madison, 1998

Lever, J. W., 'Three Notes on Shakespeare's Plants', *Review of English Studies*, 3, 1952

Loades, David, *The Tudor Court*, London, 1986

— *John Dudley, Duke of Northumberland, 1504–1553*, Oxford, 1996

Longstaffe-Gowan, Todd, *The Gardens and Parks of Hampton Court Palace*, London, 2005

McCoy, R. C., 'From the Tower to the Tiltyard: Robert Dudley's Return to Glory', *Historical Journal*, 27/2, 1984

— *The Rites of Knighthood: The Literature and Politics of Elizabethan Chivalry*, Berkeley, 1989

MacCaffrey, Wallace, *The Shaping of the Elizabethan Regime*, London, 1969

— *Queen Elizabeth and the Making of Policy, 1572–1588*, Princeton, 1981

— *Elizabeth I*, London, 1993

MacDougall, Elizabeth B., *Fountains, Statues, and Flowers: Studies in Italian Gardens of the Sixteenth and Seventeenth Centuries*, Washington, 1994

— and Naomi Miller, eds, *Fons Sapentiae: Garden Fountains Renaissance in Illustrated Books, Sixteenth–Eighteenth Centuries*, Washington, 1977

— ed., *Fons Sapientiae: Renaissance Garden Fountains*, Washington, 1978

Markham, Gervase, *The English Husbandman*, London, 1613–15

— *Cheape and Good Husbandry*, London, 1614

— *The English House-wife*, London, 1637

Martin, Colin and Geoffrey Parker, *The Spanish Armada*, London, 1988

Mascall, Leonard, *The Country-Mans Recreation, or the Art of Planting, Graffing, and Gardening*, London, 1640

— *A Booke of the Arte and Maner, Howe to Plant and Graffe all Sortes of Trees*, London, 1572

Mignani, Daniela, *Le Ville Medicee di Giusto Utens*, Florence, 1993

Miller, Naomi, *Heavenly Caves: Reflections on the Garden Grotto*, London, 1982

Misztal, Mariusz, *The Elizabethan Courtier: Ideal versus Reality Embodied in Robert Dudley, Earl of Leicester*, Kraków, 2002

Montrose, Louis Adrian, *'Curious-knotted Garden': The Form, Themes and Contexts of Shakespeare's 'Love's Labour's Lost'*, Salzburg, 1977

Morley, Beric, Peter Brown and Tim Crump, 'The Elizabethan garden and Leicester's stables at Kenilworth Castle, Excavation between 1970 and 1984', ed. Peter Ellis, *Transactions of the Birmingham and Warwickshire Archaeological Society*, 1995

Mosser, Monique, and Georges Teyssot, eds, *The History of Garden Design*, London, 1991

Melville, Sir James, *The Memoirs of Sir James Melville* (1683), ed. Gordon Donaldson, London, 1969

Mulcaster, Richard, *The Quenes Maiesties Passage through the Citie of London to Westminster the Day before her Coronacion* (1558), facs. edn, ed. James M. Osborn, New Haven, 1960

Mulryne, Ronnie, and Elizabeth Goldring, eds, *Court Festivals of the European Renaissance: Art, Politics, and Performance*, Aldershot, 2002

Nares, Edward, *Memoirs of the Life and Administration of the Right Honourable William Cecil, Lord Burghley*, 3 vols, London, 1828–31

Neale, J. E., *Queen Elizabeth*, London, 1934

Nichols, John, *The Progresses and Public Processions of Queen Elizabeth*, 3 vols, London, 1823

— 'Theobalds Palace', *Gentleman's Magazine*, 106/1, 1836

O'Kill, Brian, 'The Printed Works of William Patten (*c.*1510–*c.*1600)', *Transactions of the Cambridge Bibliographical Society*, 7, 1977

Osborn, James M., *Young Philip Sidney, 1572–1577*, New Haven and London, 1972

Osborne, June, *Entertaining Elizabeth I: The Progresses and Great Houses of her Time*, London, 1989

Parkinson, John, *Paradisi in Sole Paradisus Terrestris*, London, 1629

Pevsner, Nikolaus, et al., *The Buildings of England*, Harmondsworth [later, New Haven and London], 1951–

Phillips, John, and Nicholas Burnett, 'The Chronology and Layout of Francis Carew's Garden at Beddington, Surrey', *Garden History*, 33/2, 2005

Platt, Hugh, *The Jewell House of Art and Nature*, London, 1594

— *The Garden of Eden*, London, 1653

Platter, Thomas, *Thomas Platter's Travels in England, 1599*, ed. Clare Williams, London, 1937

Prest, John, *The Garden of Eden: The Botanic Garden and the Re-creation of Paradise*, New Haven and London, 1981

Prouty, Charles Tyler, *George Gascoigne: Elizabethan Courtier, Soldier and Poet*, New York, 1942

Read, Conyers, *Mr Secretary Walsingham and the Policy of Queen Elizabeth*, Oxford, 1925

— 'A Letter from Robert, Earl of Leicester, to a Lady', *Huntington Library Quarterly*, 1936

— *Mr Secretary Cecil and Queen Elizabeth*, London, 1955

— *Lord Burghley and Queen Elizabeth*, London, 1960

Reese, M. M., *The Royal Office of Master of the Horse*, London, 1976

Robson-Scott, W. D., *German Travellers in England 1400–1800*, Oxford, 1953

Rohde, Eleanour Sinclair, *The Old English Herbals*, London, 1922

— *The Old English Gardening Books*, London, 1924

— *The Old-World Pleasaunce*, London, 1925

— *Gardens of Delight*, London, 1934

Rooke, P. E., ed., *Theobalds through the Centuries*, Broxbourne, 1980

Trevor-Roper, H. R., 'Elizabeth and Cecil', in *Historical Essays*, London, 1957

Rosenberg, Eleanor, *Leicester: Patron of Letters*, New York, 1955

Rye, William B., *England as Seen by Foreigners in the Days of Elizabeth and James the First*, London, 1865

Salaman, Redcliffe N., *The History and Social Influence of the Potato* (1949), Cambridge, 1985

Salatino, Kevin, ed., *Incendiary Art: The Representation of Fireworks in Early Modern Europe*, exhibition catalogue, Los Angeles, 1997

Schama, Simon, *Landscape and Memory*, London, 1995

Scott, David, 'William Patten and the Authorship of "Robert Laneham's Letter" (1575)', *English Literary Renaissance*, 7/2, 1977

Scott, W. D. Robson, *German Travellers in England 1400–1800*, Oxford, 1953

Scott, Sir Walter, *Kenilworth* (1821), London, 1999

— *The Journal of Sir Walter Scott*, ed. W. E. K. Anderson, Edinburgh and London, 1998

Sewter, A. C., 'Queen Elizabeth at Kenilworth', *Burlington Magazine*, 76/444, 1940

Shapiro, James, *1599: A Year in the Life of William Shakespeare*, London, 2005

Sheeler, Jessie, *The Garden at Bomarzo: A Renaissance Riddle*, London, 2007

Sidney, Sir Philip, *The Poems of Sir Philip Sidney*, ed. William A. Ringler, Jr, Oxford, 1962

— *Miscellaneous Prose of Sir Philip Sidney*, ed. Katherine Duncan-Jones and Jan van Dorsten, Oxford, 1973

— *The Countess of Pembroke's Arcadia (the old Arcadia)*, ed. Katherine Duncan-Jones, Oxford, 1985

Sim, Alison, *Pleasures and Pastimes in Tudor England*, Stroud, 1998

Sitwell, Edith, *Fanfare for Elizabeth*, London, 1946

– *The Queens and the Hive*, London, 1962

Skelton, R. A., and John Summerson, *A Description of Maps and Architectural Drawings in the Collection Made by William Cecil, First Baron Burghley, Now at Hatfield House*, Oxford, 1971

Smith, Alan G. R., *Servant of the Cecils: The Life of Sir Michael Hickes, 1543–1612*, London, 1977

— *William Cecil: The Power Behind Elizabeth*, London, 1934

— ed., *The Anonymous Life of William Cecil, Lord Burghley*, Studies in British History, 20, Lewiston, 1990

Somerset, Anne, *Elizabeth I*, New York, 1991

de Somogyi, Nick, *Shakespeare's Theatre of War*, Aldershot, 1998

Spenser, Edmund, *The Works of Edmund Spenser: A Variorum Edition*, ed. Edwin Greenlaw et al., 10 vols, Baltimore, 1932–49

— *The Shorter Poems of Edmund Spenser*, ed. William A. Oram et al., New Haven and London, 1989

Starkey, David, ed., *Rivals in Power: Lives and Letters of the Great Tudor Dynasties*, New York, 1990

— *Elizabeth*, London, 2001

Stead, Jennifer, 'Bowers of Bliss: The Banquet Setting', in C. Anne Wilson, *'Banquetting Stuffe': The Fare and Social Background of the Tudor and Stuart Banquet*, Edinburgh, 1991

Stewart, Alan, *Philip Sidney: A Double Life*, London, 2000

Strangford, Viscount, ed., 'Household Expenses of the Princess Elizabeth . . ., 1551–2', in *The Camden Miscellany*, II, London, 1853

Strickland, A., *Lives of the Queens of England*, 8 vols, 4th edn, London, 1854

Strong, Roy, 'Federigo Zuccaro's Visit to England in 1575', *Journal of the Warburg and Courtauld Institute*, 22, 1959

— and Jan van Dorsten, *Leicester's Triumph*, Leiden and London, 1964

— *The Cult of Elizabeth: Elizabethan Portraiture and Pageantry*, London, 1977

— *The Renaissance Garden in England*, London, 1979

— *Art and Power: Renaissance Festivals, 1450–1650*, London, 1984

— 'The Leicester House Miniatures: Robert Sidney, 1st Earl of Leicester and his Circle', *Burlington Magazine*, 127, 1985

— *Gloriana: The Portraits of Queen Elizabeth I*, London, 1987

— 'Sir Francis Carew's Garden at Beddington', in *England and the Continental Renaissance: Essays in Honour of J. B. Trapp*, ed. Edward Chaney and Peter Mack, Woodbridge, 1990

— 'The Renaissance Garden in England Reconsidered: A Survey of Two Decades of Research on the Period 1485–1642', *Garden History*, 27/1, 1999

— *The Artist and the Garden*, New Haven and London, 2000

— *Feast: A History of Grand Eating*, London, 2002

Stuart, David, and James Sutherland, *Plants from the Past*, Harmondsworth, 1989

Summerson, John, 'The Building of Theobalds 1564–1585', *Archaeologia*, 97, 1959

Sutton, James M., 'The Decorative Program at Elizabethan Theobalds: Educating an Heir and Promoting a Dynasty', *Studies in the Decorative Arts*, 7, 1999–2000

— *Materializing Space at an Early Modern Prodigy House: The Cecils at Theobalds, 1564–1607*, Aldershot, 2004

Symes, Michael, *Garden Sculpture*, Princes Risborough, 1996

Taylor, Christopher, *The Archaeology of Gardens*, Aylesbury, 1983

— *Parks and Gardens of Britain: A Landscape History from the Air*, Edinburgh, 1998

Thurley, Simon, *The Royal Palaces of Tudor England*, New Haven and
London, 1993
— *Whitehall Palace: An Architectural History of the Royal Apartments,
1240–1690*, New Haven and London, 1999
Till, E. C., 'The Development of the Park and Gardens at Burghley', *Garden
History*, 19/2, 1991
Turberville, George, et al., *The Noble Art of Venerie or Hunting*, London, 1575
and 1611
Tusser, Thomas, *A Hundreth Good Pointes of Husbandrie*, London, 1557
— *Five Hundred Pointes of Good Husbandrie*, London, 1580
Uglow, Jenny, *A Little History of British Gardening*, London, 2004
Waldman, Milton, *Elizabeth and Leicester*, London, 1944
Waldstein, Baron, *The Diary of Baron Waldstein: A Traveller in Elizabethan
England* (1600), trans. G. W. Groos, London, 1981
Waller, Gary, *Edmund Spenser: A Literary Life*, London, 1994
Weir, Alison, *Elizabeth the Queen*, London, 1998
Whalley, Robin, and Anne Jennings, *Knot Gardens and Parterres*, London, 1998
Williams, Neville, *A Tudor Tragedy: Thomas Howard, Duke of Norfolk*,
London, 1964
— *Elizabeth I, Queen of England*, London, 1971
— *All the Queen's Men*, London, 1972
Williams, Penry, *The Later Tudors: England 1547–1603*, Oxford, 1995
Wilson, Charles, *Queen Elizabeth and the Revolt of the Netherlands*, London,
1970
Wilson, D. R., and J. Wilson, 'The Site of the Elvetham Entertainment',
Antiquity, 58, 1982
Wilson, Derek, *Sweet Robin: A Biography of Robert Dudley, Earl of Leicester
1533–1588*, London, 1981
— *The Uncrowned Kings of England: The Black Legend of the Dudleys*, London,
2005
Wilson, Jean, ed., *Entertainments for Elizabeth I*, Woodbridge, 1980
Woodbridge, Kenneth, *Princely Gardens: The Origins And Development Of The
French Form*, London, 1986
Woodhouse, Elisabeth, 'Kenilworth, the Earl of Leicester's Pleasure Grounds
following Robert Laneham's Letter' and 'Spirit of the Elizabethan
Garden', *Garden History*, 27/1, 1999
Woolf, Virginia, *Orlando* (1928), London, 1993
Woolley, Benjamin, *The Queen's Conjuror: The Life and Magic of Dr Dee*,
London, 2001

Yates, Frances, *Astraea: The Imperial Theme in the Sixteenth Century*, London and Boston, 1975
Young, Alan, *Tudor and Jacobean Tournaments*, London, 1987
— *The English Tournament Imprese*, New York, 1988

Unpublished works

Dix, B., and J. Prentice, *Assessment Report on the Excavations within the Former Elizabethan Garden at Kenilworth Castle, Warwickshire*, Northampton, 2007
Meeds, Gary, *Cedars: The History and Development of a Local Park*, Higher National Diploma Landscape and Amenity Management thesis, Essex, 1997
Symes, Michael, 'The Theme of the Garden and its Relation to Man in the Poetry of Spenser, Milton and Marvell', MA thesis, London, 1968
Woudhuysen, H. R., *Leicester's Literary Patronage: A Study of the English Court, 1578–1582*, DPhil thesis, Oxford, 1980

Index